Memory Is Another Country

Memory Is Another Country

Women of the Vietnamese Diaspora

Nathalie Huynh Chau Nguyen

PRAEGER
An Imprint of ABC-CLIO, LLC

A B C ☰ C L I O

Santa Barbara, California • Denver, Colorado • Oxford, England

Photo Essay: All photos appear courtesy of the interviewees.

Library of Congress Cataloging-in-Publication Data

Nguyen, Nathalie Huynh Chau.
    Memory is another country : women of the Vietnamese diaspora / Nathalie Huynh Chau Nguyen.
        p. cm.
    Includes bibliographical references and index.
    ISBN 978-0-313-36027-5 (hard copy : alk. paper)—ISBN 978-0-313-36028-2 (ebook)
    1. Vietnamese diaspora. 2. Women—Vietnam—Biography. 3. Vietnam War, 1961–1975—Personal narratives, Vietnamese. 4. Vietnam—History—1975– 5. Women—Vietnam—Social conditions. 6. Vietnam War, 1961–1975—Social aspects. 7. Women immigrants—Social conditions. 8. Memory—Social aspects. 9. Vietnamese—Australia—Interviews. 10. Australia—Ethnic relations. I. Title.
DS559.913.N46   2009
305.48′895922—dc22   2009021942

13 12 11 10 9   1 2 3 4 5

This book is also available on the World Wide Web as an eBook.
Visit www.abc-clio.com for details.

ABC-CLIO, LLC
130 Cremona Drive, P.O. Box 1911
Santa Barbara, California 93116-1911

This book is printed on acid-free paper ∞
Manufactured in the United States of America

Part of the Introduction appeared in "'Your Memories Are Your Belongings': The Narratives of Vietnamese Refugee Women," *Island* 112 (2008): 24–31. Reprinted here by permission of *Island.*

An amended version of Chapter 2 appeared as "Memory and Silence in the Vietnamese Diaspora: The Narratives of Two Sisters," *Oral History* 36, no. 2 (2008): 64–74. Reprinted here by permission of the Oral History Society www.ohs.org.uk.

An amended version of Chapter 5 appeared as "Vietnamese Women: Narratives of Cross-Cultural Marriage," *Intersections: Gender and Sexuality in Asia and the Pacific*, issue 21 (2009): 23 paragraphs. Reprinted here by permission of *Intersections.*

An amended version of Chapter 6 appeared as "'We Return in Order to Take Leave': Memory and the Return Journeys of Vietnamese Women," *Crossroads: An Interdisciplinary Journal of Southeast Asian Studies* 19, no. 2 (2008). Reprinted here by permission of the Center for Southeast Asian Studies, Northern Illinois University.

Extracts from the following poems: untitled poem by Tessa Morris-Suzuki in Tessa Morris-Suzuki, *Peeling Apples* (Canberra: Pandanus Books, 2005), 47; *The Tale of Kieu* by Nguyen Du, trans. Huynh Sanh Thong (New Haven, CT: Yale University Press, 1983), 157–158; "Famine" by Tran Thi Nga in *Shallow Graves: Two Women in Vietnam*, ed. Wendy Wilder Larsen and Tran Thi Nga, 156–157 (New York: Random House, 1986); and "He Covered Me with a Blanket" and "Searching" by Thuong Vuong-Riddick in Thuong Vuong-Riddick, *Two Shores/Deux Rives* (Vancouver: Ronsdale Press, 1995), 158 and n.p., are reprinted here by permission.

CONTENTS

ILLUSTRATIONS

PREFACE AND ACKNOWLEDGMENTS

Seamed and worn as it is by age, by experience, and by time, the face of the elderly Vietnamese woman on the cover of this book is a beautiful one. She gazes out of the frame of the picture, and appears to reflect on the past. She is emblematic of the many aged parents and relatives who were left behind and mourned as Vietnamese refugees fled their country after the fall of Saigon in 1975. This book is about the memory of Vietnamese women. Women speak of their experience of war, dislocation, and migration. They remember their homeland and those they have lost. Thirty years after the end of the Vietnam War, women reflect on their past, and the choices they have made. Their stories are framed by trauma and loss, but they also reveal a fascinating glimpse of life in South Vietnam before 1975, the changes that occurred in postwar Vietnam, and women's fortitude in rebuilding their lives in the aftermath of war and displacement.

Gathering oral narratives from Vietnamese women raises particular challenges. First, many Vietnamese are reluctant to write or tell their life stories, because it is seen as an individualistic rather than community-oriented activity and because many had experienced censorship or imprisonment in postwar communist Vietnam.[1] Second, Vietnamese women find it even harder to speak than Vietnamese men since they traditionally have had a lower level of education and are expected to remain quietly in the background. And, third, women are often hesitant to bring their private stories into the public domain. Many of these women had experienced trauma either during or after the war and during or after their escape from Vietnam. Women are reluctant to speak of rape or abuse at the hands of pirates. And within the context of resettlement, women also find it difficult to speak of violence or abuse within marriage. Once they have made up their minds to speak however, they do so with astonishing honesty. I am constantly surprised about this and about the fact that they are prepared to entrust painful and difficult events in their lives to the interviewer. The women who agreed to be interviewed for this book are doing something new and unusual. The refugee and migration experience has allowed them to reinterpret their traditional role. By agreeing to speak, women indicate that they are not only capable of articulating their stories but also that they feel they have a story to tell, and are prepared to bring it into the public domain.

This book arose out of a five-year project on "Vietnamese Women: Voices and Narratives of the Diaspora." It is based on in-depth interviews with forty-two Vietnamese women that were conducted in Australia between 2005 and 2008.[2] I approached women through the Australian Vietnamese Women's Association, which is based in Melbourne and has had twenty-five years of experience in welfare work, as well as other community groups. I made extensive use of private networks in Melbourne and interstate, since in my experience, the most detailed interviews are provided by women who have been approached in this way. I conducted interviews with twenty-one women over three years.[3] The remainder of the women were interviewed by Boitran Huynh-Beattie and Thao Ha, and I am indebted to both for their patient work. Boitran Huynh-Beattie in particular went to considerable trouble to contact women in different states. Interviews varied in length, in focus, and in intensity, and lasted from thirty minutes to more than six hours, with repeat interviews in several cases. Half of the interviews were conducted in Vietnamese, and the procedure of having these interviews translated into English and interpreting them contributes yet another dimension to the process of memory-making. All the women were provided with information on the project and on the topics that I was interested in exploring in my work. These possible topics of discussion were by no means prescriptive. Some women focused on central events in their lives, while others provided lengthy life histories that stretched from early childhood to their present lives. Overall, the interviews resulted in more than 1,300 pages of transcript in English and in Vietnamese. Interviewees were provided with a recording and full transcript of their interviews. A number of women responded with corrections and comments, or requested that some aspect of their family story not be made public because of concerns for family members still living in Vietnam. Even though they were informed that for reasons of confidentiality they would only be identified by their first name, three women withdrew after lengthy interviews because of fears relating to their families in Vietnam, or because they apprehended criticism from either their family or community for having told their life stories. Despite the fact that they had spent years living away from a communist state, a number of women were still fearful of possible repercussions on the part of Vietnamese authorities. For the most part, however, women delivered their stories as personal testimonies. They sought to convey their individual, familial, and community histories and to situate them in the broader context of the Vietnamese diaspora. A number of women reflected on how difficult it was to tell their stories to their children. They conveyed to me how glad they were that I was writing a book on Vietnamese women's experiences, and expressed the hope that their children would one day read and understand their stories. In this light, my work serves as a bridge between the different generations.

The research and writing for this book were made possible by the award of a generous five-year Australian Research Fellowship from the Australian Research Council. I am grateful to the Australian Vietnamese Women's Association, its chief executive officer Cam Nguyen, and staff members for their support. The association's community contacts proved invaluable for the project. I owe particular thanks to Ngoc Bui, Phuong Mai Ung, and Huy Luu for translating Vietnamese interviews into English, and Xuan-Dung Huynh for his work in liaising with them. Ngoc Bui, Phuong Mai Ung, and So Ung also translated supplementary Vietnamese-language material for the book. At the University of Melbourne, I am grateful for the support and encouragement provided by colleagues and friends, in particular Kate Darian-Smith, Helen Mac-Donald, John Sinclair, Vera Mackie, Kate McGregor, and Joy Damousi. Vera Mackie read a draft of the first completed chapter I wrote for the book in 2007, and both she and John Sinclair commented on the book proposal that I sent to international publishers that year.

At Praeger, I am indebted to former Senior Editor Elizabeth Demers for her immediate interest in the project and her strong support. Editor Elizabeth Potenza has responded promptly and patiently to all my queries and comments. I thank the Art Department at Praeger for their striking cover design, and their flexibility in rethinking the original design they had proposed. I am grateful for comments on the book cover by colleagues and staff at the National Library of Australia (where I was working at the time), in particular Margy Burn and Lee Christofis. I presented material from this book at a number of different conferences and venues, including the Asian Studies Association of Australia conferences in 2006 and 2008, the Annual Meeting of the Association for Asian Studies in Boston in 2007, Narrative Network Australia in Melbourne and the Watermark Literary Muster in New South Wales in 2007, and the School of Historical Studies at the University of Melbourne, the Centre for Southeast Studies at Monash University, and the National Library of Australia in 2008. I thank colleagues at these venues for their feedback on papers presented, in particular Catherine Kohler Riessman, Hue-Tam Ho Tai, and Anne-Marie Medcalf. I owe grateful thanks to Eve Herring and Gioconda Di Lorenzo for reading the final draft of the book, and to Catherine Kohler Riessman and Kate Darian-Smith for taking the time in busy schedules to write the endorsements for the book. My family and friends in Australia and overseas provided love and encouragement. Finally, my greatest debt is to all the women who provided their life stories as well as photographs for this book. I hope that I have done justice to their memories and experiences.

INTRODUCTION

Life is a reflection
that ripples with each memory.

—Barbara Tran[1]

Of the stories recounted to me in my life, one of the most memorable is that of my mother's experience as a war refugee in southern Vietnam in 1945. She was four years old, and was at the time the youngest child in the family. She saw her paternal grandfather's house in Rach Gia burned down by the communists. He had been a wealthy landowner, and had dealt fairly and generously with the local farmers and villagers. As a result, they remembered him with respect. They protected and sheltered his daughter-in-law and his three grandchildren in 1945. My mother recalls that the locals dressed her and her sisters up in peasant clothes, and hid them. With their help, my grandmother and her children made it safely back to Saigon. My mother remembers seeing one of the male villagers who had tried to defend the house coming away with a machete wound in his shoulder. Villagers tried to save as many furnishings and household items as they could. My grandmother had pleaded with the communists not to burn down the house, but to take whatever they wanted, even occupy it. It was a beautiful house, with a library, columns made of wood imported from Cambodia, and hand-carved decorations. She told them that it was part of the history and heritage of Vietnam and ought to be preserved for that reason. The communists set fire to the house. My mother watched her grandfather's house burn and the ashes of her grandfather's books drifting down to the ground. She recalls being furious about it and thinking to herself that she would later study and store all her knowledge in her head, so that no one would be able to burn it out of her. This determination saw her complete her baccalaureate degree in Saigon at the age of sixteen and an economics degree at the University of Cambridge in 1962. My grandmother, on the other hand, stressed the importance of good deeds. She said that she and her children had benefited from her father-in-law's good deeds since it was in memory of him that the villagers had protected his family.

My mother's family name is Huynh. Her father's ancestors had migrated to Vietnam from southern China early in the nineteenth century, intermarried with Vietnamese women, and established themselves successfully in the newly settled lands of the South. Her mother's family is descended from a rebel prince of the Nguyen Dynasty, who fled south from the Imperial capital in the middle of the nineteenth century. My grandmother said that this part of the family history was kept secret because her father did not want any reprisals from the French authorities. My mother therefore originated from a family of migrants, entrepreneurs, and rebels. They were prepared to resettle in new lands, adapt to changed circumstances, and rebuild their lives anew.

As for my father, one of his striking memories is that of his experience as a boy in Hanoi in the closing days of the Second World War. Every morning, my father had to deliver freshly baked bread from the family compound in Quan Thanh to the shop to sell. The city was full of snipers, and my father said that to lurk in doorways and alongside walls was a sure way of attracting notice and getting shot at by one side or another (French or Viet Minh[2]). As a result, he would always walk down the middle of the street and make as much noise as possible so that everyone could see that he was simply a boy pushing a cart full of bread. He was fifteen years old at the time. He did this early every morning before heading off to school.

My father has a different family background to my mother's. He comes from an old and traditional northern family of scholars, proud of their long history, and closely attached to their native land in the Red River Delta. The Nguyens of Kim Bai trace their history back to the fifteenth century. The family includes two brothers who succeeded at the doctoral examinations in the Imperial capital in 1511.[3] It was a rare honor, and both their names were carved on a stone stele in Hanoi's Temple of Literature.[4] The fortunes of the family rose and fell depending on the success of their sons in the examinations for the mandarinate.[5] One was sent on a diplomatic mission to China in the late sixteenth century. My father wrote the history of his family in a book entitled *A Vietnamese Family Chronicle: Twelve Generations on the Banks of the Hat River* (1991). It relates the history of the Nguyens, passed down from father to son and recorded in the family chronicles. My father left northern Vietnam in 1950 with a copy of these chronicles, written in the scholarly or Chinese script by his grandfather. Like my mother's family, my father's family is Buddhist. The women of the family played a significant role by supporting their men and keeping the family financially afloat so that their husbands could focus on their studies. It was the advent of Ho Chi Minh and the communists to power in 1945 that altered this family history, and sundered the Nguyens' centuries-long attachment to their land. In the fifties, many fled south or overseas. It was a family of patriots and nationalists who were deeply wary of communism. They saw communism as a divisive and destructive foreign creed. Tens of thousands of Vietnamese died in the communist purges of 1945–1946.[6] Members of my father's extended family were imprisoned, including three brothers in one family, the youngest of whom was sixteen at the time. After the signing of the Geneva Accords in 1954, a million northerners fled south, "voting with their feet" against Ho Chi Minh's regime. My father said that many of the soldiers in the elite ranks of the South Vietnamese Army—the Airborne Division, Marines, and Rangers—were from northern families, because northerners knew what they were fighting against.[7] My father's oldest brother served as an army officer and died in 1961. My father worked as a diplomat for the South Vietnamese government and participated in the Paris Peace Talks of 1973. We were living in Japan, where he had been posted, when Saigon fell in April 1975. For my father and for many others from northern families, the collapse of South Vietnam in 1975 was truly terrible, in that it signaled the end of their hopes for a free and democratic Vietnam. They had in effect lost their country twice.

My family background therefore encompasses the history of both North and South Vietnam. Both my parents experienced war as children and were war refugees. The central themes from both histories, apart from that of survival in wartime, are those of resilience, hard work, and adaptability on my mother's side, and of the importance of family, scholarship, and tradition on my father's. My parents met in England while my mother was a student at Cambridge, and they were

married in London at the end of 1962. My maternal grandmother rec-
ollected that my grandfather was angry when he heard that my mother
wanted to marry a northerner. He and my grandmother argued about
this, with my grandfather shouting, "Why couldn't she fall for a southerner? Aren't there enough of them around? Why did it have to be a
northerner?" He only relented when he discovered that his younger
brother was a former schoolmate of my father's father (they had both
studied at Lycée Janson de Sailly in Paris in the 1920s), at which point
my father's family suddenly became "all right," and my father became
an acceptable son-in-law.

In 1975, my family became political refugees, and my parents moved
to Australia with their four young children. More than 2 million Vietnamese left their country in the two decades following the communist
takeover of South Vietnam in 1975. The majority resettled in the
United States, Australia, Canada, and France, but Vietnamese communities were formed in countries as diverse as Israel and Norway. The
Vietnamese diaspora that came into being after the end of the Vietnam
War was one of the largest and most visible mass migrations of the late
twentieth century. Its scale was unprecedented in Vietnamese history.[8]
The toll in human lives was immense, and one of the great tragedies of
this exodus is that the number of deaths will never truly be known.
The losses of boat refugees alone are estimated at between 100,000 and
1 million people in the postwar years.[9]

As a child refugee, I grew up with my parents repeatedly underlining
the fact that our family was fortunate: we had not escaped by boat and
had not lost any immediate family members in the exodus. Although
this was certainly true, my parents' attitude also suppressed and silenced
the grief that 1975 engendered. The hidden injuries that this experience left behind were not discussed in the family. My mother was
determinedly optimistic in her attitude and busied herself with her
involvement in Vietnamese community and welfare work in addition
to full-time employment, while my father lapsed into depression.
Although he worked until his retirement at the age of sixty-five, he in
many ways never recovered from the loss of his country. He once con-
fided his belief that it was the accumulated grief and stress of exile that
were responsible for the stroke that he suffered at the age of sixty-six.
It is from this background and family story that I became interested in
the subject of memory, the memory of refugees, and the intersection of
memory, narrative, and trauma in refugee stories.

MEMORY AND NARRATIVE

The act of remembering is a means of bringing the past alive, and an imaginative way of dealing with loss. It has been the subject of much recent scholarship and is of particular relevance at a time of widespread transnational migration. For refugees, memory acquires a particular power and poignancy, since the country that they remember is now lost to them. As the Iranian American writer Roya Hakakian notes in her recent memoir *Journey from the Land of No*:

> When you have been a refugee, abandoned all your loves and belongings, your memories become your belongings. Images of the past, snippets of old conversations, furnish the world within your mind. When you have nothing left to guard, you guard your memories. You guard them with silence.[10]

The memories of Vietnamese refugees have been molded by their experience of diaspora, and many guard these memories with silence, a silence that relates not only to the departure from Vietnam and the exodus itself, but also to the impact of loss and grief on individual family members. Like the histories of the post-Holocaust generations, Vietnamese diasporic histories are often fragmented and incomplete. Members of the first generation invested their energies in adjusting to dislocation and migration, and with reconstructing lives and identities in a different country and culture. Many did this while mourning the loss of their homeland and of family members who had either died or disappeared in the postwar years. The reverberations of this experience, in terms of damaged lives, damaged relationships, and the secondary trauma that was transferred to the second and third generations still have to be fully articulated.[11] Women's stories, in particular, are still largely unknown and undocumented.[12] I wanted to record the experiences of the first generation above all because it is a generation that is aging and disappearing. It is also the generation that is the least heard in the public arena.

In a collection of Vietnamese American poetry and prose, Barbara Tran, Monique Truong, and Luu Truong Khoi write:

> We have a memory of water. Ankle deep, back bent by the sun, verdant fields. Shallow basins, eyes sealed with tears, ornate cathedrals. Salt water shrouds, lips cracked, silent flotilla. We have a memory of water. A memory that is only sometimes our own.[13]

These fugitive glimpses reflect on the significance of water in Vietnamese culture: the life-giving water of Vietnam's green rice fields, the tears of supplicants, and the watery graves of all those who perished during the exodus. The Vietnamese word for water, *nuoc*, as Huynh Sanh Thong reminds us, also denotes homeland, country, and nation.[14] To lose one's country, *mat nuoc*, "evokes an ordeal by thirst, the despair of a fish out of water."[15] Water therefore connotes life and death, home and exile. It is associated with the defining narrative of the Vietnamese diaspora: the escape by sea.[16] "Silent flotilla" refers to a collective tragedy and a collective memory of trauma. It reflects both the reality of the exodus—the great majority of those who escaped from Vietnam in the postwar years did so by boat and the majority of those who died did so at sea—as well as its more mythical dimension. Growing up in Australia, I remember notices in the local Vietnamese newspapers commemorating entire families that had drowned at sea. Stories of great loss, for example, that of the woman who watched each of her seven children die one by one on the journey, are referred to in hushed terms in Vietnamese circles. "Where there is suffering," as Oscar Wilde notes in *De Profundis*, "there is holy ground."[17]

Against this background, how do refugees remember loss? What form does their memory take? What does it reveal about their means of processing the past? How does it reflect on where they are in their present lives? Memory is flexible and adaptive, and its contradictions are inherent in its nature. We remember what we wish to remember, or what we need to remember, and our memories evolve with time and with our present circumstances. "In most acts of remembering," writes David Gross, "there is as much material from the present that is projected backward as there is material that comes authentically and indisputably from the past itself."[18] More than thirty years after the end of the Vietnam War, the memories of Vietnamese refugees and migrants bear illumination.

My exploration of intersecting issues of memory, narrative, and trauma in Vietnamese women's diasporic stories is informed by the substantial scholarship on memory, narrative, oral history, and trauma.[19] As scholars have noted, there are intrinsic concerns relating to the use of memory. Memory is unreliable and reflects a continuous process of "retranslation."[20] "Remembering the self," as Nicola King notes, "is not a case of restoring an original identity, but a continuous process of 're-membering,' of putting together moment by moment, of provisional and partial reconstruction."[21] Memory's very unreliability, however, has been identified as a strength by oral historians, since it provides clues about the relationship between past and present, and between individual and collective memory.[22] People reshape and reframe their memories to make sense of their lives. For refugees, the reappropriation of the past may reveal traumatic experiences and devastating loss, but the process of memory work may also be regenerative and lead to what Janet Carsten describes as "a restoration of the disjunctures of the past."[23] For the Vietnamese women whose life stories are featured in this book, memory is a creative process that allows them to identify not only past traumas but also the strengths that have enabled them to reconstruct their lives in another country. Women's memories reveal as much about the process of reflection in which they have engaged in relation to their lives as their actual recollections of the past. Their life stories reveal multiple truths.[24]

Women's narratives unfold in specific social, historical, and cultural contexts. I will provide the cultural and literary framework to their life stories and explore their memories through the lens of narrative inquiry. As Catherine Kohler Riessman has articulated,

> In a dynamic way, narrative constitutes past experience at the same time as it provides ways for individuals to make sense of the past. And stories must always be considered in context, for storytelling occurs at a historical moment with its circulating discourses and power relations.[25]

Narrative analysts explore how and why an event is storied, and what is accomplished by telling the story in a particular way.[26] Who elicits the story? For what purpose? What cultural resources does the story draw on?[27] I will adopt a combination of critical approaches, relying in large part on a thematic narrative analysis of the women's stories, with some reference to structural analysis. I am concerned with examining the content and form of women's narratives—the language that women use, the narrative devices that they resort to, and the structure of their stories. I searched for common themes across the narratives, as well as differences, divergences, and inconsistencies. "Narrative analysis," writes Susan Bell, "shows how structure, content, and interpretation are interwoven."[28] The women's narratives are all anchored in the diasporic experience, and several are trauma narratives that are presented as personal testimonies. "Testimony," as Judith Lewis Herman notes, "has both a private dimension, which is confessional and spiritual, and a public aspect, which is political and judicial."[29] Many women consciously position themselves in a collective framework, and interweave their personal stories with those of others in their community. They reveal a clear consciousness of their status as refugees or migrants and of the lack of visibility attached to their stories and experiences. "The process of 'bearing witness'—by refugees and other victims of social and political oppression," suggest Katharine Hodgkin and Susannah Radstone, "can . . . be empowering for individual narrators, and can generate public recognition of collective experiences which have been ignored or silenced."[30] In retelling their individual and communal stories, women reveal themselves as custodians, interpreters, and archivists of Vietnamese diasporic histories.

Many South Vietnamese households destroyed family photographs and documents in the closing days of the war—a loss that was irretrievable. Chapter 1 explores the representation of loss in women's narratives. Three women recall their lives before 1975, the impact of events in 1975, and their postwar lives. Their memories identify paths not taken and futures lost when their country collapsed; however, they also reveal women's resilience in transmuting these losses into creative and meaningful lives. Chapter 2 examines the contrasting memories of siblings. It features the narratives of two sisters, and their memories of the brother who died at sea during the exodus and the sister they lost to cancer after resettlement. Their narratives reveal distinct interpretations of past traumas, as well as the silences in their lives. Their retellings crisscross and shape each other to paint a multifaceted portrait of sibling relationships, the experience of exodus, the pain of loss, and the challenges of moving on. Chapter 3 focuses on the memories and experiences of female veterans. The histories of women who served in the Republic of Vietnam Armed Forces (RVNAF) have been largely silenced in the vast historiography of the Vietnam War. I will construct a partial history of the Women's Auxiliary Corps (WAC) and Women's Armed Forces Corps (WAFC) from the few written sources available and examine the life stories of four former servicewomen. Their narratives reveal that while few may be aware of their stories, female veterans are able to successfully construct individual discourses of their war service and their postwar lives, and, in the process, are creating and preserving the histories of RVNAF servicewomen. Chapter 4 explores four narratives in which women reconstruct wartime lives and remember wartime losses, as well as postwar traumas. Women not only remember different aspects of war, but also formulate and articulate these experiences differently. Their individual "traumascapes"[31] manifest themselves not only in the content of stories, but also in the shape and structure of their narratives. Chapter 5 studies the accounts of four women who have intermarried with non-Vietnamese men. The contexts for these marriages range from Asia in the 1960s to Australia in the 1990s. Women reflect on the significance of their choices, family responses to their relationships, and the challenges and rewards of having a partner from a different cultural background. On another level, their narratives reveal women's relationship with memory and with their Vietnamese past, and the complex of social, cultural, and familial factors that underlie their choice of a partner from another culture. Chapter 6, lastly, focuses on women's return journeys to Vietnam. It features the narratives of four women who have made the return trip, and those of two women who have chosen not to journey back to Vietnam. I will explore how women have managed and negotiated their return, and how they have dealt with the disjuncture between past and present, and modified their conception of home and the homeland.

In a lecture delivered in Berlin in 1996 on the importance of memory, the writer Elie Wiesel notes:

> If there is to be one word that defines the fragility, the vulnerability but also the invincibility of the human condition, it is memory. . . . To remember is to acknowledge the postulate that time does leave traces and scars on the surface of history, that all events are intertwined, all gates open to the same truth.[32]

The narratives of Vietnamese women are intrinsically valuable in their own right.[33] Their memories redress the perceived "silence" of women in the wider Vietnamese diaspora.[34] Their experiences not only illuminate the stories of Vietnamese refugees and migrants, but also point to essential truths relating to the human condition.

CHAPTER 1

Lost Photographs

In the closing days of the Vietnam War in 1975, my family was living in Tokyo, Japan, where my father was working. He had been appointed the Republic of Vietnam's Ambassador to Japan the previous year. My maternal grandmother flew over to visit us, and stayed on as the situation in South Vietnam worsened. My aunt in Saigon, my mother's oldest sister, had the presence of mind to send two boxes to Tokyo via ordinary post as circumstances deteriorated further: the first box, which reached us, contained my grandmother's jewelery (my aunt had sent the jewels in tins and they reached us intact in Tokyo); the second box, which never reached us, was full of family photographs. I have always wondered what happened to that box of photographs, and whether it lay abandoned in some post office or on an airport tarmac in those last days, as South Vietnam collapsed, and I have always regretted its loss. Those pictures of my mother and her sisters, my grandparents, and other relatives would not have held any meaning to others, but for my family, as we began our new lives as refugees, they signified a link with our past, our family history, and our lost country. As Janet Carsten notes, photographs are "artefacts of memory . . . compressed and made portable."[1] They are of particular significance to refugees and migrants, since they embody a sense of past place and belonging that is all the more important in the aftermath of displacement. Photographs are also a potent reminder of those who were lost.

In an essay entitled "Lost Photos," the Vietnamese American writer Andrew Lam remembers:

When I was eleven years old I did an unforgivable thing: I set my family photos on fire. We were living in Saigon at the time, and as the Viet

Cong[2] tanks rolled toward the edge of the city, my mother, half-crazed with fear, ordered me to get rid of everything incriminating.

   Obediently I removed pictures from album pages, diplomas from their glass frames, film reels from metal canisters, letters from desk drawers. I put them all in a pile in the backyard and lit a match. When it was done, the mementoes of three generations had turned into ashes.[3]

Lam's words convey the finality of that act of destruction—a destruction that mirrors the collapse of South Vietnam and carries in its wake a similar sense of irretrievability. His words bring to mind those of my sister-in-law, who was ten years old when she escaped from Vietnam by boat in 1980. When I asked her whether she had any photographs of herself as a child in Vietnam, she said very few, because the family photographs and the family book were burnt by her oldest sister. Her father had already destroyed family documents in 1975, but it is the loss of the photographs and especially the family book that my sister-in-law regrets the most. This act of destroying photographs and documents, an act that was repeated in countless South Vietnamese households in 1975, as the country fell to communist forces, underlines the fragility of tangible mementoes of the past and of loved ones.

   One of my sister-in-law's most beautiful photographs—one of the few of her family that she keeps stored in a box—is that of her sister Hoa, taken in 1970 when Hoa was eighteen years old. In this picture, Hoa is portrayed with her cousin Ngot in Saigon. It may be that, as Inga Clendinnen writes, "all photographs are melancholy; the vanished moment caught at the moment of its vanishing,"[4] but I find this photograph particularly poignant because I know Hoa's story. Hoa disappeared at sea with her children, two daughters who were then ages seven and three, and two siblings in 1978. According to my sister-in-law, Hoa had married a soldier for love, much to their father's chagrin. Hoa's husband left with the Americans in 1975. She stayed behind with their children because her father refused to leave the country. Three years later, just after she had in turn left Vietnam by boat with her children and her younger sister and brother, her family received Hoa's sponsorship papers from her husband in the United States. But it was too late, she had disappeared, as had her children and siblings, and more than 200 people on their boat. Hoa's husband waited for years, hoping against hope for news of his wife and daughters. After ten years, Hoa's family told him that he should move on with his life and marry again. He finally did so but is still haunted by nightmares of his lost family. The following lines by Tessa Morris-Suzuki, while they relate to a more recent tragedy off Australia's shores, are a powerful evocation of boat people lost at sea:

> And are we still too high above the clouds to see them now
> as they float, like birds on the water?
> Or in unsleeping moments do the faces rise from fathoms deep?
> The thirst beyond quenching for drowned laughter,
> The ache of unrecoverable dreams.[5]

The story of Hoa and of her family is one of love and loss, of hope and denial. It is most of all a story of lives prematurely destroyed, and of futures obliterated. It is this "ache of unrecoverable dreams" that I wish to address in this chapter, through the narratives of three Vietnamese women who are now resettled in Australia. How do women cope with loss, especially the loss of hope? I will explore women's memories of their early lives, their recollection of events in 1975, their postwar experiences, and how they have reconstructed their lives "on the other side of sorrow."[6] Their stories describe life paths that were ruptured by personal and community traumas, and the corrosive sense of despair that could and did ensue, and that at times seemed to overwhelm their existence. The stories also reveal, however, the effort that women expended on reshaping and redirecting the course of their lives, even in the face of repeated failures or setbacks. Their narratives illustrate in this way the regenerative aspects of memory-making. Women not only identify the extent of losses sustained and the depths of grief experienced, they manage at the same time to author meaningful and purposeful lives. In "Lost Photos," Lam describes his metaphorical effort to retrieve his family photographs from the ashes of the family home (in the form of a dream). He fails in this, but concludes:

> Precious things lost are transmutable. They refuse oblivion. They simply wait to be rendered into testimonies, into stories and songs.[7]

His observation resonates in the following narratives.

EARLY LIVES

The first narrative is that of Hoang,[8] born in 1948 in Sa Det, southern Vietnam. Her father and grandfather were involved in politics, and were anti-French as well as anti-communist. The family was strongly Buddhist. Her grandfather was assassinated by the communists in 1951, and his death was reported in Vietnamese newspapers of the time. It left a lasting imprint on the family. As for Hoang's father, he worked for the government and also ran private businesses to support a large family of twelve children. Hoang was the eldest. Her life before 1975 combined her love of music (she was a member of the Vietnamese Red Cross Women's Association band from 1964 until the end of the war), her work in acupuncture, and her medical studies. She went to Japan in 1968 and spent two years studying acupuncture. On her return to Vietnam, she practiced it while studying medicine. Her father actively supported and encouraged her in all her artistic and scholarly endeavours. She recollects:

> Being the eldest daughter of a rebel politician who was constantly being harassed by the government, I was given every opportunity to expand my knowledge. My father's life was very unstable so he invested everything in his children. I was allowed to study whatever I desired. At the age of nine, I started to learn music. Then I started to learn how to play an instrument. After three years, the teacher's children and nieces and my siblings and I got together and established a band of fourteen members. My father did not allow me to perform with the band for money but only for fun at end-of-year school functions. Then around 1964, we were invited to join the Vietnamese Red Cross Women's Association (VRCWA). I played the accordion. We went to soldier outposts, to entertain the soldiers who did not get leave to go home to their families at Christmas or the New Year. We brought them gifts. At the time of the [Nguyen Van] Thieu presidency, his wife was a member of VRCWA and we visited Hue and Da Nang. We often played in Vietnamese and American hospitals, and at military barracks. I also participated in supporting disabled veterans and their families. We usually got around by military jeep, helicopter or airplane. After 1968, I performed less frequently as I went to Japan to learn acupuncture for two years.

She relates her memory of the following incident involving her father, and it is a telling one in light of her later reflections on him:

> One Sunday, Mr Tran Van Huong, the Vice-President [under Nguyen Van Thieu], invited my father and me to dinner to thank us for the acupuncture treatment he had received. It was raining very hard and there was a knock on my door. The maid came in and said that there was a

woman with a young child wanting to see me. I told her to tell the lady that it was Sunday and that I did not make appointments with anyone. The lady told the maid that my father had said that if the child got sick, she could bring him here at any time. I again told the maid to tell the lady to come back another time as it was Sunday and I was busy. When my father heard what I said, he came out and slapped me on the cheek. He had never hit me before. I was so angry with him that I refused to go to the dinner with him. I was not going to obey him. He was trying to control me because he was my father. I would never see a patient on Sunday. My father did not go to the dinner. I went by myself wearing sunglasses to hide my red eyes. When Mr Huong saw me he was surprised by my late arrival. He asked me what was wrong. I told him that I had sore eyes. I was extremely upset with my father. That particular child had been written off by the hospital. At four years old, he could neither sit, stand, nor talk. After one year of intensive acupuncture treatment, he had started to sit, walk and talk. His family was ecstatic. As a result, my father told the mother that if there was any urgent change in his condition, she should contact us right away, no appointment required. On that day, the child fell sick and the mother was worried so she brought him to us. When he saw me refuse to see a patient, he was angry. He asked me: "Why did you regard your dinner outing as more important than the life of the little boy?" He valued the welfare of patients. Everyday, when I returned home from the university, there were always people waiting for treatment. I was often very tired and did not wish to see people but my father encouraged me to soldier on to help people.

Hoang's narrative portrays a coming-of-age story in which she features as a young woman who learned to be conscious of her social responsibilities and felt confident of her future prospects. She anchors this life trajectory against a family background of mingled privilege and tragedy. Her father had seen his own studies in Japan interrupted by war in 1945, and he wanted to do all he could to enable his children to complete their education. He was a formative figure in his daughter's life and was instrumental in shaping her career interests and work ethics. Hoang's detailed reconstruction of the incident involving the acupuncture patient reveals not only the lesson that she drew from it (the importance of service) but also the level of attachment between father and daughter. Hoang relates that she held high hopes and ambitions before 1975: she wanted to complete her medical degree and eventually become hospital director.

The second narrative is that of Tran, who was born in 1957 in Bien Hoa, southern Vietnam. Tran's parents were Vietnamese Chinese, and owned one of the largest bookshops in the South. The family lived above the premises and Tran describes the fascination that the bookshop held for her as she grew up:

> I was the first-born and one of the things I remember clearly was that everyone expected me to be a boy. I was not happy about this, so I decided that I had to do something to get people's attention. I decided to study. I wanted to get high marks and win a scholarship to go overseas. I've wanted to study overseas since I was fourteen.
>
> My parents were half-Chinese but they were born in Vietnam. We were a big family, eight children. My father had two bookshops in Bien Hoa, and one was the second largest bookshop in South Vietnam before 1975. I loved the big bookshop. I read Tolstoy, Romain Rolland, Balzac, Thomas Hardy, I read all the Western writers before I read any Vietnamese books. I'd started Year 9 when my parents opened this second shop. I was supposed to keep an eye on the cash register but I spent all my time reading. My aunty would come in and knock on my head and say, "Is this the way to mind the business?" My parents' bookshop was a meeting place for high school students. They pretended to look at books but would actually stand close to each other and whisper. And I really didn't like that [laughs]. School finished at about 4.30 P.M. so those young couples would come in and stay for an hour or two. And because the bookshop was quite long, after five we needed to turn the lights on to light up the back of the shop. So I always turned the light on very early [laughs] to chase off those students. I don't know if anyone remembers that.

Tran's narrative is structured as a quest narrative, in which she presents a younger self who was aiming for a specific academic objective. Her words illustrate her early awareness of gender bias in her family and in wider Vietnamese society, a bias that was the legacy of a thousand years of Chinese influence on social mores. She was determined to struggle against this form of discrimination, and she focused on education as the best avenue to personal and social empowerment. Her narrative demonstrates her early love of books and of reading, and the opportunities that her parents' bookshops, and the wealth of books that they contained, afforded her during her school years. Books represented an opening into other cultures and other societies, and in this excerpt, Tran provides a marvelous portrayal of her absorption in reading and concomitant haphazard shopkeeping skills. Like Hoang, she was the eldest and came from a large family. Her life story reveals not only that she decided at age fourteen exactly what she wanted to do, but also that she resolutely worked her way through high school to reach her goal.

The narrative of the third woman, Le, differs considerably from the first two. Le was born in Buon Ma Thuot in 1964 (she is unsure of her date of birth), and grew up in the Central Highlands of Vietnam, among the Ede and Jarai people. She relates that her mother was from a Chinese ethnic minority, with possible connections to indigenous Taiwanese communities, but that she does not know her father's background. She has only vague memories of him. He died when she was young. She provides the following glimpses of her childhood:

> I have a memory of a grown up man in my life when I was very little. My mother and he were selling food like pawpaw salad. One night, in the light of an oil lamp, I was sitting on the floor, and they were making chilli sauce and one drop of the sauce jumped into my eye so I cried, that was one of my memories about that man. The next memory was that he got a huge stomach and he died and I was wearing a white hat for mourning and my mother was crying, and there were gongs and drums playing in the village.
>
> I hardly heard my mother talk about him, only sometimes she'd hold me and cry and say: "Poor kid, you no longer have a father," and that was it, and I didn't hear much about him. And then after that my mother still carried me around with a piece of cloth wrapped around her body. She walked up and down the rocky hills very early in the morning and it was dark at night when we came back.
>
> She came from China and belonged to a minority group—the language is now very rare. I still want to find out where exactly she came from.

Le's mother earned her living moving from place to place and working as a cleaner, cook, and housekeeper in various schools and shops. Le relates:

> My mother worked in a house that was selling coffee. We were staying at the back of that house, sharing the room with the family dog. The room was so small, even smaller than a single bed here, that we couldn't sleep side by side, so we had to sleep head to toe. And another thing I remember is the rough concrete wall. It didn't have a proper seal, but had lots of holes and those holes were full of ticks. I often used a

toothpick to kill them one by one, and the wall became like a bloody wall. And I had a great time out of it, yes. And then the dog was following me everywhere, even when I went to school. My mother made lots of nice clothes for me by hand and often I came home dirty with dog paw prints all over my clothes because of that dog.

This life of poverty was enlivened by frequent trips to the cinema. This means of recreation, however, was not without risk since cinemas, like other places where people congregated in South Vietnam during the war, were targets for terrorist attacks. She recounts one such incident:

My mother and I often went to see movies, and we would often see the same movie four or five times. The local cinema was in the middle of the market place just on the other side of the street and she loved movies. They were mostly Hong Kong movies and they had subtitles. I was sitting on her lap, reading all those subtitles and half guessing the meaning of what was said, and I just whispered translations into her ear. She couldn't read, she was learning at night and writing some words. As mother and child, we spent many good times like that in the cinema. Some people sitting next to her found it annoying but I wasn't shy. I just kept whispering in my mother's ear, trying to tell her the story.

The cinema was bombed twice, you know. It happened in the middle of the film, one time I remember it was a Japanese film. There was a blind heroine, and she had a really long sword. It was nearly at the end of the film and it was very exciting. She was trying to fight with the enemy, turning around with the sword, and all of a sudden "Boom," you know, there was the bomb, the fumes, all the electricity was cut off and all the people started to scream and my mother put her body over me. We were trapped in between seats and she used her body to cover me because people just stepped over us, other people just tried to jump up and get out, and she was injured because she protected me. I was eight and this was around 1972. I heard that the seats in the last row were supposed to be the best seats. There were some important people sitting there so that's why the Viet Cong tried to kill them, but they killed innocent civilians.

Her mother died the following year. Le was spending the night at her aunt's when she was told the news. She remembers:

In the morning at about three o'clock I think, the old man came knocking on the door and said that my mother had passed away. She woke up looking for me and cried: "Where is my daughter? Where is my daughter?" But I wasn't there, there was no phone [in the hospital]. Even now, I can't imagine how she suffered, or how sad she was. I always regret that I wasn't there for her.

When I went back to Buon Ma Thuot, I really felt a sense of loss. I felt like nobody's child. Nobody wanted me, my aunty didn't want me and I cut myself off from my friends, I didn't want to see them and avoided them even when they called to me outside the door. I spent my time reading books and I started to write poems. I also started to translate Chinese novels into Vietnamese just for fun and I learnt to read music. I also did a lot of drawings.

Le's narrative is not only set against a framework of significant loss but also identifies the means with which she learnt to cope with bereavement. She provides a wealth of visual imagery in her recollections—the oil lamp at night, her mother carrying her Highland fashion over rocky hills, the narrow room with its pockmarked walls where she lived with her mother. While she is eloquent in conveying the tragedies and deprivations of her childhood, she also relates its joys: handmade clothes by her mother; cinema outings; and the remembered closeness between mother and child. Her reconstruction of the terrorist incident that she witnessed—the bombing of the local cinema—is vivid and detailed, but even here, the focus of her narrative remains on the interaction between mother and daughter (Le whispering translations into her mother's ear, and her mother sheltering her with her body in the panic and confusion following the bombing). The majority of victims of communist terror in South Vietnam in 1968–1972 were ordinary civilians.[9] Although orphaned at the age of nine, Le found a new family in the form of "the old man," the last shop owner that her mother had worked for. He took her in and became a father figure for her.

THE EVENTS OF 1975

All three women have vivid memories of events in 1975 and their sequels. The loss of the war represented a watershed in their country's history, and a significant marker in their own lives. Hoang's narrative reflects a life path that took an abrupt turn after the fall of South Vietnam. She relates:

Before 1975, I was in medical school. I was finishing my third year when the Viet Cong took control of the country. I was deemed to have an unfavourable family history and was expelled from the university.

My father was arrested on the second of July. He was taken away in an unmarked car. My brother followed the car on his motorbike and saw that he was taken to Police Headquarters. They told us he would be released after four or five days. But when my mother went there the following day, she was told that there was nobody of that name there. Only one visit per month was allowed. The next month, the same thing happened. After five or six months, we were told that he had been transferred to Phan Dang Luu prison. My mother went there but once more, they said that there was no such person there. On the fourth attempt, they finally admitted that he was there. We could only send him food. We weren't allowed to visit him.

He was held in Phan Dang Luu prison for four years, then sent to Chi Hoa prison for four and a half years. My mother was allowed to visit him twice before he died. I sent money home so that my mother could bribe the prison authorities. Throughout all this time, my father was never brought to court for trial or convicted of any crime. When my father died, we were not told until a week later. On the death certificate, it stated that the cause of death was liver failure and blocked arteries. The time of death was also recorded. The body was buried at Ba Queo.

Hoang in fact begins her life story with the collapse of her country and its aftermath. It provides the focal point to her narrative and she returns to it episodically. All other aspects of her life revolve around this central tragedy. This extract not only conveys the grief of her father's absence on a personal level, but also a series of endings: the end of South Vietnam, the end of her university studies, and the end of her hopes for a medical career. Her father's arrest and his later death in prison constituted the second major tragedy the family experienced at the hands of the communists.

Tran, for her part, has the following memories of April 1975:

My parents' house was on the same street as the biggest hospital in Bien Hoa and all the trucks carried corpses or injured people. All I saw as I looked out from our balcony on the first floor was all the corpses bouncing up and down when the trucks went over some holes. Ambulances traveled along the main street many times during those days and then I saw open fire at the airbase and rockets falling in. I could see all the explosions. They went on at night as well. I read somewhere about the destruction of Troy and it was a very vivid experience for me to see the destruction of the war but at the same time I also saw its beauty, it was a strange phenomenon. All the houses shook and you could feel the ground shake from the explosions.

After 1975, all the books were confiscated and taken away by the government, including all the textbooks of biology, mathematics, physics, chemistry, all the dictionaries and you know things that are not ideological. Mathematics is mathematics whether you're communist or capitalist, Russian or American. They came in trucks and took everything away, they even confiscated all the stationery my father had, compasses, pencils, pens, colors, rulers, they were all gone.

I . . . to be honest, I was brainwashed by all the politics after 1975 and particularly after I started university in 1976. I believed that in order to create a fair society, a socialist society, individuals had to make sacrifices so my father's bookshops happened to be in the pathway of history, and history had just crushed my father's business in order to make everyone enlightened.

Tran relates that her father was not bitter about the closure of his bookshops—he even supported the new regime initially. But disillusionment soon set in:

My father had an incident involving his typewriter. Our neighbour went to the local police and reported that my father was working for the CIA because he heard Morse typing from my parents' house. My father was investigated by the police. He said, "All I did was use a typewriter" but they told him "You have to hand the typewriter in," so he did. So one after another event gradually revealed the way the government intimidated citizens, and since we were southerners and not directly involved in the "just cause" [the communist cause] we felt very much like second-class citizens. My father started to rethink the ideals of socialism and at that time in 1977, we had to register either as *Viet* or *Kinh* [ethnic Vietnamese] or as *nguoi Hoa* [ethnic Chinese] and my family put *nguoi Hoa* and we were discriminated against. At university, my class was the first class of Art History in the reunited Vietnam. We were told that we would be sent to Hanoi. I was the first student in every subject, politics, history, art history, and English, and when the list was declared my name was not on it [laughs]. It was only later on that I realized that it was because I'd said I was ethnic Chinese in my CV. So you know my belief, my utopian belief in socialism started to fall apart just like that, like ice melting under the summer heat. That's why I wanted to escape.

Tran provides a striking illustration of war and the destruction wrought by war in the closing days of South Vietnam. Her literary interests are evident in her allusion to the destruction of Troy in Euripides' *The Trojan Women*. The political consequences of life under the northern regime became apparent when the authorities closed down her family's bookshops and confiscated their contents. Her narrative reveals that father and daughter initially believed in the ideals of communism, and wanted to adapt to a brave new socialist world after the end of the war. Successive events, however, and the extent of state repression after 1975, were soon to disabuse them of those illusions. The final straw for the family was the discrimination directed against ethnic Chinese in the late 1970s. This was to lead Tran and her family to make two attempts to escape from the country.

As for Le, she recalls that war suddenly intruded into her life in 1975:

That day one of the stores on the other side of the street had smoke coming out the windows, it was hit by gunfire or something so that's how the fire started. The whole market was built of timber and burned. Then late in the afternoon, smoke started coming inside the shop, I lost my voice and it was so hot and people were yelling: "*Le oi!* You have to get out of the house now, your house is burning!" So we quickly threw a few things together. I had a few photos of my mother and we got a blanket and that was all. I had to help Truong [the old man] to walk. He had asthma, and he couldn't breathe. We could hear people running and shouting, and the sound of shooting outside in the streets, it was very scary.

For two nights the whole market block was just like a sea of fire and the smell of salted fish was everywhere. The next morning, you could hear the fighting reach the other side of the street. Then came loud knocking at every household. It was the Viet Cong, the *bo doi*. They said: "Get out of the house, get out of the house!" So for the first time in my life I saw a *bo doi*. Many of them seemed very young. They were dressed in black, holding guns, and telling us: "Get out, get out, this way, this way." We were told to walk to a remote area outside the town. On the road I saw dead bodies and dead animals. Young men and their fathers and brothers were kept aside, and wives and kids were crying because they got separated. I was crying too but Truong, he was old and sick so he was allowed to go on and so we kept walking with a group of people from that area that we knew. We walked fast you know, we kept walking very fast and crying. After two hours, we arrived at a place with a storeroom where we could stay. Truong had a little storage space to hide his opium. Our next-door neighbours were Teochew people and we ended up staying with them. They were making rice wine and had lots and lots of old rice for making the wine. They stopped making the wine and used the old rice for cooking.

Le reconstructs the events of 1975, the fire that engulfed the market area where they lived, the arrival of northern troops—the *bo doi*—people being forcibly removed from their houses and being marched in groups outside the town, and men being separated from the women and children, and taken away. Le's narrative conveys the shock of that experience, and the sense of disorientation that affected townspeople as the war, which, until then, they had mostly experienced at a remove, erupted into their neighborhood, bringing with it destruction, separation from their menfolk, and displacement from their homes. Buon Ma Thuot was encircled by communist forces and fell on March 11, 1975.[10] Despite this experience, however, like Tran and her father, Le and "the old man" were hopeful that all would be well under a reunified Vietnam. As she relates:

> Before 1974, Truong often listened to communist broadcasts from the Chinese mainland, so he believed in the communists even before 1975, and he said: "It's a good thing, under the communists, everybody is equal, no rich people, no bullying, no racism." And I thought, "Oh my God I wish my mother were still alive, she would be so happy."

The reality of life in postwar Vietnam, however, with its political and ethnic tensions, was to disrupt these beliefs.

POSTWAR LIVES

Hoang's life was subjected to dramatic changes after 1975. After the arrest and detention of her father, and her expulsion from the university, she made the decision to escape from Vietnam with her husband. She was able to see her father once more before she left the country, and describes visiting him in prison:

> In 1977, after the birth of our first child, we decided to try to escape Vietnam. We asked to see my father again to discuss moving to the New Economic Zones and handing the house over to the Viet Cong. It was only then that they let us visit him. We were asked to wait in a little room and two soldiers led my father in. My mother went over to the soldiers and offered them some sugarcane juice while I whispered to him that I was planning to escape from the country. My father told me that it was a good idea but that I must be careful not to get caught. Then my mother came back to our seat and from then on, we could not say anything

anymore. We only did small talk for ten minutes. After that, I successfully escaped from Vietnam and came here but my father was still in prison.

Hoang's first years in her new country were marked by hardship, isolation, and the de-skilling and downward mobility that many refugees and migrants were subjected to. De-skilling was widespread in Vietnamese diasporic communities in Australia, Canada, France, and the United States.[11] She remembers:

It was really tough. The first job that I was referred to was at an abattoir in Flemington. All my life, I had never harmed or killed any living thing. When I saw the meat, the slaughter, I was terrified. I ran out of the place and never came back. I was then referred to an ice cream factory. It was winter at the time. I did not have sufficient warm clothes to wear. I had no car. Every morning, I woke up at 4 o'clock; I had to prepare the food and clothes for my son to go to childcare. I did not have money to buy disposable nappies for him so had to use cloth ones instead. I had to walk to the train station, take the train then walk from the station to the factory. The uniforms provided were too big for me. I had to wear rubber boots like firemen. With a university education, having to work in a factory was very depressing for me. My weekly wage was only $105; I had to pay $45 for childcare. The childcare centre closed earlier than my working hours so I had to pay another $10 for the extended hours. I received a letter from my mother asking me whether I was still continuing with my medical studies. She imagined me wearing a white coat like a doctor. I cried when I read her letter. I got so upset that I did not focus on my work and the ice cream spilled all over the bin. My supervisor rushed to my spot yelling, "What happened?" When he saw my red eyes, he calmed down. He told me to go and wash my face. He gave me an aspirin to calm my nerves. Then he asked me whether someone had done or said something to upset me. He was worried that I might be the victim of workplace bullying. I told him that I was depressed. Every three months, I sent money to my mother so that she could buy supplies for my father in prison.

I arrived here as a refugee. I know that there are many people who are less fortunate. As a refugee living in Australia, I'd like to show to the rest of the Australian community that Vietnamese refugees are decent people. We are here to contribute to society. We don't want to be a burden to society.

I was extremely sad at the news of my father's death. He taught me everything. He ensured that I had the best education that I ever wished for. He taught me to treat everyone with respect whether they were rich or poor. He encouraged me to treat people whether they could pay or not. I think I inherited characteristics from both parents. Here in Australia, I am a Home and Community Care worker; I help the Vietnamese elderly and the disabled to lead independent and dignified lives.

Hoang's retelling interweaves her personal losses with the loss of her country. The bright future that she had envisaged for herself was destroyed by the collapse of South Vietnam in 1975. Her narrative shifts from a coming-of-age story to one of suffering and endurance. The former medical student and musician became a refugee and an unskilled worker in an Australian factory. Her account reveals that her depression over her condition was made worse by her mother's continued hopes for her. She provides a portrait of her breakdown and the reaction of a sympathetic supervisor at the factory. Her father's death served to underline the scale of all that she had lost. Her words, however, also convey the fact that his example helped to sustain and inspire her in her later life and work.

As for Tran, she made two failed escape attempts in 1977 and 1978. She tried to leave Vietnam by boat and then by land. Her family could not afford any other attempts so she had to resign herself to making the best of her postwar circumstances. She became a teacher at Dong Nai Art School. Her adolescent dream of winning a scholarship and going overseas eventually became true, but not until twenty years after the momentous events of 1975. She refers to the element of "fate" in the way her life eventuated:

> I went to Australia the first time in January 1995 and it was also the first time I had travelled overseas after two escape attempts and after dreaming of studying overseas since I was fourteen years old. If South Vietnam hadn't collapsed in 1975 . . . had it collapsed say four months later my fate would have been very different.

She completed her graduate studies in Australia, and her life is one that is closely linked to the arts and the art world. She reflects in the following way on her sense of belonging in her new country:

> This is my present and my future. After my first semester here, I went back to Vietnam and I didn't feel that I belonged to Vietnam anymore. I don't know if it's because I read many Western novels before I read Vietnamese novels or because as a person, a curious person, I found that Australia offers everyone a chance whereas in Vietnam everything must

be in a box. You are born Chinese Vietnamese you're stuck in that box, you're born in a *bourgeois* family, you're stuck in that box, you're born a southerner, you're stuck in that box, and I hate that. To me Vietnam has too many restrictions that I just can't stand. Vietnam as a country is a lovely place, but as a regime, as a nation, there are so many things wrong there that need to be corrected. I don't know if a revolution or gradual reforms could improve the country . . . you know it's just like with horses, people have to cover part of the eyes of the horse so that the horse can go straight, and Vietnamese people have part of their eyes covered by the Party and government so that they can only see one way, they don't have any other options. To me Australia provides other options, Australia provides alternatives and I like that fact, I like living in Australia.

As a Vietnamese who was not able to leave her country until the 1990s, she is also critical of the lack of acceptance that some of these later migrants have met from the earlier waves of refugees in the 1970s and 1980s:

Those who see all the Vietnamese coming out of Vietnam recently as Viet Cong, that is a very wrong assessment, because living in Vietnam was not our choice. If we could have had a choice we would have picked another country. You must have heard of the saying: "If everyone had a choice then the electric poles would walk out of Vietnam too."[12] I would have left if I could have. I tried my best and my family with all eight children but after two attempts, we ran out of resources full stop, and we were stuck there.

In my first year of residency in Australia, I had nightmares all the time. I saw myself being arrested and interrogated by the police or questioned by my colleagues in Vietnam or losing my passport and being late for the plane. And then I'd wake up at 3 or 4 o'clock in the morning and think, "I'm in Australia thank goodness." In Vietnam, I'd lived with trauma for so long, I'd dealt with suppression for so long. I didn't say a word about the loss of my parents' business. Who could I talk to? What could I say? I couldn't trust anyone. So all the losses stayed inside, just like an infection.

Tran's narrative reflects in essence a series of quests, with an underlying objective that she did eventually reach. She tried twice to reshape her life in the postwar years: first, by adapting to life under the new regime; and second, by joining the mass movement of refugees leaving the country. It was the third reshaping that finally would enable her to

fulfil, after two decades, her dreams of completing her education overseas. The cost of those intervening years is evident in her recounting of
the nightmares and insomnia she suffered from after she left the country, and her belief that these were delayed reactions to the suppressed
traumas of her postwar life.

Le, for her part, joined a performing troupe after the end of the war.
Her narrative describes the political indoctrination that she and other
young performers were subjected to:

> I love music, that's why I joined the troupe, because I love art and music
> and dancing and all of that. And in the beginning, the songs were the
> old songs from the jungle, and were really strong in spirit. When I first
> joined the troupe, I had no idea about politics, although during the war
> I saw American soldiers walking past shops, big, tall, white or black
> Americans, and sometimes I ate their biscuits and tin foods. When I
> joined the troupe we had classes, and they taught us about how bad the
> South Vietnamese government and the Americans were, and used words
> like *nguy* (renegade) and *dich* (enemy). So we thought of the worst
> things to say about the old government, and good things to say about
> Ho Chi Minh and North Vietnamese heroes. And then we learnt to sing
> and perform on stage. Of course my friends hated me and avoided me.
> They called me names like *bo doi*.
>
> In '75, in the early years, we were taught that China and Vietnam
> were like brothers, they were "close like lips and teeth." And then in
> 1978, those teeth and lips were biting each other. China and Vietnam
> had war on their border. And during that time, those of us with Chinese
> blood had trouble. You know that at that time, there were loudspeakers
> everywhere, just about on every street corner and in every workplace. It
> didn't matter if you wanted to listen or not, it was loud in your ears and
> you could hear the news about China and Vietnam fighting. It was terri-
> ble, really terrible. People said, "You bastards. Chinese people are
> bastards." There were songs about this. I was given a song about "You
> bastards," and I couldn't sing it. I just stood there and cried. Some peo-
> ple hated me and one of the other performers gave me a hard time and
> any time the speaker was on she said: "Why don't you just get out of my
> face, you bastard," and I'd cry in my mosquito net at night. I remember
> one time, we were travelling in the North, and that day we had to serve
> a group of people from Russia. It was around '79, '80. I had to learn Rus-
> sian and [East] German songs and other songs I didn't know the meaning
> of. I just memorized the sounds by heart. I was upset, I was crying, but
> somehow I found strength from within, maybe from my mother. Anyway

I did my best performance on that day, singing to those Russian people. And they came up and asked especially for me. Other people like the boss or the director or the mayor in the Central Highlands were all very kind to me.

I left Vietnam when my husband's family sponsored us. The papers started in 1982 or 1983, and took a few years to get done. I was very sad because performing was my passion, and also I didn't have a good marriage. Later on domestic violence came into my life.

Le's words reveal that she was able to carve a new life for herself after 1975. Her account relates that neither she nor her fellow performers paid much heed to the political implications of their work. It was only when war broke out between China and Vietnam that ethnic and political tensions came to the fore. As Le narrates, this attitude affected her, even in her relatively sheltered position in a government troupe. The troupe, however, signified not only a career but also a way of life for her. By 1985, she had spent nearly half her life—ten years—as a troupe performer. Membership in the troupe allowed her to express her love of music and provided her with a sense of belonging. Her account makes it clear that although she left the country in 1985 after being sponsored by her husband's family, it grieved her to do so, since it meant the end of her performing work. She has the following reflections of adjusting to her new life in Australia, a life that has been marked by personal setbacks but one that has also granted her fresh insights into artistic freedom of expression:

When I first came here, I struggled a lot against racism. That's why my art is about anti-racism and the human condition, it's like a healing for me to do this kind of art. For more than twenty years I've watched Australia growing. People are more accepting, more tolerant and more understanding towards each other even though there are still groups who have a negative attitude towards other people. Australia is such a beautiful country. It has so much to give. There are so many good people here, people who've brought their experiences from other countries and also their understanding. It's like a great contribution, creating a beautiful picture out of all these little things.

Vietnam will always be a special place in my heart—the people, the music, the culture. When I hear about people there being suppressed by another culture, like people from North Vietnam coming to the Central Highlands, taking over the land, chopping down trees and destroying the forests. . . . Highlanders wouldn't be Highlanders without forests or trees and they've been pushed to the edge of Vietnamese society. I feel very sad about that and I want to say something about it in my art. I don't know what I can do for refugees. I can't give them a visa, but at least their voices, their faith, and their suffering can travel around the country through my art.

I went back to Vietnam for the first time in 2002, seventeen years after I'd left. It's still a strong place for me but I knew I couldn't live there as an artist. I need freedom to express myself and I wouldn't have that kind of freedom in Vietnam. And I was kidding myself that I could live there and work as if I was in Australia, but that's impossible. Now I feel Australia is my home. The word "my place" is very strong in my heart.

Le's narrative reveals that the one constant element in her life throughout these turmoils has been her art. Music and art provided forms of therapy for her. Her early life was marked by successive losses, and her postwar experiences were marred by the ethnic tensions of the late 1970s. She has had to rebuild her life several times: after her mother's death, following the collapse of South Vietnam in 1975, and after her migration overseas. In Australia, she acknowledges that she has the freedom to fully express herself, as well as her political beliefs, through her artwork.

NARRATIVES AND TESTIMONIES

The women's narratives illustrate personal stories of loss and displacement that are encompassed within a wider collective framework of loss. The collapse of South Vietnam signified not only a national tragedy but also one that had its repercussions in the lives of individuals and families. Its echoes continue to be felt in the Vietnamese diaspora today. The narratives explored here reveal lives that were marked not only by major traumas such as war and postwar repression, but also by a series of cumulative adversities. The women's life histories reveal the damage caused by these traumas, and the grief and regrets that they engendered. They illustrate life paths that were interrupted and fractured by succeeding tragedies, and that had to be rebuilt and then rebuilt again. Like Lam's "Lost Photos," the women's acts of remembrance are a means of transmuting past lives, past hopes, and past losses into testimonies. "Where the state has claimed a monopoly of truth," as Vieda Skultans notes in *The Testimony of Lives*, "individual lives bear witness against the state."[13]

Most people in South Vietnam tried to make the best of their changed circumstances after 1975. After thirty years of war, they did not want to leave their native land, and they hoped to adapt to life in a reunified Vietnam. It was only when the state imposed repressive measures that southerners began to reassess their choices. The postwar years saw the restriction of free speech and movement, and the curtailment of religious and artistic liberties.[14] More than 1 million former soldiers, civil servants, and teachers were subjected to "re-education."[15] The regime executed more than 65,000 citizens.[16] Another million were forcibly de-urbanized and relocated to the New Economic Zones.[17] The regime nationalized businesses and industries, collectivized agriculture, imposed currency reform, and confiscated much private property.[18] Chinese businesses and schools were closed down in 1976, and Chinese Vietnamese had to register their citizenship.[19] The families of those related to the former South Vietnamese government were discriminated against in terms of education and employment, as were those of ethnic Chinese and Amerasians.[20] Family networks were disrupted or ruptured as relatives disappeared in re-education camps, the New Economic Zones, or as escapees. By the middle of 1979, more than 700,000 people had left Vietnam.[21] These factors, along with Vietnam's invasion of Cambodia in 1978 and border war with China in 1979, contributed to the destabilization and erosion of southern society.[22] Communism, which, until the war's end, had remained a largely nebulous concept for many South Vietnamese, became manifest in its material cruelties, and it is at this point that the mass exodus from Vietnam truly got under way. As Tran's narrative reveals, for all those who escaped overseas, many more gave up after repeated failures or perished. In the final analysis, despite widely differing backgrounds and divergent life stories, the women's resilience in reconstructing their lives after repeated traumas, and to do so in a diasporic context, forms the common thread binding these narratives.

"Remembering," writes David Gross, "enables one to see . . . roads not taken in one's life, possibilities cut short, potentialities left undeveloped. Memory permits an individual not simply to visit again these futures that did not happen, but actively take them up once more if one so chooses."[23] The act of remembrance and its ability to revisit possibilities stifled and futures lost distinguish the narratives of the first two women, Hoang and Tran. Hoang lost her father, her home, her country, and her hopes of a medical career. As she states, "April 30th was a momentous day for Vietnam and for me. I lost my motherland and I lost my family."

Her narrative circles back constantly to April 1975 as the catalyst to the losses in her life, describing, in the words of Toni Morrison, "circles and circles of sorrow."[24] This elliptical structure reflects the centrality of this tragedy in her memory. Although Hoang was able to escape the country with her husband and child, and survive a twenty-day journey at sea, her early years overseas were marked by privation and depression. Her narrative reveals that she still perceives herself as a refugee living in another country. It expresses a lingering malaise about her place in her new country, a country in which she does not want to be "a burden to society." Her words imply that the refugee experience undermined her sense of place and belonging, and that she is still not fully "at home" in her new land. The three great markers of her life are all associated with tragedies in Vietnam: her grandfather's assassination when she was three, her country's collapse when she was twenty-six, and her father's death in prison when she was thirty-four. Her narrative indicates that she still grieves for him. His death is linked in her memory with the loss of her homeland, and with the death of her early dreams and hopes. Yet, as her words reveal, it is also her memory of him, and the work ethics that he instilled in her, that have enabled her to persevere in her efforts to reconstruct her life. Although she was never able to complete her medical studies, she is working in the health and welfare sector. Her life story draws a continuing thread between her work for disabled veterans in Vietnam during the war and her care for the elderly and disabled in contemporary Australia. In this way, she acknowledges the strengths that were imparted to her by her father, and her desire to pay tribute to his memory.

As for Tran, she and her family experienced firsthand the regime's "Campaign to exterminate decadent literature" in 1975–1976, during which time books and newspapers were confiscated or burnt, and South Vietnamese writers, intellectuals, and artists were arrested and sent to prison camps.[25] One of the first acts of the campaign was the destruction of the well-known Khai Tri publishing house in Saigon and the arrest of its general manager.[26] The suppression of "decadent material," including music and film tapes, was still ongoing in May 1981, when the Executive Committee of the Ho Chi Minh Party Committee launched a three-day campaign across eleven districts that resulted in the seizure of "more than 2,500 phonograph records and cassettes, dozens of movie reels, and over four tons of reactionary books."[27] Even though the regime closed down her parents' bookshops and took away all the books, Tran reveals wryly that she was "brainwashed" by communist propaganda after the war, and especially after she began her tertiary education. Her narrative implies that many others were similarly "brainwashed." It was only following a succession of incidents involving the authorities (her father was also accused of "supplying rice to the enemy hiding in the jungle" after he had bought a ten-kilogram bag of rice to live on in the New Economic Zones) that the full realization of what life under Vietnam's communist regime entailed finally set in. The loss of the bookshops clearly resonated with her. Its importance is reflected in the structure of her narrative, in which she refers periodically to this incident and to other instances of discrimination on the part of the regime. These act as reminders of the reasons why she sought to leave the country. Throughout the privations and injustices of the postwar years, Tran never quite lost sight of her dreams of studying overseas, and this underlying sense of purpose provides a framework for her life story. Her narrative reveals how much she had chafed under the political constraints of Vietnam's postwar regime, and the lengths to which she went to conceal and suppress the extent of her losses. She makes a clear distinction between Vietnam's culture and the politics of the postwar government, and she articulates her appreciation of the freedoms that life in Australia has afforded her.

Le, for her part, had a life marked by a succession of tragedies. She lost her family at a young age, witnessed the destruction and death of war when Buon Ma Thuot fell to communist forces in 1975, found transitory happiness in working for a government troupe in the postwar years, and then was faced with a series of adversities after migration. Her narrative illustrates that, as a child, she dealt with grief by seeking refuge in books and in creative expression, and this creative urge forms the central trope of her life. It explains why she joined a performing troupe after the war, and why she was later reluctant to leave the country. The troupe provided her with a sense of community after the loss of both parents and the isolated life that she and "the old man" were living. She was eleven years old when the war ended, and her narrative relates that she and other young members of the troupe were swayed by the fervor of revolutionary songs and were happy to chant slogans from the new regime. In this they were not alone: many Vietnamese who were children in the postwar years remember enthusiastically singing songs to "Uncle Ho" at school (while their parents were planning to escape the country). As one of the women explained,

> As a child, I have to say that I was somehow "brainwashed." I was excited about singing all the propaganda songs at the time, all the pro-communist songs. I didn't really know what I was singing—I loved the opportunity of being with the peer group, so I did everything other kids did. I loved *Bac Ho* (Uncle Ho) [laughs]. I didn't feel as if I was betraying my grandfather and uncle who were in re-education camps, I didn't think about that at the time—I was just caught up in the moment.[28]

For Le, this creative urge was an adaptive measure that enabled her to deal with her mother's death, adjust to the changes in postwar Vietnam, the pressures of immigration and resettlement in Australia in the mid-1980s, and a series of abusive relationships in her adult life. Migration features in her life history as another challenge to overcome, and one that was followed by significant personal losses. She escaped an abusive marriage, her son was taken away from her for a number of years, and she recently suffered another major loss when her Australian partner died unexpectedly of a heart attack. However, her narrative also reveals that migration has allowed her the space and freedom to fully express her beliefs through her art and to articulate her advocacy of the minority peoples of Vietnam's Central Highlands. Her story ends, as it begins, with the Central Highlands, demonstrating in this way the importance of the Highlands as a reference point in her memory and consciousness.

"Narrative," suggest Lewis and Sandra Hinchman, "emphasizes the active, self-shaping quality of human thought, the power of stories to create and refashion personal identity."[29] For both Hoang and Tran, the reappropriation of the past has enabled them not only to identify the paths that they did not take and the projects that were derailed by the larger traumas of 1975, but also to acknowledge the determination and fortitude that saw them reconstruct their lives in the aftermath of war and displacement, and to recapture, even if in damaged form, a portion of their earlier hopes and visions. For Le, the act of re-memory has allowed her to articulate her true vocation and to recognize the unexpected gifts that migration to Australia has brought her. Lost photographs, lost loved ones, and lost futures live on in the memories and narratives of these three women, transmuted into the resilience and creative energy essential to rebuilding shattered lives.

CHAPTER 2

Sisters and Memories

Sibling relationships are among the most pervasive in life.[1] Exploring the memories of siblings regarding their shared pasts is therefore likely to uncover a rich source of perceptions, recreations, and insights that stretch over their lifetimes. In this chapter, I examine the memories of two sisters who escaped from Vietnam in 1978 and lost their only brother at sea during the journey. A third sister also escaped successfully but has since died of breast cancer. The remaining two sisters therefore remember not only their brother, who disappeared at sea nearly thirty years ago, but also their sister, who had shared the experience of diaspora with them. The different perceptions of these two women, their retellings of their family story, and their memories of loss, embody not only individual reactions to significant and traumatic events of the past, but also individual interpretations and communications of this shared past. The events of the past influence the present, and the present in turn shapes memories of the past. As Katharine Hodgkin and Susannah Radstone note, "contests over the meaning of the past are also contests over the meaning of the present and over ways of taking the past forward."[2] The women's recollections interconnect and diverge at different points. Their retellings crisscross and shape each other to paint a multifaceted portrait of sibling relationships, the experience of exodus, the pain of loss, and the challenges of moving on in the lives of these women.

Within families, sisters usually share the longest relationships. As the following observation by Monica McGoldrick suggests,

The relationships in life that last the longest are those between sisters. Our parents usually die a generation before we do, and our children live on for a generation after us. Our spouses rarely know us for our first 20 or 30 years, and it is rare for friendships to last from earliest childhood until the very end of our lives. Thus, our siblings share more of our lives genetically and contextually than anyone else, and sisters even more, since sisters live longer than brothers.[3]

Siblings often remember the past differently, depending on their personality and characteristics, their position in the family hierarchy, their gender, and the family's structure and circumstances at any given point in time.[4] Their memories reveal distinct approaches to understanding past selves and histories, as well as the history of their family. Differences in perceptions "don't invalidate an account," writes Marcia Millman, "in fact, they offer especially valuable information because they suggest that the speaker is driven primarily by wishes and illusions, which is crucial to understanding anyone's behavior."[5] When siblings have experienced major upheavals in the form of war, loss of country, and exodus, their memories convey individual recreations and interpretations of shared events, as well as their family dynamics. They also, however, situate the siblings' experiences within a wider framework of collective loss and mourning. In such a context, memory can reveal broken and traumatic pasts. Yet memory can be empowering, in that "it may also be an agent for reshaping and reinvention of that past into more acceptable shapes."[6] For those who seek to reconstruct their lives, this ability to reshape memories is a positive and affirmative means of dealing with the traumas of the past.

The siblings who are the subject of this chapter were born in southern Vietnam: Anh, the eldest, in 1943; Kiet, the only boy, in 1946; Nga in 1949; and Suong in 1952. Their mother died of tuberculosis when Anh was eleven. Their father was a businessman and remarried twice after their mother's death. The siblings were close as children, and remained close as young adults. Anh was a pharmacist, Kiet and Nga worked in the family business, and Suong, the youngest, studied law at Saigon University. The fall of Saigon and the collapse of South Vietnam in 1975 proved to be a watershed for the family, initiating a chain of events that led to the siblings' escape by boat in 1978, Kiet's death at sea, the sisters' stay in refugee camps in Malaysia and Thailand, and their eventual resettlement in Australia. Their father died in Vietnam in 1987, and Nga died of cancer in Australia in 2004. The two surviving sisters are Anh and Suong, the oldest and the youngest, and it is their narratives that are examined here.

Vietnamese society is strongly family centered. David Haines' study of kinship in South Vietnamese households between 1954 and 1975, a time span that covers the family life of these sisters in southern Vietnam, reveals a close degree of relationships between siblings, with a third having contact with a sibling on a daily basis, and three quarters on at least a monthly basis.[7] Sisters and brothers were as likely to be close as siblings of the same sex.[8] For the Vietnamese siblings whose stories form the focus of this chapter, the relationship acquires additional significance since it is one that is marked and tested by the experience of exodus, loss, trauma, and migration. For they lost not only their home and homeland, and what James Freeman terms "meaningful sources of identity,"[9] they also lost two of their siblings.

In Vietnamese literary culture, sibling relations are often portrayed in a traumatic framework. One of the best-known stories of sibling devotion is that of "The Betel and the Areca," in which two devoted brothers fall in love with the same girl.[10] One brother marries her, and the other pines and eventually leaves home. He reaches the banks of a river, dies and turns into a stone. The remaining brother is heartbroken and goes in search of his sibling. He reaches the shores of the same river and also dies. He is turned into a tree (the areca). His wife in the meantime searches in turn for him, and she too dies by the river and is turned into a vine (the betel). Together, their stories symbolize brotherly and spousal devotion. The stone crumbles when heated and is mixed with the areca nut and the crushed leaves of the betel to produce a red paste that initially was chewed by newlyweds or siblings as a sign of felicity and affection, and whose usage then quickly spread.

As for sisterly relations, the most famous historical example is that of the Trung sisters, who led a rebellion against the Chinese in 40 C.E. Although the rebellion was short-lived and the two women died three years later, the sisters had succeeded in defying the Han Dynasty. They "were immortalized in song and story"[11] and came to symbolize national independence and pride. A striking literary evocation of sisterly devotion is that between the sisters Kieu and Van, the central female protagonists of Nguyen Du's great nineteenth-century classic *The Tale of Kieu.*[12] Here, too, the sisters' stories are set within a context of separation and grief. Both sisters are models of beauty and virtue, and when the older sister Kieu sells herself into prostitution to save their father from debtor's prison, she begs her younger sister Van to marry her fiancé Kim in her stead. Van fulfils her sister's pledge and marries Kim. When, after many years of trials and tribulations, Kieu finally returns to her family, Van tells her sister of the years of waiting and grieving, and advises her that it is time for her to marry Kim at last:

> Day after day, we hoped and prayed for Kieu—
> with so much love and grief these fifteen years.
> But now the mirror cracked is whole again:
> wise Heaven's put her back where she belongs.
> She still loves him and, luckily, still has him—
> still shines the same old moon both once swore by.
> The tree still bears some three or seven plums,
> the peach stays fresh—it's time to tie the knot![13]

Kieu does marry her former love, but she insists on the relationship remaining unconsummated. It is her sister Van who bears Kim's children. The two sisters and Kim form a felicitous three-way relationship that enjoys "weal and wealth,"[14] a relationship that points not only to the polygamous nature of the society portrayed but also to the continued attachment of the sisters toward each other. These stories and tales illustrate examples of sibling devotion that endure even parting and death.

Writing about the relationship between sisters in 1993, the writer Helen Garner refers to the "imagined map" of her family and notes that "[i]t was unsettling to learn that each sister has her own quite individual map of that territory: the mountains and rivers are in different places, the borders are differently constituted and guarded, the history and politics and justice system of the country are different, according to who's talking."[15] These individual maps that characterize each sister's memory and experiences, are, in the case of the two Vietnamese sisters discussed in this chapter, also strongly marked by the impact of diaspora. The maps track the sisters' geographic journeys from their homeland across the sea to other Southeast Asian countries, and then finally to Australia. They trace the sisters' metaphorical journeys through life's reverses and challenges. Their individual and family stories unfold within the wider narrative of the Vietnamese exodus, and their personal losses within the wider context of loss of homeland.

The sisters' narratives are remarkable in that they reveal not only where their memories converge or diverge in relation to specific episodes in the past, but also the extent to which pivotal events remained unspoken in the family.[16] The sisters recollect their early lives in Vietnam, as well as their later lives overseas. They speak of the memories of those they have lost: their brother, father, and sister. And yet much of their familial interactions are characterized by silence. Siblings remained silent about central events in each other's lives, either because to speak was too painful or too difficult, or because silence allowed a measure of control over events and was judged to be the best way to protect a loved one. Silence emerges as one of the most striking aspects of family connectedness. This may seem contradictory, but as these narratives will reveal, silence indicated solidarity and love, as well as the desire to control and to hide. I will explore three central events that illustrate each sister's interpretation of the past, and the texture and shape of the silences in their lives.

FAMILY DRAMA

The first event occurred in 1968 or 1969. Anh remembers the clashes that occurred between the middle sister, Nga, and their stepmother, clashes that were severe enough to lead to the following:

It affected Suong, and she attempted suicide in her last year in high school, because she was upset about this family clash. She took medication (Tylenol) and was in a coma for at least ten days. She was in the hospital for a few months and she did her Baccalaureate exam while she was still in the hospital.

My father was very upset about this, because he wanted a happy family, and when this happened, he saw it as some sort of failure on his part. We practically lived in the hospital with her. At first it was a public hospital, but then they put her in bed no. 13 [which the family considered unlucky], so we took her to a private hospital—she was still unconscious at that stage. She was in a coma for quite a while, ten days or a few weeks. At that time I was studying Pharmacy at the university. And Kiet went to Binh Trieu, a shrine to the Lady of Fatima, and he took some holy water back to Suong. And she recovered and did the exam. Maybe she doesn't remember any of this. Even after she recovered consciousness, she had to stay for a long time in the hospital, because she developed gangrene from lying down for so long. We were worried that she wouldn't recover and we all prayed. We were a Buddhist family.

After this, Kiet, Nga and I showed more affection towards Suong and we were more considerate towards her. When you almost lose someone, you regret that you didn't do more for them. It brought us all closer in a way.

Suong's account of the same event differs considerably from her sister's. She relates:

> I have to say that I had a very good and peaceful childhood. I felt very protected because I was the youngest one, and our mother died very early. She was about forty-two when she died and I was two and a half. Everyone just poured their love and attention into me, so I was actually a spoilt little girl, and when I went to primary school, I didn't do very well [laughs].
>
> I started to become interested in study at a later stage, and surprisingly, I did very well in secondary level. The system there was the Baccalaureate Parts 1 and 2. You did Part 1 at the end of Year 11 and Part 2 at the end of Year 12. So I did Year 11 when I was sixteen, and just a few months before I sat the exam, I had a terrible accident, and nearly died, so my family didn't think that I could go to the exam at all.
>
> I had a car accident and a head injury, so was unconscious for several weeks, or several days, I can't remember now, so my family prayed and went to a place called Binh Trieu on the outskirts of Saigon, and well, people believe that Our Lady of Fatima appeared there once, and since then they have gone there to take holy water home to cure their relatives, and my brother did the same and brought back a bottle of holy water and applied some to my face, and the day after that I woke up [laughs], and everything was intact, including my brain, so then a few days later I started to study for the exam, because I was determined to sit for it, and nobody had any real hope for me, but I did it and did very well, and then moved on to Year 12. I did very well in my final exams and was approved to go to Belgium to study medicine.

The sisters' narratives converge on a number of aspects: that Suong was unconscious in hospital for several days or a few weeks, that the family prayed for her, and that her brother Kiet went to the shrine of Our Lady of Fatima and brought back holy water, which he gave to Suong, and which led to her return to consciousness and recovery. Suong then went on to study for and do the Baccalaureate exam. The sisters therefore relate the same chain of events that culminated in Suong waking from her coma, and then successfully sitting for her exam (although Suong specifies that it was at the end of Year 11, while Anh remembers that it was in Suong's last year at high school, but this is a minor point). Where their narratives diverge radically is in the stated cause of Suong's coma, and their reactions to her illness and recovery. Anh relates that Suong attempted suicide by taking an overdose of pills, and that this was the result of tensions within the family. Suong, on the other hand, remembers her family as being close and loving, and her coma the result of a car accident. Her main concern was to make sure that she succeeded in her exams, since they eventually led to study overseas.

This family near-tragedy stayed in Anh's mind because it highlighted problematic issues within the family relating to their father and stepmother, their father's expectations, tensions between Nga and their stepmother, and finally the fact that this state of affairs was fraught enough to have led to the attempted suicide of the youngest, Suong. Suong's gesture brought these familial issues into the open. Anh's reactions, and those of Nga, Kiet, and their father, are characterized by self-blame and guilt. As Suong's elders, they believed that they had failed her. They should have played closer attention to her, and they should have been aware of her distress. For Anh, Suong's illness was an important family milestone because it brought the siblings and their father closer together. The outcome of this event was a positive one, since all the siblings rallied to their sister's side ("we practically lived in the hospital," says Anh), and the father realized that he had expected too much of the relationship between stepmother and stepchildren.

For Suong, this event was pivotal because she "nearly died." The cause of her coma is remembered as an accident, and passed over quickly, because its sequel was of so much greater import to her. She not only survived, but she more than compensated for her illness by triumphing at her exams. In their work *Contested Pasts*, Katharine Hodgkin and Susannah Radstone note that "if at times people claim memories of what never happened, or happened other than how they remember it, this does not mean their memories are invalid or irrelevant, but that different questions need to be asked."[17] This is what I would now like to do in relation to the sisters' memories, and the reasons why each sister needs to remember the same event so differently.

Anh's reconstruction of the cause of Suong's coma is plausible. She has no reason to create such a story. It was an incident that affected the entire family and brought tensions between the stepmother and stepchildren to the fore. It allowed the father and his four children to draw closer together (the stepmother features only on the periphery of this narrative). As the oldest child, Anh clearly felt a strong sense of responsibility toward her youngest sister, and she describes the feelings of guilt that not only affected her but also her father, Kiet, and Nga. They felt that they "should have done more" for Suong. On the other hand, Suong's memory of the incident also makes admirable sense from her point of view and fits within a narrative that emphasizes a positive and constructive approach to life. For Suong, the cause of her coma is dwarfed by its consequences, and by the fact that she was able to present a story of triumph over adversity. In this context, the silence in the family surrounding Suong's attempted suicide is explained by her father and siblings focusing their energies on helping her to recover fully from her long illness. It was a silence driven by love and the desire to protect. And with Suong's recovery, the passage of time, and the other major events that affected the life of the family, the cause of Suong's coma did not come up for discussion. Anh's narrative reveals that she is fully aware of the fact that Suong may have been too ill to remember what had happened. As for Suong, her memory of events may have been the result of the trauma that she suffered, but also reflects a plausible interpretation of what may have led to her coma and hospitalization. Her reconstruction prioritizes her family's support for her, her remarkable recovery, and her scholarly accomplishments. As Hodgkin and Radstone remind us, "memory itself covers up: it reshapes, attempts to comfort, addresses changing needs."[18]

Anh reveals that the family's desire to protect Suong extended to another incident, in which the three older siblings conspired to bring Suong home from Belgium a couple of years later, on the pretext that their father was ill. Anh relates:

> We didn't want her to stay overseas, we were concerned about her, about her staying alone in Belgium, so we, Nga, Kiet and me, we decided to call her back to Vietnam. We told her that our father was sick, but in fact he wasn't. We just did it so that she would come back.
>
> Looking back now, it seems to have been a childish thing to do, that we called her back because we wanted her in Vietnam again. If she had stayed in Belgium and completed her studies there, her life would have been very different after 1975, she could have married a Vietnamese man there, she could have lived in Belgium, you never know. But after her stay in hospital, she truly became our baby sister. We cherished her and wanted her home, so we all, all three of us, Nga, Kiet and me, we planned this and got her home. I don't know whether she remembers this or remembers why we called her back.

Suong, for her part, gives the following account:

> I decided to go to Lièges a few months before the start of the university year. The first two months, well, that's the time to look for accommodation and study French. And then the university year began and I did

two weeks, and then my father was sick. He was a diabetic person, and his diabetes played up and he was admitted to hospital, so the family informed me in Lièges and wanted me to come home just for a short time, and I thought well this was a good excuse to go home and meet up with my boyfriend again and be close to my father in case anything happened. So I went back, and my father got better, and then, I changed my mind, I didn't want to go back to Lièges, it was too lonely, and I didn't want to go back, I wanted to be in Vietnam with my family. So I decided to stay, and enrolled in the Law Faculty. So I did Law for four years, and just one month before I sat for my final exams, the communists took over South Vietnam and closed down Saigon University, especially the Law Faculty. They didn't want the Law to operate, the communists were against the legal profession.

It seems that her older siblings' ploy worked. They succeeded in bringing her home from Belgium. She accepted at face value the news that her father was ill, and then she decided she wanted to stay anyway. Anh's narrative indicates that Suong's three older siblings still felt guilty over the earlier incident and that their overprotectiveness was driven by the near loss of their youngest sister a few years back. Their actions in bringing her home and Suong's decision to stay in Vietnam all entailed consequences in that it meant that Suong was with them when their country collapsed, instead of being safely overseas. Anh is aware of this and expresses regret for this, but Suong clearly asserts that it was her choice to stay in Vietnam with her family.

A BROTHER'S DEATH

The second central event in the sisters' lives is the exodus from Vietnam, and the resulting loss of their brother Kiet. Both Anh and Suong remember that Kiet enjoyed spending time with his sisters and that he was unusually considerate. Anh remembers: "He used to dress up like a girl because the rest of us were girls, he didn't wear a real dress but would put a blanket on top of his head and play with us. Later on, after the fall of Saigon, Kiet helped us a lot." Suong says of him: "My brother was the only son and the only man in the family apart from my father. He was gentle, thoughtful, feminine." The siblings had planned to escape from the country together, but as with many other escape accounts, their plans went awry. Nga, Suong, and Kiet left together on the same boat, while Anh, who had two small children by that time, failed to make it to the rendezvous in Can Tho. Suong remembers:

> We waited and waited and waited, but there was no sign of them. There were other small boats, but their group didn't turn up. We were very concerned about their wellbeing, and then the boat owner decided, well, he had to, you know, to keep going. Otherwise, the police would have discovered our escape plans. So we kept going.

Their boat was approximately twenty-four meters long and held 124 people. Most were hidden in secret compartments under the deck. The men and women were in separate compartments, with the men lodged close to the fertilizer. Suong gives the following account of the circumstances surrounding her brother's death:

> Just before we reached international waters, the water pump broke down, and the skipper encouraged all the young men to bail the water out of the boat by hand. And our brother took his turn during the night, and he just fell overboard and disappeared. My sister and I were sleeping underneath the deck and someone made an announcement that Kiet had gone. And you know, the announcement woke everyone up, and we all got up to the deck, and looked around, and there were sharks swimming around the boat. He just disappeared, in the middle of the night. I think it was about 2 A.M. I remember vividly that it was a very dark night, very dark, there was no moon. For three hours, before we set off again at about 5 A.M., the people in the boat tried to console us. My brother died on the eighth day out, and we arrived at the refugee camp sixteen days later.

While Nga turned her grief inward and withdrew below deck, Suong sought to occupy herself with work on the boat. She was given the job of chopping wood and cooking rice. She says of her sister:

> Nga became quite sick. She would stay there, in bed, crying all the time, so I would go up to the deck and then go back down to see if she was still alive, because one of us had already gone and I just wanted to hang on to her. And I remember that she said, "Don't go again." I think that she was afraid that she would lose me as well and that if I was on the deck, a wave would wash me overboard.

Suong, for her part, was emotionally numbed by the double blow of her brother's loss following on so closely from the lack of news regarding their sister Anh and her children. She also continued to hope that her brother had somehow survived and would rejoin them later on.

> Whenever I was on the deck, I would look out at sea, and whenever I saw another ship—for my brother disappeared in international waters—I would hope that he had been picked up by that ship and that one day we would be reunited. Because it's hard to come to terms with the fact that someone, who just a few hours before was sitting next to you talking, then disappeared.

She related that her brother had a premonition of his death, what she referred to as his "sixth sense" and that, just a few hours before he died, he gave them the cheque that had been entrusted to him. He told them, "Keep the cheque with you, just in case." When the sisters reached Pulau Tengah refugee camp in Malaysia, Nga's depression lifted, while Suong had a delayed reaction and fell ill. However, she carried her hopes for her brother's survival throughout her stay in the refugee camp and into the years of resettlement overseas: "I went on hoping even after arriving in Australia. I kept on hoping that one day we would get a letter from him saying he'd arrived safely somewhere."

As for Anh, she had last seen Kiet just before their planned escape and initially believed that all three of her siblings had made it to safety. She heard the news of her brother's death just a few days before she left the country:

> My cousin received a letter from her sibling that told her that my brother had died. She told us about it. We were just told that he had fallen off the boat and that was it. There were no more details. I think they said that Nga was very ill, but I didn't know anything much else.
>
> I remember that I heard the news just days before I left—at that time, in my mind, I didn't want to tell my father because I knew that he couldn't accept that my brother had died and that we were going as well and that he may loose a daughter and grandchildren as well so we (my cousins and me), we decided not to tell my father. Because at that time, I thought that if my father knew that my brother had died, he would have tried to keep us in Vietnam. I was worried about Nga and Suong, and about them still being ill after what had happened and I thought that I should go and support them.

Anh made it to a refugee camp in Thailand and eventually rejoined her sisters in Australia. Echoing Suong's words, she states,

> It took me a long time to accept that my brother had died, that he was no longer alive. We hoped that he would come back and see us. I knew on one level that he had died but I still hoped that he may have somehow survived.
>
> From time to time, I think about Kiet, and I see him as a young man.
>
> Normally I don't dream much, but I saw him once in a dream a long time ago, more than twenty years ago, I just saw him in a normal family setting here in Australia, as if he hadn't died and that he was here in Australia, like Nga or Suong, that he was here.

As Maria Tumarkin notes in *Traumascapes*, "the absence of the body creates a profound crisis for mourners. For one, it makes it difficult to let go of the possibility that the person presumed dead is wandering somewhere."[19] It was a hope that the sisters shared with many other Vietnamese refugees who lost loved ones at sea. Many families still think of family members as "missing" rather than "dead" even decades afterward.[20]

The sisters' narratives converge on several points: they remember Kiet as a particularly caring, thoughtful brother, perhaps atypical among Vietnamese men, and both had difficulty believing that he had died. Both carried hopes that he was still alive and would somehow get in touch with them, even years later. More important, the sisters reveal that they agreed to keep silent about Kiet's death, a silence that was directed, this time, toward their father in Vietnam. The three surviving siblings never admitted Kiet's loss to their father, and their silence lasted until his death nine years later. As Suong explains, "our brother was the only son in the family, so the loss of the only son was just too much for our father to bear." She also acknowledges:

> But in the end, I think he somehow knew what had happened, for he wrote to us, and kept on saying, "Ask Kiet to write," or "Send photos of all of you," and we deliberately didn't send them. We ignored his request. Nobody was really brave enough, to be the one to tell him.

As with the earlier silences, this silence was motivated by a mixture of emotions: guilt, love, and the reluctance to hurt their father. Their silence may also have reflected a wish to somehow keep alive their own hopes for Kiet's survival, as if the open admission of his death would have made it final. Reflecting on this silence twenty years later, Suong admits: "Now that I think about it, and know about the grieving process, it might not have been the right thing to do." This silence underscores the grief underlying this family tragedy, with the sisters unable to reveal and therefore share their loss with their father, and the father never having the news confirmed and therefore unable to mourn for his son. This death, the greatest trauma to affect their lives during the exodus, remained unvoiced between the generations, and the sisters' narratives illustrate in this way "the precariousness of family communication in the wake of trauma."[21] In her work on Holocaust survivors and their children, Ruth Wajnryb writes of the difficulty of communicating traumatic experiences across the generations:

> It is bound up with the complexity of how to tell a story when the story is wracked by trauma. From the parents' perspective, the dilemma was how to tell what they could not bear their children to have to hear. From the child's perspective, it was how to hear what they could not bear their parents to have to tell.[22]

This silence in the case of these Vietnamese sisters is the reverse of the silence portrayed in Jewish narratives of the post-Holocaust generations. It is the younger generation here that finds itself unable to communicate loss to the older. In consequence, the sisters' experience of exodus, bereavement, and trauma is accompanied by a great silence between the generations.

A SISTER'S LOSS

The third event that I wish to discuss in the sisters' lives is the death of their sister Nga in 2004. Both Anh and Suong acknowledge that Nga lost a great deal after 1975. She had been in charge of the family business and finances, and lost much of her status with the collapse of their country and the siblings' escape from Vietnam. Anh remembers that Suong and Nga were particularly close as sisters—they were close in age and shared a bedroom as girls. Anh says of Nga:

> Nga was very strong. Even though she was younger than me, she acted as if she were my older sister. Because when I got married, it was as if I'd relinquished my power as older sister. Nga took on the role of older sister. She looked after the business and the finances.

She was strong and straightforward and a little bossy. She had her own philosophy, her own view of what was right and what was wrong. Things would have been easier for her if she had been more flexible, but people loved her, and we loved her too.

Suong, in particular, shared a lot with Nga. Aside from their shared childhood and adolescence, the sisters experienced the escape from Vietnam with Kiet, Kiet's loss, the refugee camp in Malaysia, and the early years of resettlement overseas. As Suong relates, "we were two sisters living together, grieving for our brother, having a hard time, trying to survive." Suong gives the following portrayal of Nga:

> She really was the big sister and took on the role of big sister. Anh didn't do that—she is easygoing. Nga was not happy in Australia, she was in a deep depression because she had a lot of power and control in Vietnam—she controlled our father's business and she had a lot of authority. She lived more in the past and was sad in Australia—she had lost her profession, her status, her identity.

Both Suong and Anh, however, acknowledge the happiness that Nga found in her children, and her children's achievements in Australia. Anh says, "She was not really happy, but she was pleased with what she had. It seemed to me that all her life she was very devoted to her family. She was a devoted mother."

Nga's loss was another milestone in the sisters' lives in that it not only brought up memories of the past and of their former lives in Vietnam, but also allowed them to reflect on the experience of migration and the implications of loss on a personal level as well as in terms of their former country. Each recollects different facets of Nga's illness and death. Suong narrates:

> She was diagnosed with breast cancer Grade 2 in June 2002. She had a mastectomy four months after the diagnosis—followed by two treatments of chemotherapy.
>
> Nga was a very active person normally. She was very negative about her illness. It was a death sentence and she gave up. She told me that cancer is like wheat in the garden—you can't get rid of it. She had no trust in her treatment, became depressed and went downhill. She never recovered. The second chemo treatment knocked her down. The cancer spread to her liver and bones and was very painful. She died in March of 2004.

I tried to see her and visit her and be close to her. As a nurse, I could see that it was the end. I tried to be positive and cheerful, I "performed" but driving home I'd be crying, I'd be a wreck.

When her cancer spread to her bones, she wanted to stay at home but her husband wanted to send her back to the hospital against her will. He was a lovely man but he couldn't care for her at home. She went to the hospital, and there was talk of radiotherapy and palliative care, but she said: "Please let me go home." I talked to her husband and the doctor and they agreed. This was in mid-March. She went home on Monday or Tuesday. On Thursday she went downhill, and wanted to see everyone. On Friday, we thought it was going to be her last day.

After her mastectomy, we had applied for our oldest sister [she is referring to Nuong, their cousin and adopted sister who stayed behind in Vietnam to look after their father] from Vietnam to come over. But the visa was delayed and there were various checks. When the cancer reached her bones, we got her oncologist to write a letter of support and sent it to the Australian Consulate in Ho Chi Minh City. It sped up the process and Nuong arrived on the Saturday, four hours before Nga died. I think that Nga tried to hang on to see her. She was unconscious most of the time. She was being treated with morphine and was heavily sedated, but when our sister arrived, she held her arms out to her and then fell back. Nga died at 4 P.M.

Anh's reconstruction diverges from Suong's in a number of ways:

Nga had her first operation, the mastectomy, followed by chemotherapy, and then she got better. My niece Joanne [Nga's daughter] went to Adelaide to study first year Medicine and we went there to visit her in September of 2003. Nga looked very healthy.

And then in December of 2003 or January of 2004, the cancer came back, and spread to the liver and bone. I didn't expect the cancer to spread so quickly. I was hopeful, and Nga was very hopeful because she wanted to see her children at least finish university.

When I heard that the cancer had spread, I knew that there was no more hope. We just tried to make her comfortable. I think that she still wanted to take anything that could help, such as herbal medicines.

For almost a year, I came every week to see her. But when she was in the hospital then I tried to come everyday. At one stage I took annual leave so I could be with her.

Nga passed away on Saturday, but early on Friday, we knew that she was almost gone. I still remember that she wanted the Republic of Vietnam flag so we had to ask the President of the Vietnamese Community

Association for a flag, and when he brought it to the house, she held it to her chest, so we buried her with the flag.

That night, the Friday night, everything was very bad, her legs were very swollen, and we stayed with her, and she was very tired, and we were waiting for Nuong to come to Australia, and she arrived Saturday morning just in time to see Nga before she died. When she was about to die, Nga couldn't let go, she kept on struggling to breathe, like she was still holding on to something, and we calmed her down and told her to let go, and that we would take care of the children, and then she went.

The sisters' narratives concur on the issue of Nga's personality and character traits. They both say that she had responsibilities in the family business in Vietnam and that she took over the role of older sister. She was opinionated, motherly, and loving. Where the sisters' narratives diverge is in their reconstructions of her illness and death. Each remembers a different facet of her sister in the latter's final months. Nga's alternating emotions of hope and despair are remembered separately by each sister. While Suong remembers her sister's anguish, Anh remembers her struggle to live. And while their memories also differ in terms of Nga's last wishes before her death (seeing her adopted sister from Vietnam, according to Suong, and holding the flag of the former Republic of Vietnam, according to Anh), both of these have as their common point their symbolic link with home and the lost homeland. It seems that in her dying hours, Nga sought the solace and comfort of a loved one and a loved object from her lost country. Both Suong and Anh recognize this, even if their memories highlight different manifestations of this aspect of their sister's last hours. At another level, these narratives also reveal the fact that the sisters retained their own strong personal memory of Nga's loss. Unlike the silences that surrounded Kiet's death, the sisters talked about Nga after she died. Suong states:

Nuong stayed in Australia for three months. We (Nuong, Anh and me) we talked about Nga—how domineering, vocal, talented and organized she was. She was a rebellious child, a typical middle child. We had problems with our stepmother because of Nga. Everyone loved and respected her and was devoted to her. At times it hits me and I still miss her.

In a memory as painful as the death of a sister, Patricia Foster reminds us that "to know a sister is to know paradox; to try to describe her is to tangle with the subjectivity of language, the inherent lies of story."[23] Each sister brings the subjectivity of her own memory, as well as the subjectivity of language, to her description of Nga, her life, her illness, and her passing. In the case of these sisters, their story is not only a personal story of loss, it is also the continuation of the story of exodus, the loss of country, and the effort expended in recreating new lives in another country.

SISTERS AND MEMORIES

These narratives evince the different means with which each sister dealt with loss and trauma. The collapse of their country, Suong's aborted university studies, the confiscation of their family business by the communist authorities, the escape from Vietnam, and resettlement overseas are upheavals that they shared with many others; however, within the wider story of the Vietnamese diaspora, the sisters articulate their own stories of separation, resilience, and survival. They are aware that they were more fortunate than many others who escaped by boat. As Suong relates:

> In the camp, with the boats that came afterwards, some people lost their entire family. I felt lucky. I felt that the loss of the one brother was minor compared with other people's losses. I remember one particular young man, in his mid-twenties, who lost his entire family. His boat sank and he was picked up by a fishing boat. Most of the people on his original boat died. He lost his parents and all three siblings. Only a few others were picked up along with him.

Anh, the oldest, believed that her role was to care for and protect her younger siblings. This was brought home to her most directly with Suong's attempted suicide, coma, and lengthy convalescence in hospital. Anh is aware that there is much that she has not communicated to her sister. Her memories of her sister are punctuated with "I don't know whether she still remembers this" and "She probably doesn't remember this." Her narrative evinces a clear understanding that these reconstructions are her own and that her sister may remember otherwise or may have no recollection of the same incident at all. Anh's narrative is quiet and contained. She states that she has learned to deal with events in a restrained manner. As she relates,

> I don't respond much to emotion. I don't seem to get angry, and when good things happen, I don't react much either. I have always been like

that. When we were young, we were taught that as a girl, you shouldn't show much emotion. We can't shout when we're happy, we can't cry much, we're supposed to be calm and well-behaved, and I've been like that all my life.

I don't think ahead. It's part of the way I look at things. If something is bad, I don't see it as being bad forever, if something is good, I take it easy, slowly. I see it as a coping mechanism.

While Anh's reaction may be a response to trauma—what Wajnryb refers to as "the phenomenon of suppressed emotion [as a] management strategy adopted by survivors to enable them to speak, without which words would be drowned by emotion"[24]—Anh is also aware that she has internalized the lessons from her past. Vietnamese women were traditionally brought up to abide by the Four Virtues: Right Occupation, Right Speech, Right Appearance, and Right Conduct.[25] They were instructed to be modest, hardworking, and quiet, and not to indulge in unseemly displays of emotion. In Anh's case, this restraint on her emotions has enabled her to deal with successive losses in her life: her mother, her business, her home, her country, her brother, her father, and last, her sister. This restraint also means that she does not express great happiness or joy, which she acknowledges, but on the other hand, and of greater importance to her, it has granted her the fortitude to bear many reverses. This life philosophy reflects the lessons taught in Vietnamese classics, such as Nguyen Du's *The Tale of Kieu*, and in Vietnamese tales and legends: that fate is harsh and virtue often goes unrewarded. Andrew Lam has captured this attitude aptly in the following words:

> Back home, they accept that noble deeds are rarely rewarded with happily-ever-afters, that broken love is the norm, and that those who do good can be and often are punished. These stories are concerned with their young listeners' spiritual growth, not with convincing them that they live in a benevolent universe. Considering how the country has been war-ridden for thousands of years and how disasters have a way of destroying hope, Vietnamese tales have evolved to prepare the next generation for cataclysm and grief.[26]

As the oldest sister, Anh is the one who has been most influenced by traditional expectations of women's role and behavior in society, but it is also clear that she is cognizant of this and that she is able to articulate the strengths that this has given her as well as its drawbacks.

Suong, nine years younger, was twenty-five years old when she escaped from Vietnam to seek a new life overseas. In her narrative, she expresses emotions more openly, whether they be happiness or grief. Her narrative reveals a positive construction of life story and identity, and much of her affirmation deals with the consequences of her brother's loss. She says:

I am not a superstitious person, but I have to believe in something, because to plan our escape, our brother went to a fortune-teller and she said that for this escape to be successful, two chickens would have to be sacrificed. Now in Vietnam, when you plan a major event, you always celebrate with something really grand, like a whole roast pig. When my brother told the skipper that maybe we should have two chickens instead, the skipper said, "Oh no, we have 124 people on the boat, we can't just have two chickens, we have to have a roast pig." Well, the two people who died on our trip was our brother, who was born in the Year of the Rooster, and the skipper's brother-in-law, who was a heroin addict, and he screamed, you know, he had no heroin, he screamed and screamed, and the doctor on the boat gave him morphine, and he died of an overdose, and he was also born in the Year of the Rooster. This means that two roosters were sacrificed for the safety of the boat. How else would you explain that?

She believes that the deaths of her brother and the skipper's brother-in-law were the payment exacted for the safety of the 122 other people in the boat. She preferred to give the deaths of these two young men meaning rather than interpret them as tragic and senseless losses. "This preoccupation with questions of meaning," suggests Vieda Skultans in *The Testimony of Lives*, "is shared by many trauma victims. It is 'the need to make habitable meanings from uninhabitable truths.'"[27] Furthermore, Suong believes that it was her responsibility to not only survive but also to take full advantage of the chances that a new life in Australia gave her. Her brother had died during the exodus. She, therefore, needed to live to give meaning to his death, and by extension meaning to the deaths of all those who had lost their lives while escaping from Vietnam. Her life was gifted to her by her brother, and to give thanks, she had to live and live well. She had already paid too much for this chance at a new life. She states:

I remember the day we left Pulau Tengah, and I looked back and saw people standing there, still in the camp. I felt so sorry for them and thought how lucky we were not to have to stay there any longer, and I decided I'll have to make it worth it, it had cost too much to get to where I was, so the rest of my life, I'd really have to make it worth it.

This assertion that she had to "make it worth it" drives much of her approach to life and to resettlement overseas. She emphasizes: "Here in Australia, we found freedom, independence, we could live our own life. I am happy here."

The sisters' narratives reveal two central tropes in their lives: silence, both as a sign of solidarity between family members and a means of protecting a loved one; and responsibility, in terms of what they believe is owed towards other family members. The silences that feature, first, between the sisters, and second, between the sisters and their father, are framed by trauma and loss. They represent a means of exerting a degree of control over overwhelming events and an attempt to delay or push away the direct acknowledgment of death or loss. As Luisa Passerini suggests, "it is easier to think of the positive meanings of silence in the personal and private sphere."[28] The sisters dealt with traumatic events in the family by adopting a measure of silence, a silence motivated by love but also by a complex of other factors. In her work on silence in the wake of trauma, Wajnryb writes:

> Silence is as complex as spoken language, as differentiated and as subtle. Sometimes it is self-imposed, sometimes, other-imposed. Sometimes it is driven by the urge to protect or salvage or cherish; other times, as a weapon of defence or control or denial. One thing that underscores all instances: it is rarely unproblematic.[29]

While silence could be positive—a symbol of shared responsibility and a means of caring for a loved one—it could also be negative, in the sense that only certain family members were privy to the truth or truths behind significant and traumatic family events. Both Anh and Suong express regret for some of these silences. Anh does so in relation to recalling Suong back from Belgium—a recall that was motivated by a selfish desire to have a much-loved younger sister home. Suong regrets hiding the news of Kiet's death from their father, a silence that was partly motivated by love for their father, but also by a measure of cowardice on the part of all three surviving children. No one wanted to be the bearer of bad news, but the silence in relation to Kiet's death also meant that their father could not grieve for him openly and that the family as a whole could not mourn for him nor give comfort to all its members. Suong relates that this silence was particularly difficult for their adopted sister Nuong, who stayed behind in Vietnam to look after their father. While it was easier for Anh, Nga, and Suong to remain silent about Kiet because of their geographic distance from their father, Nuong had no such convenient distance. She had to keep her knowledge of the truth and her mourning secret from the adoptive father with whom she lived. These are silences that the sisters needed to keep at the time, but that they no longer need to resort to now, a lifetime after the events that they remember. As Passerini writes, "silence can nourish a story and establish a communication to be patiently saved in periods of darkness until it is able to come to light in a new and enriched form."[30] The sisters can now expound on the different events that affected their lives and reflect on the reasons why they kept silent on certain issues.

The sisters were at different ages, and stages in their lives, when their familiar world was overtaken by wider events in history. When Saigon fell, Anh, the oldest, was married with a young family, while her three younger siblings were single and the youngest, Suong, was still a student. The siblings were united in their desire to leave their country and build a new life for themselves overseas. Their father spent the last of his savings on getting them out of Vietnam, and despite her knowledge of Kiet's loss at sea, Anh persisted with her own escape plans, and also left the country by boat with her two children. All the sisters were affected by the weight of events—the collapse of their country, the disappearance of their brother, their refugee status, the uncertainties of camp life, and the difficulties and challenges of resettlement overseas. These earlier losses were then compounded by the grief of losing their sister to cancer. Yet they were able to construct coherent life narratives based on these shaping events and traumas in their lives. Their attachment to their family and their determination to construct new lives for themselves impart a structure and meaning to their narratives. For them, "wider cultural and historical narratives (as well as the storytelling context itself) provide the frames of reference within which individual narratives can be either constructed or understood."[31] It seems that the sisters found comfort in the fact that theirs was a story among many and that this in turn helped them to adjust to the different stages of mourning. Nancy Boyd Webb writes that

> some traumas are so intense that their force continues to reverberate through time and place, making it impossible for people to escape their

horrible memories. Nonetheless, it is the *meaning* of the event, not the trauma itself, that gives it power—and the attribution of meaning is very personal and unique.[32]

These intertwining strands in the sisters' lives, of silence and responsibility, of the desire to shield and to hide, of the urge to care for and to control, reveal the strong attachment between the sisters, even though their personalities and approaches to life differ quite markedly. Their perceptions of their shared past indicate the way in which each found it most expedient to process events, experiences, and losses. Although the sisters highlight different aspects of Nga's death and have diverging memories of her dying, their narratives converge on the issue of her loss being linked to the loss of homeland. Their private grief is in this way linked to the collective grief of the diaspora, and their loss to the wider losses of the diaspora. "Storytelling and mythmaking," writes Joan Laird, "help us to bear witness, to see ourselves mirrored in a collective identity, at once both subject and object."[33] Through these narratives, the sisters articulate their interpretations of their own story, their family, and their place within the wider story of the Vietnamese diaspora. "Hearing more than one version of a family history," as Millman informs us, "is a powerful reminder that sisters may live in the same house but they live in different families."[34] In the end, each displayed her own strengths and was able to provide comfort and aid to Nga during her final months. The features that emerge the most strongly from these narratives—which intermingle survival, loss, grief, and hope—are, in the writer Drusilla Modjeska's words, "the gift, and the vexation, of sisters [and] love as abiding as blood."[35]

CHAPTER 3

Women in Uniform

My interest in the women who served in the former Republic of Vietnam Armed Forces (RVNAF) stems from a conversation with a Vietnamese friend in Oxford several years ago. He had just completed a doctorate at Edinburgh University and was working as a research fellow in Oxford, while I had just begun my own studies there. He had been a boat refugee, and dedicated his doctoral dissertation (in physics) to Vietnamese boat people. In the course of a discussion on his family history, he spoke with pride of his mother and her sixteen-year service in the South Vietnamese army. He said that she was in the Parachute Division and that a photograph was taken of her parachuting out of a plane. It was a fascinating account and I never forgot it. When the opportunity arose of conducting research on Vietnamese women in Australia, I contacted him and informed him that I would like to explore his mother's story, and that of other women like her who had served in the RVNAF. His mother was the first former military woman to be interviewed for this book.

This chapter will explore the oral narratives of four women who served in the RVNAF. The women each served between eight and twenty-two years in the armed forces. Yet their histories and those of thousands of other RVNAF servicewomen have been omitted from the extensive historiography of the Vietnam War. Inheritors of a Confucian culture in which women were traditionally abjured to abide by the Three Obediences and the Four Virtues,[1] servicewomen had to negotiate and mediate their disparate roles and responsibilities as daughters, wives, mothers, and soldiers. Their narratives reveal the disjuncture between public and private memories of the war. While many women remember their war service, keep in touch with former army colleagues, and join reunions and memorial marches, historians of the war have remained largely silent on their participation.

In a 2004 review of Lam Quang Thi's *The Twenty-Five Year Century: A South Vietnamese General Remembers the Indochina War to the Fall of Saigon* (2001), military historian Jeffrey Grey writes:

> The Vietnam War impacted primarily and most directly upon the Vietnamese, but the Vietnamese themselves, and especially those former soldiers and citizens of the Republic of Vietnam, are largely invisible in the extensive published literature on the war. The people, the nation, and the cause on whose behalf we fought have yet to be consciously and effectively written into the history of their own war.[2]

The few monographs that do focus on the RVNAF privilege the experiences of men and remain silent on the women who served. Dong Van Khuyen's *The RVNAF* (1980), published by the U.S. Center of Military History in Washington, D.C., is a detailed study of the RVNAF from its formation through to its demise in 1975, but it contains only brief references to the Women's Auxiliary Corps (WAC) and the Women's Armed Forces Corps (WAFC). In the preface to his monograph, Dong thanks Pham Thi Bong, "a former Captain in the Republic of Vietnam Armed Forces"[3] for her work on the manuscript, but she is the only servicewoman he refers to by name in the study. He presents neither the history of the WAC or WAFC, nor their composition. In his book *ARVN: Life and Death in the South Vietnamese Army* (2006), Robert Brigham refers to North Vietnamese women who served in the People's Army of Vietnam (PAVN).[4] South Vietnamese women, however, only feature as Army of the Republic of Vietnam (ARVN) "wives and companions."[5] Books on Vietnamese women soldiers in the war such as Karen Gottschang Turner's *Even the Women Must Fight: Memories of War from North Vietnam* (1998)[6] and Sandra Taylor's *Vietnamese Women at War: Fighting for Ho Chi Minh and the Revolution* (1999),[7] as their titles indicate, focus solely on those who fought on the communist side.[8] South Vietnamese servicewomen therefore fail to feature either in the handful of books on the RVNAF or those on Vietnamese women soldiers. This chapter sets out to address this imbalance by exploring the life stories of four former RVNAF servicewomen. Their narratives will uncover and illuminate some of these hidden histories.

The suppressed histories of South Vietnamese servicewomen, like those of South Vietnamese servicemen, are linked to the collapse of South Vietnam and the loss of the war in 1975. Their war service is denied by postwar socialist Vietnam. Unlike their northern counterparts, southern soldiers are not inscribed into a heroic postwar national narrative of resistance to foreign invasion. As noted by Heonik Kwon:

> The postwar Vietnamese state hierarchy put great emphasis on controlling commemorative practices and propagated a genealogy of heroic resistance wars, linking the death of a soldier in the American War to a line stretching back from the French War to the legendary heroes of ancient victories. Every local administrative unit in Vietnam has a war martyrs' cemetery built at the center of the community's public space, and the reminder, "Our Ancestral Land Remembers Your Merit," is inscribed on the gothic memorial placed at the center of this place.[9]

This problematic postwar narrative not only omits South Vietnam and its twenty-year struggle against the communist North, it also occludes the fact that North Vietnam fought the war with the massed support of the Soviet Union and China. The partial release of archives in Russia and China is allowing some of this history to be uncovered, but much still remains to be written.[10] In consequence, while North Vietnamese women soldiers[11] may be publicly inscribed into the tradition of historic Vietnamese heroines such as the Trung sisters, who led a revolt against the Chinese in 40 C.E., and to more recent revolutionary female heroes, the service of South Vietnamese women is remembered in the more circumscribed spheres of veterans' associations or their homes and families. I am here referring to former RVNAF servicewomen who now live overseas. In Vietnam, as Hue-Tam Ho Tai notes, southern war losses "have been erased from public memory."[12] Tai writes:

> The remains of those who fought on the other side in the Armed Forces of the Republic of Vietnam had to be taken away when its military cemetery was razed after 1975. . . . [S]outhern dead, absent from national commemoration, often go unmentioned in the collective narrative of their extended families. Condemned to the shadows, they refuse, however, to remain unmourned. Their demand to be recognized, however, threatens the peace of the community at the level of family, community, and nation.[13]

While there may be no public memorials in Vietnam to the quarter million South Vietnamese soldiers who died in the war, their service is remembered by the aging communities of war veterans and their families in the Vietnamese diaspora.[14]

Southern female personnel served in the armed forces from 1950 until the fall of Saigon in 1975, but it is extraordinarily difficult to obtain information on their history. The following partial history is reconstructed from a detailed article on "Servicewomen" by Ho Thi Ve, published in the RVNAF *Servicewomen's Magazine* in the United States in 2001,[15] and Phung Thi Hanh's "South Vietnam's Women in Uniform," published by the Vietnam Council on Foreign Relations in 1970.[16] It is supplemented by the few brief references to the WAC and WAFC in Dong's *RVNAF*. Ho Thi Ve stresses in her article that she might have missed many details, that this was partly due to the lack of reference materials, and that she was as careful as she could be in terms of consulting with her colleagues and cross-checking the information that she obtained.[17] Her article notes that she would welcome additional comments or corrections. Ho grew up in Hue, central Vietnam, and joined the *Viet Binh Doan Trung Viet* (Army of the Center) in 1950. She states that female personnel in the *Viet Binh Doan* worked as typists, secretaries, accountants, military nurses and nursing aids, and numbered in the hundreds.[18] The *Viet Binh Doan* ceased to exist in 1952, when it was integrated into the National Army of Vietnam. Ho then joined the WAC and was transferred to Saigon. She notes that WAC consisted of five specialized branches: Staff, Medical Corps, Communications, Military Supplies, and Social Work. In 1959, the Ministry of Defence cut down these branches, and only two were left: the Medical Corps and Military Social Work. Members of the WAC who wanted to continue in the service had to join one of these two branches after appropriate training. Otherwise, they were demobilized. There were no promotions in the WAC during this time: lieutenants, for example, had to "stamp their feet at the same place" for nine years.[19] This bears out what Phung notes on the WAC in her article: "Almost without recognition, the Women's Auxiliary Corps continued through the years with little support."[20] As the war escalated, Phung writes that:

In spite of considerable opposition from military leaders, the Women's Armed Forces Corps (WAFC) was formed on January 1, 1965, around the nucleus of 600 women then enrolled in the Women's Auxiliary

Corps. Patterned after the Women's Army Corps (WAC) in the United States, the WAFC was placed under the command of the Vietnamese Joint General Staff.[21]

The shift from WAC to WAFC in South Vietnam signified a shift from a French-inspired military model to an American one. The office of the chief of WAFC and the training center for WAFC were located in Saigon, and the first chief of WAFC was Major Tran Cam Huong.[22] A colonel when she reached retirement age on April 1, 1975, she was succeeded by Luu Thi Huynh Mai, who had been promoted to lieutenant colonel on January 1, 1975.[23] The WAFC Training Center recruited women over the age of eighteen who volunteered to join the armed forces. The WAFC were not tasked with combat duty. After basic military training, WAFC personnel were dispatched to different branches according to the needs of the Ministry of Defense. They received specialized training at different schools: General Administration, Medical Corps, Finances, Military Supplies, and Military Social Work.[24]

In 1967, the WAFC Training Center became the WAFC School. Female troops were enlisted from 1968. Five years of basic schooling were required for enlistment while officer candidates were required to have eleven years.[25] Enlisted women soldiers worked as security guards and drivers, and priority was given to the widows of soldiers killed in action.[26] Phung writes that after the 1968 Tet Offensive, "a bill was introduced in the National Assembly to draft women between the ages of 18 and 25 . . . but the legislators, more conservative in their views, quickly vetoed the proposal, feeling that women were needed at home."[27] Dong refers to 1,025 enrollments in the WAFC School in 1970, out of a programmed input of 1,400.[28] The School trained seven classes of female officers—the eighth class was interrupted by the events of April 1975.[29] Ho notes that a small number of WAFC personnel also received training in several different Army Schools in the United States: Army Officer Training at Fort McClellan in Alabama, Civil Affairs at Fort Gordon in Georgia, Psychological Warfare at Fort Bragg in North Carolina, and Administration at Fort Benjamin Harrison in Indiana.[30] Fort McClellan was home to the U.S. Women's Army Corps, and this was the reason that WAFC officers were sent there.[31] Before April 30, 1975, the WAFC consisted of 6,000 women out of a theoretical strength of 10,000, including 600 officers.[32] These figures tally with those provided by Phung, who refers to 4,000 women in the

WAFC, 3,000 in the National Police, and more than 1 million in the People's Self-Defense Forces (PSDF) by the end of 1969.[33] Phung, in fact, refers to Ho as Major Ho Thi Ve, the commander of the WAFC Training School.[34] Both women state that South Vietnamese service-women were not trained as combat troops.[35] Phung writes:

> There are no women in the WAFC trained as combat troops. The purpose of the WAFC, according to Lieutenant Colonel Tran Cam Huong, its woman director, is to provide "woman-power" to release men for assign-ment in combat areas. Most of the women serve as typists, supply clerks, switchboard and teletype operators, social workers, nurses, and medics.[36]

The women's role, in effect, was to act in a support capacity to South Vietnamese men in uniform. I will now explore the memories and experiences of four former servicewomen.

The first woman, Thuy, was born in Kien An, northern Vietnam, in 1936. Her parents were traders. Her father was arrested by the French in 1947, and the family never heard from him again. In 1949, the mother and six children walked from Cai Nang to Haiphong, where they stayed until 1954. They moved south at that point, forming part of the mass movement of refugees from North to South Vietnam. Thuy joined the army in 1955 and served for sixteen years, seven of them in the Airborne Division. She retired in 1971. The second woman, Hoa, was born in Bien Hoa, southern Vietnam, in 1935. Her parents were also traders. Hoa joined the armed forces in 1953 and served until 1975. She worked in a military hospital for ten years before going to the United States for Officer Training in 1968, after which she joined the WAFC School. She was pregnant with her second child when she was interned in a re-education camp after the communist takeover of April 1975. She was released after fifty days. The third woman, Quy, was born to Vietnamese parents in Kratie, Cambodia, in 1936. Her father was a civil servant, and the family returned to Vietnam in 1945. She joined the army in 1956. She served for twenty years until the fall of Saigon in 1975, and like her male counterparts, was sent to a re-education camp, where she was incar-cerated for two and a half years. The fourth woman, Yen, is the youngest. She was born in Saigon in 1945. Her father was a lawyer. She trained in the WAFC School and graduated in 1968. She worked as an instructor at the school until 1975. Like Hoa and Quy, she too was interned in a re-education camp after the end of the war, in her case for three years. Thuy was sponsored to Australia by her sons in 1989, Hoa and her husband migrated to the United States under the Orderly Departure Program in 1993, Quy was sponsored by her brothers to Australia in 1986, and Yen escaped from Vietnam in 1981 and is now settled in Australia.

THE DECISION TO JOIN THE ARMED FORCES

What motivated these four women to join the armed forces? Unlike many men, South Vietnamese women were not drafted into the army. They made a conscious career decision at a time when army service for women was not an obvious choice despite the later extensive mobilization of South Vietnamese men.[37] Some women faced considerable opposition from their families for entertaining thoughts of an army career. Yung Krall, author of *A Thousand Tears Falling*,[38] recalls wanting to join the army to defend her country against the communists as a seventeen-year-old but was told it was a "no-no" for a girl to join the army as far as her family was concerned.[39] Frustrated in her efforts, she opted for the closest alternative, and became an army radio journalist. In 1964, at the age of eighteen, she joined G5, the propaganda and communications section of IV Corps, and worked as a journalist for "The Voice of the ARVN." This work allowed her to "feel closer everyday to the war zone and realize how much [they] owed the soldiers who were fighting, keeping places like Can Tho safe."[40] Family resistance to the notion of women joining the army was the experience of Thuy, despite the fact that both her older brothers served in the armed forces. One of Thuy's brothers was in the Eighteenth Division, and she states that the whole division moved south by air in 1954. While Thuy encountered opposition from the male members of her family, the other three women report family reactions that differed considerably from hers. All four women provide distinct motivations for joining the armed forces, and their decisions are set against specific familial and social backgrounds.

Thuy had opened a tailor's shop in Saigon when she heard the following radio announcement in 1955:

> I heard that the government was recruiting female army personnel. My two older brothers were already in the army. If I joined with my older sister then we would be four siblings out of six in the army. I applied to join. I enticed my sister and some of my friends into applying. I joined the army so that I could give a helping hand, and hasten the possibility of returning to North Vietnam. I was nineteen then. I worked as a nurse in the paratroopers' division. Since I was under twenty-one, I had to

have my mother's consent. She had to go to the district administration to sign the approval.

I heard that with the armed forces you could go here and there, to lots of places. I liked to travel, so I joined up. I was like a tomboy. My father said: "If she were a boy she would be very active." Even now, I still like to go here and there, I like risky adventures like men.

She underwent military training and learned to parachute:

Many people in the division encouraged me to learn parachuting and I took the course. There was no compulsion. I liked taking risks, I felt I had some spare time, and I felt that I could make it. Learning to para-chute was very hard. There were ten of us including Tam, Hoanh and Vui, and there were other women who were from the North. Anyway, Hoanh, Vui and the others are all dead. We had to practice jumping from a wooden cage, four meters high, it was exhausting. On my second jump, when I opened the front of the parachute the jerk was so strong that I lost my mind for a while. When I went home, I passed my home without realising it. My mother was so surprised at seeing me passing by that she called out "Where are you going?"

Of her older brother's reaction to her army service, she states:

He did not want me to join the armed forces. He worked in military communications and he rarely came home to visit my mother. I lived with my mother and younger sibling. Every time he came home, I had to hide my uniforms in my neighbour's house. The jeep sent to take me to work had to pick me up at another place instead of in front of my house like usual. I had to change at my neighbour's, I did not dare to wear the uniform in his presence. Once I had lunch at my friend's house and her parents said, "Thuy, you look very tanned lately because of your parachute training." My brother said immediately, "Let's go home, it is late." Once we got home, I received a terrible beating. Now he is in America, he's become very gentle, he no longer minds other people's business. My other big brother also forbade me to join the armed forces, but my mother did not voice any opinion about my career so I could still do what I liked, in spite of the fierce opposition from my brothers.

Hoa's experience differed considerably from Thuy's. She provides the following prosaic reason for joining up in 1953:

My family was not well off and I had to work to support my family. Before that I worked as a secretary in the French Army for a year, and then I heard that the National Army of Vietnam at that time . . . to tell the truth, paid a higher salary. The pay was double what I was earning in the French Army, so I changed over. I was accepted immediately; I had to fill up an application form then got an appointment for a test. A lot of us turned up for the test—it was the First Cycle of Secondary Education and was based on the French educational program. I took the test and passed, and was then called to present myself for work. I asked for one month's delay because I had to apply for leave from my previous work: we had to let them know in advance. One month after I gave notice at my old job, I went to my new job without having a day off.

Of her training she says:

We had to train, just like male soldiers. We trained in a football stadium, and for shooting practice, we would go to Quang Trung Training Centre. We had to practice everything, for we had to know everything but we never used it. In our work we did not need the use of guns. Army women were not required to go to the front.

The third woman, Quy, provides yet another motivation for joining the armed forces:

In 1952, while I was studying at Gia Long Girls' High School, there was a big flood. Due to this flood, the Viet Minh could no longer stay where they were and some came to our village. There was one guy who had a crush on me but I did not know about it. I was very naive. Before he went out on mission, he had asked a neighbour to approach my parents for their consent to our marriage. She said to him that I looked older than I was and that she did not think that my parents would approve. He threatened my family and said that if they did not agree to the proposal then he would notify the authorities that we were Viet Minh and we would all be put in jail. This threat worried my mother a great deal and she contemplated moving house. While we were looking for a new place, we heard the news that he had died on his mission. In Vietnam, if one does not have a decent status, one can easily be taken advantage of. It would be hard to live in a society like that so I was determined to obtain a decent social status for myself so that I would not be a pushover. I joined the armed forces in 1956.

Yen, the youngest of the four, states that she was influenced by the following: the escalation of war in the 1960s, the inspiration provided by a woman who served in the National Police, and recruitment drives for female army personnel:

> I finished high school—I passed Baccalaureate I but failed Baccalaureate II. I wanted to continue to try for Baccalaureate II but I was affected by the war situation in 1964. The Americans began coming. There was a young woman—she was a student like us but in reality she worked for the National Police. I think I was influenced by her to a certain degree. When I was young I dreamed of going overseas for my studies and then going to different places. One day I saw an ad on TV about recruiting female officers and I applied. It was in 1967, I forget what month but I think it was the beginning of 1967. I attended the training for female officers that lasted about eight months. After graduation, I received the rank of commissioned warrant officer and I was kept on to work for the school. It was the beginning of the formation of female troops and therefore graduates of the first classes were kept at the school to train following classes.

The four women are forthright about their reasons for joining the armed forces. Their narratives encompass two generations of female army personnel, from the first three who joined the forces when the women's corps was still an auxiliary corps in the 1950s, to the fourth, Yen, who joined the WAFC at the precise juncture that signaled the start of female troop enlistment. Their reasons for choosing the army range from youthful idealism and enthusiasm, to a practical desire to earn money and make a living. The women situate their lives and work within individual familial and social frameworks, and their narratives reveal that their reasons for joining stem from a combination of personal and familial circumstances.

Thuy's narrative is initially structured as an adventure story. She underlines the fact that she was "a tomboy" and that she "liked to travel." She encouraged other women to join up and abided by her choice despite at times violent opposition on the part of her older brothers. Her hardy spirit is reflected in a tough physique, since she voluntarily engaged in parachute training. Her decision to join the army is presented as an act of agency and an assertion of independence. It was also shaped, however, by her family's circumstances as refugees from communism, and by the fact that her two older brothers served in the army. She joined up because she wanted to contribute to the war effort. Army service therefore fulfilled not only a personal desire for adventure and change, but also a wish to form part of a broader struggle against the

North Vietnamese regime that had displaced her family and a million other northern refugees.

Hoa, on the other hand, presents army service as a practical means of earning a living, and of aiding her family's depressed circumstances. In 1953, the National Army of Vietnam provided a better salary than her secretarial work for the French Army, and she explains candidly her reasons for transferring armies and beginning what became a twenty-two year career in the military. For Quy, joining the armed forces was a means of bettering her family's social status as well as her own. An army career signified an avenue to individual and familial empowerment. She perceived it as an effective means to protect not only herself but also her family. If she were a serving officer, it would be much harder for anyone to accuse her family of being Viet Minh, or to threaten to do so. For both Hoa and Quy, the army enabled them not only to engage in a rewarding career but also to fulfill the Confucian concept of filial duty by serving their family.

As for Yen, her narrative refers to four factors: first, the escalation of the war; second, the influence of an attractive and inspirational female police officer; third, campaigns to recruit female personnel, although in her case the medium was television rather than radio as it was for the earlier generation of army recruits; and last, like Thuy, a youthful yearning for adventure and travel. The effects of recruitment drives have been recorded by other female soldiers. In an article entitled "I Joined the Army," Dang Kim Hoa writes of the indelible effect that a pretty young officer named Xinh had on her decision to join the army after finishing high school in 1967. After she completed her training, Dang discovered that that same officer who had inspired her to join up, had been murdered by the communists. Dang took over her position at the military academy, but forty years later, the memory of the pretty young female officer remains poignant in her mind.[41] For the women whose narratives feature here, the South Vietnamese army represented a broadening of choices, options, and horizons. All four express different motivations for joining up over a time span stretching from 1953 to 1967, but all made the army their career and three served until the collapse of their country in 1975.

SERVICE IN THE ARMED FORCES

The experience of Vietnamese women who served in the RVNAF reflects that of women in other armed forces of the twentieth century: women were not combat soldiers but rather served in a variety of administrative and support roles that enabled the functioning of the army. As noted by Gerard de Groot in his work on British women in the First World War, "service to the cause was often an extension of what were seen as natural womanly duties."[42] South Vietnamese female army personnel served in a similar capacity and saw their role as adjunct to that of male military personnel. Many worked in traditional areas such as nursing and communications.

Thuy worked as a nurse in the Airborne Division and then later became a military social welfare assistant. She relates of her experiences and postings:

> I studied nursing for six months, and then sociology for another six months. I went to the battlefield at remote sites to bring the injured back to our facility for treatment. I was overwhelmed with emotion when I saw the injuries our soldiers sustained. Some of the injured did not survive. When I worked at the military hospital, sometimes there were not enough beds for injured soldiers, and they were left out on the veranda. Also there were times when I had to bring the bodies back to their families.
>
> I worked in the parachute division until '61. I had my second child and was assigned to distribute drugs in medical clinics and to help soldiers' families. I also worked for three other units close to my home. I was promoted to the position of chief of social services of the Medical Corps not long before my demobilization in '71.
>
> My nature is the nature of an adventurer; I like to go here and there. As a military social welfare assistant, I could go to any place where there were garrisons to help soldiers and their families. I liked that kind of work.

Of her training in the Airborne Division, she states:

> Well, the training lasted for months. We learnt to run and to do physical exercises to promote our physical strength. I always managed to complete the circuit, but lots of women could not make it. We learnt how to react once we got out of the plane. For example, if the parachute deviated from the planned course, which rope you had to pull in order to correct it. Once you approached land you had to avoid landing on one foot; you had to draw your legs together tightly so as to land on your bottom. There were so many things to learn. There was one girl, named Chau, she worked in general headquarters and she also registered to follow the training. She broke her leg on landing and was brought to Cong Hoa General Hospital. Her wound teemed with maggots, it was horrible.

It was highly dangerous, we had to train like men but men had to complete seven jumps before receiving the certificate while girls needed only
six jumps.[43]

She relates of military discipline:

Military discipline was very strict; especially at the parachute division.
On the way from Phu Tho to the place where my company was garris-
oned for example, I came across a very wicked superior. He is now a
colonel and he is in America. I did not dare to wear the red beret while
riding on my Velosolex motorbike; he saw me holding the beret in my
hand and he penalised me by compelling me to work that Saturday and
Sunday. I had to change four uniforms in one day; a white uniform, a
khaki one, a green one and one for practice. I had to present myself every hour with a different uniform. He just wanted to maltreat people.
Even now, sometimes, I still dream of changing uniforms in a hurry to
present myself to my superiors in time.

She states that when she joined the army, she had no intention of marrying. As she remembers,

I did not think of getting married. When I went out with my married
friends in my spare time, I often heard complaints about their married
life. One of them told me that her mother-in law compelled her to have
children when she did not want to. I also heard about frequent disputes
between husband and wife. I did not know anybody, I had no boyfriend.
Moreover, I like to go here and there, and a family would be a hin-
drance. I decided not to get married. But in the end it was fate.

Her account conveys a strong desire for independence and freedom.
The phrase "I like to go here and there," with its connotations of
autonomy and mobility, features repeatedly in her narrative. She
resisted social pressure to marry and have children—and in a family-
oriented culture like Vietnam, such pressure was intense—but finally
acquiesced to her older brother's wishes. Her narrative reveals that
marriage, and especially motherhood, altered her perceptions and her
priorities. The mobility that she had appreciated earlier in her career
became a source of frustration and difficulty for her once she had her
children:

When my children were born I loved them so much, I realised that
should I continue with my way of life, I could not care for them. While

other people could stay home to care for their children, I had to wander around. It was miserable.

It was very hard to ask for permission to be absent from the workplace, even for a valid reason like doing paperwork for the children. You had to apply to be absent for two hours, you had to present the permission at the gate; we were not free to go out at will like civilians. It was very hard.

I was in the armed forces for a long time. When I got out my children were already grown. As you know, children in Vietnam are not as healthy and chubby as children in this country. My children fell sick very often, I had to work during the day; at night, I had to go care for them at the hospital. It was miserable.

As for Hoa, she gradually worked her way up from commissioned warrant officer to captain between 1953 and 1975. Like Thuy, she was at first opposed to the idea of marriage, but for different reasons.

First I was with a Signals unit and stayed there until 1957 when an order came from Madame Nhu stating that army women could only continue serving in two branches.[44] Army women could only be in the Medical Corps or in Military Social Service. Before that, we could be in many branches. Many of us worked in the offices of Military Ordnance or Military Supplies, but after 1957, we could no longer do so.

When the order was promulgated I chose to join the Medical Corps. I was sent to Cong Hoa General Hospital to train to be a military nurse. After six months or one year of study I worked at Cong Hoa General Hospital for about ten years. I was supposed to work as a nurse but I was designated to do office work for Supplies. I was chief of section of Supplies, but I had to be on nursing duty too: my official profession was nursing. We had to be "ready for combat duty" two days a week. When there was heavy fighting, more wounded soldiers arrived at the hospital and the regular team could not cope with the extra workload. We would be called to assist and had to be available 24 hours a day. There was a room with four beds where the four of us on duty stayed.

The work at the hospital was very difficult. To tell the truth, during my ten years there, I was so frightened that I did not dare to think of marriage. I saw so many women, very young women, crying over their dead husbands. I could not stand the sight of widows in mourning headbands holding young children and weeping. I found it unbearably sad. During those years, I thought that I would never get married, no, never.

Her career took a turn for the better in 1968 when she went to the United States for officer training:

> In '68, I was sent to the United States to follow the Officers' Basics class. Upon my return, I was assigned to the WAFC School; this work was better suited to what I'd learnt. I worked there until 1975.
>
> When I first came to the School, young cadets there complained about the commissioned warrant officer who'd returned from the United States and was too strict. I wanted to teach them what I'd learnt over there. They kept complaining but we had to be strict because as female army officers, our behaviour had to be exemplary. My commanding officer was a woman but she was like a man, from the way she walked to the way she did anything. She was very capable, and spoke English and French. She fully deserved to be in the command post. She was exemplary, she was a real leader. Her name was Ho Thi Ve, Lieutenant-Colonel Ho Thi Ve, and she died last year.

Hoa relates that she has many positive memories of her army service:

> One week before graduation we took the cadets to visit many places in order to learn about different methods of working or commanding. During that week the whole staff of the WAFC School went with the cadets. The commanding officer of the School and her deputy, the battalion commander and her deputy, the company commander, the platoon leader, we all went. I really enjoyed those occasions. We were glad that staff and cadets were on friendly terms.
>
> To tell you the truth, even now at my age, after so many years in the army, I am still fond of the military life. I have many good memories and many bad ones too, but more good than bad. I do not know about other people but as far as I am concerned I found military life extremely interesting, even now I still feel the same way. For this reason I feel glad every time I see anyone in uniform. At the WAFC School, we kept working during March and April 1975, we worked until 28 April.

As for Quy, she, too, became a captain. She relates:

> I trained for six months. Instructors were both male and female. There were many female military personnel before me. Graduates could become officers as well. The number of military personnel in the battlefield increased, so they had to increase the number working in administration, just like America. Some were doing work that was predominantly female-oriented like nursing and social work. The women

performed work that the men could not do as well. Usually it was 10 percent female, but it was quite hard to recruit enough women to reach that figure.[45]

First, I worked for the General Staff in Saigon then I was transferred to the Medical Corps at Cong Hoa General Hospital, where I worked as a laboratory technician. I specialised in biochemistry. After that I was sent for officer training and after graduation worked at the WAFC School. At the time of the Tet Offensive, I was working at Navy Headquarters. Upon my return from training in the United States, I moved to Can Tho, where I worked at IV Corps Headquarters until 1975.

Everywhere I went I had male fellow-workers alongside me. They were courteous and respectful. There were no problems.

Like Thuy and Hoa, she remembers war casualties in military hospitals:

In the old days, hospitals had a mortuary but afterwards mortuaries were moved to the cemeteries. Every time there were many dead soldiers their relatives came and wept; the sight of this demoralized wounded soldiers at the hospital. That was the reason why mortuaries were moved to the cemeteries.

Working at the hospital, everybody had to take turns at the patient reception desk, and the postoperative room, three days a week. All the hospitals followed the same schedule. Besides the three days of duty, we had another day when we were on stand-by and could expect to be called up anytime when more staff were needed.

When I worked in the military hospital, I witnessed too many deaths. I'd see a healthy, good-looking youth one minute then the next minute, I'd find him in the morgue. That was considered normal in a time of war. I saw a beautiful girl of about eighteen or twenty being maimed by a bomb. Nothing can restore beauty lost.

She never married, but she does not ascribe this to life in the military. It was just the way things eventuated. She speaks of female military personnel and of her life in broad and mythic terms:

We were similar in that we all wanted to serve our country. We all wanted peace for our nation, families living in harmony, and the war to end.

My whole life frankly has always been affected by wars. There were strong and powerful heroes and villains. Our country was continually struck by wars. Consequently, life for the Vietnamese people was precarious, like waves ebbing in and out of shores.

In later life, she has sought refuge in Buddhist meditation as a means of coming to terms with her life experience, in which the reverses in fortune that she and her family experienced are linked to the successive tragedies her country was subjected to, including the collapse of South Vietnam in 1975.

Yen, for her part, says of her experience and training:

> I graduated as an officer in 1968 and stayed there until 1975. The basic training was at the WAFC School then I was sent to the Instructor School at Thu Duc.[46] After that I followed the course for vice-commander of the political warfare battalion in the Le Van Duyet army barracks. All these courses were basic courses and two years later I was sent to Vung Tau to follow the middle level course at the Signals School.
>
> I was also detailed for one year to teach a course entitled "Training government employees to become cadres." This program was created to replace the unsuccessful program by Madame Nhu to "para-militarise" women. We were four officers and five non-commissioned officers responsible for training female government employees. . . . I am pretty forgetful now. I cannot even remember clearly some of the tasks I performed while I was with the armed forces.

She states of the work of female military personnel:

> We did a good many tasks. For example, some of the officers after basic training were sent to the United States to train in Air Force Nursing. They learnt how to provide special care for pilots and flying crews. A great number of us trained in nursing and worked in military hospitals. Some did bookkeeping work for military supplies and others were typists. Others trained in communications and operated the central switchboards of various army corps. There were many more jobs but I cannot remember them all.
>
> We trained altogether seven classes. The last class, the eighth class, had to be dismissed halfway through. In total, we can say that there were on average about fifty students in each class; that amounted up to about 400 officers. There were about 6,000 or 7,000 non-commissioned officers and soldiers.

She remembers how proud her father had been of her accomplishments and her army career (he was a lawyer and died in 1972):

> I was the eldest child in the family, I had five brothers after me, and for that reason, my father loved me most. He always supported me, he

considered me the elite of society. I was proud of myself. As an army officer, I was ready to fulfil my duty, even if it meant death.

The women recollect different tasks and responsibilities, and provide
individual perspectives of army service. Thuy worked as a nurse before
becoming a military social assistant. Her work was interesting and varied in that it enabled her to travel to different garrisons. Her experience of army service was tarnished only by the remembered petty
cruelties of certain officers, and her feelings of guilt regarding her perceived failure in her duty of care toward her children. She states that
she wanted to leave the army after ten years but had to complete
fifteen years of service before she could afford to do so.[47] Thuy's narrative of army service initially expresses her pride in her physical courage,
and her resilience. She was a pioneer in many ways, being one of the
first women to volunteer for and successfully complete parachute training. Marriage for her was not only unexpected, it was an institution
that she was at first strongly opposed to. Motherhood, however, altered
her priorities, and her remembered grief regarding her children shifts
the tone and texture of her narrative. She expresses self-blame for not
spending more time with them when they were young, and recalls how
"miserable" this forced distance from her family was for her. Her narrative reveals a tension between her evident pride and joy in her service,
and her grief and guilt relating to her children. Like British women
during the Second World War, Thuy had to "find [her] own solution
to the problems of combining war work with domestic tasks,"[48] and
from her account, she failed to find a satisfactory solution to her
dilemma.

As for Hoa, her narrative reveals a long association with the army,
from its early days in 1953 to 1975. She adjusted to the changes in the
armed forces over the years. She found her ten years of work at Cong
Hoa General Hospital traumatic and haunting, and was thankful to go
overseas for training and then teach at the WAFC School until the
end of the war. Like Thuy, she refused to contemplate marriage initially, but in her case it was as a result of witnessing war casualties during her years of service in a military hospital. She was profoundly
marked by the mourning of young war widows and did not want to
subject herself to such grief. She believes that if she had continued
to work at the hospital, she never would have married. In her case,
the opportunity of going to the United States for officer training

represented a significant and positive shift in her career prospects, and she clearly found her work at the WAFC School rewarding.

Quy, for her part, worked in several different units, and was part of a minority of women who served in the Navy. As noted by Phung, of the 4,000 women in the WAFC by 1969, only forty-five were attached to the Navy.[49] Like Hoa, she was marked by the war casualties she saw in military hospitals, and the scale of wartime losses. As Neil Jamieson notes,

> In nine years, about one in every five soldiers, perhaps one in every twenty adult males, was killed or seriously wounded while fighting for the government. . . . Since virtually every soldier who was killed or wounded had a wife, parents, children, brothers, sisters, and friends who were affected, there were few people in the society whose lives were not blighted by deep personal loss.[50]

Quy frames her life and army career against the backdrop of thirty years of war in Vietnam. Her words allude to the overwhelming impact of larger events on the lives of individuals, and the arbitrariness of fate in such a context. Her narrative reflects her efforts to achieve a sense of detachment from the tragedies that she witnessed. Last, Yen provides details of her training at the WAFC School in 1968, the multitude of tasks carried out by women in the armed forces, and her subsequent career as an instructor until the end of the war. She stresses how proud her father was of her accomplishments and of her status as an army officer. Her family viewed the service of women in the armed forces in a different light to that of Thuy's.

RE-EDUCATION IN POSTWAR VIETNAM

What were the consequences of army service for women in postwar Vietnam? Thuy was demobilized in 1971, and she states that she was fortunate in this respect, because it meant that she avoided the internment that other army women were subjected to after the communist takeover in 1975. The other three women, all of whom were still serving officers in 1975, were imprisoned in re-education camps after the end of the war.

Hoa recalls in detail the events of April 28, 1975, and their aftermath:

> My husband worked for the Air Force at Tan Son Nhat. He came into the WAFC School and shouted loudly, "Why are you all still working?"

He went to the commanding officer's office—she was still working as usual—and he said: "Oh my God, they are already at Tan Son Nhat, you have to bury or burn all the files of army women right away. You can't leave them here!" Then he took me home, and instructed me to take some clothes, take the baby, and go. I told him that we couldn't leave my parents behind. I decided to stay, so he did likewise. On the night of 29th, a young couple next door asked us to leave with them on the last ship that was moored at Bach Dang Quay. My husband asked me to go too, but I still refused, and in the end we stayed. I don't know whether that couple made it to safety. We never saw them again. On the 30th we listened to the radio and heard President Huong handing power over to Duong Van Minh, then Duong Van Minh announcing the capitulation of the South.

My husband was so shocked that he became ill and had a fever, he said that now the communists were coming, we would all die. My mother consoled us by saying that nothing would happen, and that it was nonsense to think that they would kill us all. But later on when we were sent to re-education camps and communist prisons . . . my mother heard communist officers speaking of a truck carrying re-education camp prisoners that had overturned, killing all those onboard, and she cried bitterly. The neighbours took pity and asked her why she cried, and she said that her daughter might have died in that accident. Later on my neighbours related this story to me, and I felt great pity and love for my poor mother.

I was pregnant with my second child at the time, but I still had to go to re-education camp. They forced me to go, many pregnant women also went. ["They spared nobody" (her husband's voice)]. They spared nobody [she repeated the sentence].

At first I was at Long Giao for twelve days, and then with twelve of my colleagues I was transferred to Quang Trung. They incarcerated only officers. We were required to go to class to be re-educated. We were glad because we thought that we could then go home. We hadn't the slightest idea about what we were getting into. We had to start by writing self-confessions about all that we had done, from what year to what year, and where. The day after that we had to write self-confessions again. We thought they would make us do it once or twice but they kept asking us to do it again and again, day after day. We were so scared that we kept a draft for the next time, we were afraid that if one self-confession differed from another, we would be in trouble. And this process continued on and on until the day of my release.

One day they gathered all the women for a meeting, and said that whoever was in difficulties could write these down. I wrote down that my husband was in re-education, I was in re-education, and that my old and frail parents and my three-year-old child were uncared for at home. I was pregnant and delivery was very difficult for me. My first child was born by caesarean section, and doctors had told me that the second child would have to go through the same process. After reading my petition they investigated my home district. When what I had declared proved to be true they gave me fifty days, and they released me. I was still under what they call it . . . house surveillance. Then one day they asked me to come to a communal meeting. All the local people were there. They put me up before the whole audience and asked them whether they knew that I was an army captain. They encouraged people to talk about my activities so that I could be judged. Do you know that I was loved by the locals? Everybody raised their hand demanding to speak; they all testified that I was very good, and that if anyone needed help, I was always ready to help. Because everybody said only good things about me, they had to grant me my freedom. My husband was released only three or four years after the birth of our second child.

Quy, too, was interned in 1975 and spent two and a half years in detention:

While I was there no one knew about our release date. We were all kept in the dark. I would say that I was hoodwinked. They asked us to make self-criticism statements and they kept on asking us to do so, I can't remember how many times. They would compare different statements, so they could detect it if we lied. I had nothing to hide so I just kept stating the truth. I was moved around four or five different camps. We went from Hoc Mon to Quang Trung and then to Long Giao. The majority of soldiers were maltreated in re-education camps, especially when management of the camps was transferred from the military to the Interior Ministry. Luckily, the manager in charge of our camp was from South Vietnam so she was quite empathetic towards us. She knew that we were all educated people who were being imprisoned for political reasons and that we were not thieves or law breakers. Consequently, we were treated with dignity and kindness. Even though we were there in large numbers, there were no problems.

Yen, like Hoa, also remembers clearly the events of April 1975:

In Saigon as you know, at the last moment, Mr Huong assumed the post of president and ordered the break up of the ranks. On the last day, the 30th of April, I stayed at the school until midday and we received the order to dismiss. I felt extremely sad. Everything was over [she pauses for a while]. However, I think we were still lucky because there was not much bloodshed.

This "luck," however, was short-lived:

Sometime in May, if my memory is correct, it was on the 15th of May that the communists ordered all officers to present themselves for re-education. According to the communiqué we were to go to the camp for ten days and we had to bring enough food and clothes for ten days. I took food and clothes for ten days but I returned only three years later.

When we were first interned, we were taken past Tay Ninh and we went past the border with Kampuchea to a place called Katum or something like that, I did not know the place. They moved us only by night, so we lost our sense of direction easily. I was with a group of females and there were not many of us at first: only about a dozen or so. Then other groups of women joined ours, and we then numbered about sixty. They then transferred us back to Cu Chi, where our group merged with a group of policewomen. We stayed there for about a year then we were transferred to a place that used to be Quang Trung Training Centre, the site of the old military barracks. We spent the remaining two years in this location. It was very hard the first few weeks because they were not sure where to incarcerate us, therefore they kept moving us from one place to another.

There was no sexual harassment. I have to assert that that kind of treatment never happened to us. However, we were harassed mentally. We had to work very hard during the day and attend political indoctrination classes two or three times a week. They taught us the principles of communism, demonstrated why communism was good, showed us how they had triumphed over us, and concluded that we were parasites and traitors to the motherland. Every week, we had to write a review, we had to write down that we recognized our past mistakes and promised to make amends. We had to repeat this process week after week.

It was a form of mental torture. We did it in the hope of being released because all of us wanted to return home as soon as possible. We kept writing review after review saying the same thing over and over again. We wrote that our eyes were now opened, and promised that once we were released we would do our best to build an ideal communist society. We all lied.

While we were in prison, we had no idea of how things were outside the camp. They kept any news of the outside world from us. After my release, I experienced even worse depression than when I was in the camp because what I saw in society was completely different from what

I'd been told in the camp. I was not allowed to live in Saigon. My mother had to give up her house in Saigon and return to our ancestors' land in Bac Lieu or Ca Mau. I then had to present myself to the village cadre and write weekly reviews. All this led me to meet the village police officer and it was because of him that I fled overseas. I was thirty-three and still single. When he saw me he courted me and he acted very rudely. I was so upset that I forgot all my fears and lashed out at him, and that very night I fled to Saigon. I stayed in Saigon until I could escape. During the six months that I was there, I befriended a teacher. She was a communist cadre but she liked me very much. I liked her too and as a result, I wrote to tell her the story of the village police officer when I escaped. She brought the letter to my village to denounce him and he was demoted and transferred to another place.

In 1981, I succeeded in escaping from Vietnam.

Like many others who were interned after 1975, these three female officers presented themselves for ten days of "re-education." Hoa was released after fifty days, but Quy and Yen found themselves subjected to two to three years of imprisonment without trial, during which time they were transferred to different camps. This is a common refrain in refugee memoirs. Former military and civilian subjects of the South Vietnamese regime registered for re-education believing the new government's assurances that they would only be away from their families for a short time. They were also lulled by the fact that most noncommissioned officers and privates who registered for re-education were released after three days.[51] Hence Quy's remark, "I would say I was hoodwinked." It was not only former military personnel and civil servants who were required to register, but teachers had to do so as well.[52] In this way, in the words of Tiziano Terzani, "some 250,000 people disappeared into the remote jungle concentration camps that [were] distributed over the whole country."[53] Actual numbers of those interned are difficult to gauge, since the regime released contradictory information on the number of detainees held in its prison camps.[54]

The re-education camp system first came into operation in northern Vietnam during the Indochina War (1946–1954).[55] Nguyen Van Canh writes:

All political prisoners in communist North Vietnam had to undergo *cai tao tu tuong*, or thought reform. In official documents it was always referred to as *cai tao* ("thought reform" or "re-education") or simply *hoc tap* ("education" or "study").[56]

After Vietnam was reunified in 1975, the bamboo gulag became an extensive network of camps spread throughout the country. Nguyen refers to more than 100 camps containing an average of 3,000 prisoners each,[57] but a more recent study by Nghia Vo posits the existence of more than 1,000 camps of varying sizes in postwar Vietnam, holding between a few hundred to more than 20,000 prisoners.[58] One of the most notorious, Katum Camp, was located in Tay Ninh, close to the Cambodian border, and housed 10,000 prisoners.[59] Camps not only took in detainees at the end of the war, but continued to receive new prisoners over the next two decades. The practice of illegal arrest and detention was still common in 1988.[60] There were not only camps for political prisoners but also camps for escapees (those who attempted to escape the country either as boat or land refugees after 1975) as well as camps for women and children.[61] In his 2001 memoir, Vietnamese Amerasian Kien Nguyen describes being interned at the age of thirteen in "Re-education Camp No. PK 34" after a failed escape attempt.[62] He spent two months doing hard labor before his mother was able to bribe authorities for his release. He stresses that his was "a specific camp for women and children."[63] Several memoirs of camp life have been published in English and in French.[64] The most famous Vietnamese camp detainee is dissident poet Nguyen Chi Thien, who spent a total of twenty-seven years in internment in North Vietnam. He was first imprisoned in 1961 under "Re-education Act No. 49."[65] His poetry received international recognition when he managed to smuggle a handwritten collection of 400 poems into the British Embassy in Hanoi during a brief period of liberty in 1979.[66] He had composed these poems in prison and memorized them. He was arrested by Vietnamese security agents as he left the embassy.[67] Adopted as one of six "prisoners of conscience" by Amnesty International in 1986, Nguyen Chi Thien was finally released in October 1991.[68] His poetry collection *Flowers from Hell*[69] was awarded the International Poetry Prize in 1985.

While a number of memoirs and poems by Vietnamese male detainees have appeared in English and in French, and are thus available to an international readership, no such writings by Vietnamese female detainees have as yet made their way into print.[70] And yet, many women were interned in the postwar years. Their numbers include not only those who served in the RVNAF as either soldiers or civilians, or who worked as public servants under the former Saigon government, but also those who were caught attempting to escape the country after

1975. Many were interned in prison camps with their children. Vietnamese authorities did not appear to have a uniform policy in relation to escapees. Those who were caught were either fined if they were lucky, or imprisoned for lengths of time varying from a few weeks to more than a year after failed escape attempts.[71] Women, however, have rarely spoken about their experience of internment in postwar Vietnam.[72]

The narratives of Hoa, Quy, and Yen are among the few that provide a glimpse of camp existence for southern women after 1975. Some common features of camp experience emerge from their accounts: first, prisoners registered for re-education in the belief that it would only be for a short time; second, they were not told how long they would be detained; third, they were shifted to different camps; fourth, they were subjected to political indoctrination and had to write regular "confessions"; and, last, they were isolated from any news of life outside the camp. However, the women's narratives also register differences in their camp treatment. Hoa was under particular strain because she was pregnant when she was interned. She stressed that the regime did not make concessions to anyone ("They spared nobody") and that other pregnant women were similarly imprisoned. It was an act that profoundly affected not only her but also her husband. The phrase "They spared nobody," from both husband and wife, emphasizes the impact of these events. Hoa, however, was successful in seeking special exemption from the camp authorities, which led to her release from re-education after fifty days, and eventually, with the support she received from her local community, to being granted her freedom. Quy, for her part, underlines the fact that she was fortunate in having a female camp manager who was a southerner, and who treated political prisoners with respect and decency. As Vo notes, "the treatment of prisoners varied depending upon the location of the camps, proximity of towns or populated areas, and behaviour of the staff members and wardens."[73] Yen asserts that no sexual harassment occurred in her camp, but she describes the relentless insistence on prisoner "confessions" as "a form of mental torture." Her narrative reveals that while she objected to the behavior of the local police cadre that she had to report to after her release, another communist cadre that she befriended in Saigon—a female teacher—ensured that the policeman who had harassed her was later reprimanded, demoted, and transferred. It was an unusual action for this cadre to undertake on behalf of a former female soldier and escapee. Female friendship and solidarity appear to have overcome political barriers in this instance. Hoa's and Yen's narratives also reveal that women in the WAFC School stayed at their posts until the end of the war.

WOMEN IN UNIFORM

"Women's narratives," suggests Penny Summerfield, "include a dialogue between the present and the past, between what is personal and what is public, between memory and culture."[74] These four female veterans have rebuilt their lives overseas and have adjusted successfully to their new countries. They have given sober appraisals of their army service and their postwar lives. They were candid in providing a variety of motives for joining up, and their experiences reflect Phung's words from 1970:

> Why do women join the WAFC? Last year a questionnaire was distributed to find out. "Half of them said they joined to have a job and make a living," said Colonel Huong. "As for the rest, I think they like military life, and they want to be able, in some way, to help the war effort."[75]

Although they came from different family circumstances, all four were subjected to years of political instability and decades of war. They may have had different reasons for joining up, but all made a career of their army service. The women have reflected on their lives and work, and acknowledged the highlights as well as the drawbacks of their chosen careers. Their experiences reveal the ways in which women negotiated the pressures of being soldiers as well as daughters, sisters, wives, or mothers in South Vietnamese society. They have identified the skills that their war work equipped them with, such as resilience and self-reliance, as well as the emotional scars of their service, such as their memories of injured and dead soldiers. All four witnessed the collapse of the army and the country that they had served. The travails and tragedies of the postwar years and the extent of state repression after 1975 tested their resilience and endurance.

Thuy's narrative reveals a core of determination. As she states, "It is my nature. Once I decide to do something, I have to finish it by all means." She overcame considerable family opposition in order to undertake her army duties. After 1975, she concentrated her efforts on getting her children out of the country, and she persisted despite a number of failed escape attempts. She resisted intimidation by the Vietnamese authorities in the postwar years, and recalls that when a cadre pulled out his pistol in her house, she told him to put it away because otherwise she would not speak to him. She refused to leave her home and move to the New Economic Zones, thereby ensuring that her family kept a roof over their heads. She notes that she is the disciplinarian in her family: "When I say something, it is immutable like a nail driven into wood." This persistence and resolve saw her withstand the hardships of the postwar years.

Hoa, for her part, expressed considerable distress about being interned even though she was pregnant, and speaks of a personal loss after the war:

> I do not know how many of my friends died in communist prisons. I know of the death of one friend who was my former classmate. She was still single, and while she was in the re-education camp, she had a fever. They did not let her family know, so she wasn't provided with medicines, and she died in prison. I'd been released some months before that. She died on the first day of Tet.
>
> When she died, no one knew. I learnt of her death from another person. It was in the evening, I was selling foodstuff at the end of an alley, when a woman came and asked me whether I knew of such a person. I told her that she was my friend. Then she said, "I will tell you softly." She said that she had been released from the camp and she let me know about the death of my friend. She asked whether I could advise the family that she had died on the first day of Tet. It was one month ago. She said, "If you know the family, please let them know so they can go and look for her grave."
>
> I rode my bicycle to the house of my friend's brother-in-law, Dr Thuong. I told them the bad news. When he heard this, Dr Thuong said, "These people, we cannot live with them under the same sky, they are so cruel. People get sick and they don't allow the family to bring medicines. They let people die like this and don't even advise the family."

She underlines the regime's lack of humanity in failing to notify the young woman's family of her illness and death. After her release, Hoa had to struggle alone to support her two children and aging parents, while her husband spent a total of five years in various prison camps. She worked as a street hawker in the postwar years. Like Thuy, she resisted pressure to leave her home and move to the New Economic

Zones, and she stayed steadfast in her refusal to submit to the authorities. She is forthright in expressing her anger toward the regime: "There are no words for their behaviour." She concludes with an impassioned defense of the RVNAF:

> I was in the armed forces and I know that our army fought bravely and tenaciously. They were not lukewarm in their fighting. But because of the strategic situation, the Americans had to let go, they no longer supported us, while on the communist side, the Russians and the Chinese continued to help the North Vietnamese. Do you see that? Two allies helped them.

As for Quy, she remembers many military deaths in 1975, and experienced difficult years after her release from re-education camp. She was forcibly relocated to Suoi Day 2 in Tay Ninh, one of the New Economic Zones. She made numerous unsuccessful attempts to escape the country from different locations—Ca Mau, Ba Ria, Vung Tau, and My Tho—before finally being sponsored overseas by one of her brothers. Like Thuy and Hoa, she displayed fortitude in refusing to give up on her efforts, and she persisted despite several failures. In her later years, she has sought to come to terms with the reverses and tragedies of her life through the practice of Buddhist meditation. She avers that she feels no resentment or hatred toward the regime.

Yen, like her older colleagues, displayed strength of mind in organizing her escape from Vietnam after her release from prison. She asserts that she became stronger as a result of her trials:

> After careful reflection, I don't think I have much to regret. I think we have to undergo many trials in our life, but we can draw lessons from such experiences. If I had boarded that ship at Saigon port and escaped in 1975, I would not have had to endure the hardships that I did. But during those three years in prison, I acquired many new skills and many virtues. In fact, I do not regret the decision to stay in Vietnam, I accept life as it is and believe that I can overcome any adverse condition by sheer power of will.

She conveys how fortunate she is to have been given a chance at a new life overseas, a chance that she terms a "rebirth." As she relates, "once you have experienced hardship, you enjoy life more."

Thuy, Hoa, and Quy served as military nurses in the 1950s and 1960s, and all three were marked by the nature of their work and by the extent of military losses. Yen notes that the majority of female army personnel worked as nurses. They were too few, however, to cope with the scale of military casualties in the South. Dong's *RVNAF* states that

> According to statistics, in 1966 South Vietnam had only 1,000 medical doctors; 700 of them were already serving in the RVNAF. As a result, medical doctors were assigned to hospitals and medical units to the regimental level only. There were no medical doctors at the district or battalion level, except for the Airborne and Marine Divisions. . . . Medical treatment at military hospitals was also affected by the lack of a professional corps of nurses. The supervision and training of nurses were usually the responsibility of ward physicians but very few could spare the time for this task. To overcome this shortcoming, a nurse corps was activated in 1971 and courses were conducted to train officers and NCO's in nursing duties. . . . Still, requirements far outgrew the availability.[76]

Dong omits any reference to the many women in the WAC and later WAFC who served as nurses or medics. In her narrative, Thuy refers to the lack of sufficient beds in military facilities, with injured soldiers having to be laid outside. Dong notes in this respect,

> With regard to facilities, most hospitals needed repair and rehabilitation. Except for the new 500-bed ward built for the Cong Hoa General Hospital, most field hospital wards built after 1963 were of the semi-permanent type with roofs and walls made of corrugated iron sheets. . . . Running water and sanitation were two permanent problems.[77]

Thuy recollects that she was so busy when casualties were particularly heavy that "[she] had no time to eat." An army career signified in essence, a life of service. As she sums up: "It is a job that involves helping others in one way or another." This is clearly how Thuy perceived her role. Her responsibilities consisted of assisting doctors to treat the injured, and helping the families of the injured. As a military social assistant, she distributed supplies and medicines to the families of soldiers. She fulfilled in this way the principal role of women in the WAFC, which was to bring relief and succor to male soldiers, and to assist soldiers' families. As noted by de Groot, "the most important point about female service was that it freed men for more important tasks, namely combat."[78] Even though their work blurred the distinctions between the home front and the military front, the four women draw a clear distinction between their own work and that of male soldiers on the frontline.

The women acknowledge the fallacies of memory and stress that their recollection of events may be faulty or unreliable. As Inga Clendinnen has noted, "our memories are essential; our memories are unreliable. Most of us live with that discomforting paradox."[79] A number of differences and inconsistencies emerge from the women's recollections and interpretations of past events, as well as between the oral narratives and the written sources. Hoa and Quy, for example, state that it was President Ngo Dinh Diem's sister-in-law, Madame Nhu, who was responsible for reducing the WAC to only two branches in 1957, while Ho writes that the Department of Defence decreed this change in 1959.[80] Neither Ho nor Phung make any reference to Madame Nhu in their articles on South Vietnamese servicewomen. Hoa refers to two days of "combat duty" in military hospitals per week, while Quy remembers that it was three days a week, with a fourth day on standby. Estimates of the number of female officers range from 400 to 600. Estimates of the overall number of female troops range from 6,000 to more than 7,000. Yen stresses how unreliable her memory is, but she then provides a detailed account of the range of tasks carried out by women in the WAFC. While the women may make a point of underlining how much they have forgotten, despite fluctuations in details and statistics, their memories of army service have a level of congruence. This may reflect the fact that many army women do congregate, even if it is only once a year, to attend memorial marches or reunions. These occasions provide them with the opportunity to reflect on the past and on their war service. Memory and the connotations of memory and narrative are all the more important in the case of South Vietnamese servicewomen since there is a dearth of available documents on their history.

The narratives of these four former military women may succeed in establishing a dialogue between past and present, but they reveal a problematic relationship between the personal and the public, and between memory and culture. The women have no public history against which to contextualize their personal memories and experiences of army service. They and other female military personnel have been omitted from histories of the war, and they fail to feature in statistics or "facts" relating to the war. Although thousands served in a variety of roles throughout the duration of the war, women who served in the

RVNAF appear to have been forgotten by allies and enemies alike. The fact that these women all volunteered to serve in a time of war has gone unremarked. Their actions are all the more notable since South Vietnam neither expected nor encouraged the large-scale mobilization of women into its armed forces. "Women's experiences," writes Summerfield, "are, routinely, omitted from public accounts of the construction of national identity through military activity, and hence from accounts of war, which is reproduced as (inevitably) predominantly masculine."[81]

While others may have failed to acknowledge them or their service, female veterans remember their past careers and remember those who have died. They do so within the close circles of veterans' groups. The first international reunion of RVNAF servicewomen took place in California in 1998.[82] Female veterans from countries as diverse as Denmark and Australia attend these reunions. The *RVNAF Servicewomen's Magazine* commemorates female colleagues lost in three different postwar contexts: in communist prisons after the war; at sea while trying to escape; and overseas. The 2007 Special Issue of the *Magazine*, for example, refers to Colonel Tran Cam Huong, the first chief of WAFC, who died of illness after ten years in re-education; Captain Nguyen Thi Van, who died in a communist prison; Lieutenant Nguyen Thi Thinh, who was executed for revolting against the regime; and Major Trinh Thi Tam and Captain Tran Thi Kiem Hue, who died at sea while trying to escape Vietnam, among others.[83] Former members of the WAFC work together to contribute funds toward the support of female war invalids in Vietnam. Hoa speaks of this in her narrative:

> Now in the United States, some of the army women volunteer to care for old female veterans. We do what the men do: we send money to war invalids. One army woman volunteered to coordinate the help we provide to our old colleagues at home. She sends the money over to the needy once a year. We send her a contribution every year. Her name is Nga. She lives in Sacramento and devotes her time to doing that.

Female veterans acknowledge that theirs is an aging population and that fewer march or join reunions every year. Many women suffer from poor health as a result of their years of privation and hard labor in re-education camps. Former servicewomen, however, continue to establish a public presence by participating in memorial marches in their adopted countries—on Memorial Day in the United States, and Anzac

Day in Australia. All four women whose narratives feature here have taken part in memorial parades. As Quy relates:

> Being part of the army in the past is something that can never be erased. I feel obligated to participate in the march. It is my duty to take part in the march. I had enjoyed the experience of being in the army in the past, now I must share the responsibility with the rest of the troops. I don't know how long I can keep on marching but I will continue until I can no longer do so any more.

Their presence in commemorative marches signifies their determination to inscribe their experiences and that of other South Vietnamese servicewomen into the national narrative of their adopted country. Their narratives reveal that while few others may be aware of their stories, these female veterans have succeeded in constructing individual discourses of their war service and postwar lives, and are, in the process, creating and preserving the forgotten histories of RVNAF servicewomen.

Plate 1
Hoa with her cousin Ngot (in the foreground) in Saigon in 1970. Hoa disappeared at sea in 1978 with her two daughters, ages seven and three, and her younger sister and brother.

Plate 2
Hoang playing the accordion as part of the Vietnamese Red Cross Women's Association Band at a concert for the Department of Ammunition and Logistics in 1966.

Plate 3
Tran's mother in the family bookshop in Bien Hoa in 1974. In 1975, the communist authorities confiscated and removed all the books, and the bookshop was closed.

Plate 4
Le in the Central Highlands, circa 1969.

Plate 5
Le in Buon Ma Thuot in 1983.

Plate 6
Front row from left to right: Nga, Kiet, and Suong with their cousin Nhan behind them in Saigon in 1957.

Plate 7
Anh in 1970, shortly after she obtained her degree in pharmacy from the University of Saigon.

Plate 8
Suong on the day of her graduation as a nurse in Melbourne, Australia, in 1984.

Plate 9
Thuy with her parachute pack on her shoulder at Cu Chi, a jumping training site, in 1957. She was in the Airborne Division for seven years.

Plate 10
Thuy as a military social assistant giving presents to a soldier at the Department of Army Security in 1969.

Plate 11
Quy in her army uniform in 1970. Note the rank insignia that she removed from the photograph.

Plate 12
Yen (seated in the front row on the right) with army colleagues in 1972. Hoa is seated in the front row on the left.

Plate 13
Bon in Saigon in 1971.

Plate 14
Hoa (second from right) with her classmates at Gia Long Girls' High School in 1956.

Plate 15
Kieu (front row, second from right) with her classmates at Lycée Descartes in Phnom
Penh, Cambodia, in 1960. She remembers a vibrant cosmopolitan upbringing in
Phnom Penh in the 1950s and 1960s.

Plate 16
Kieu and Claude in South Vietnam in 1973.

Plate 17
Tuyet and Terry at Ky Hoa Lake, Saigon, in 1992.

Plate 18
Hanh and Sammy in Vietnam in 1999.

Plate 19
Vinh as a high school student in Hue in 1961.

Plate 20
Vinh with her daughter Anh in 1975.

Plate 21
Tien (on the left) with her friend Mai by the banks of one of the smaller branches of the Saigon river in 1973. Mai drowned at sea while escaping the country by boat in 1978.

Plate 22
Ngoc (on the right) with her sister Thanh in Galang refugee camp, Indonesia, in 1980.

CHAPTER 4

Fragments of War

Vietnam was at war for thirty years from the end of the Second World War to the fall of Saigon in 1975.[1] War left its imprint on generations of soldiers and civilians, and lasting scars in the lives and memories of individuals and families. "War," as noted by Michael Humphrey, "involves the destruction of people and their worlds. It involves laying waste life and property. And when the war is over its legacies live on in personal memories, bodily scars and destroyed cultural landscapes. People and landscapes remain contaminated by war for the long term."[2] In South Vietnam, the damage caused by three decades of war was then compounded by state repression after 1975. This chapter explores four narratives in which women reconstruct wartime lives and remember wartime losses, as well as postwar traumas. They include those who formed part of the million Vietnamese who fled south as refugees when the country was partitioned into two following the Geneva Accords of 1954, those whose relatives served in the Republic of Vietnam Armed Forces, and those who retain sharp memories of witnessing or bearing deaths in wartime. Women experienced further traumas in the aftermath of war when their families were subjected to political discrimination, when family members were imprisoned by communist authorities, and when they made their escape from their homeland as refugees.

As these narratives will reveal, women not only remember different aspects of war, they also formulate and articulate these experiences differently. Wartime and postwar losses and traumas in these narratives manifest themselves not solely in terms of the content of stories, but also in the shape and structure of women's narratives.

War features in many Vietnamese novels, short stories, and memoirs. The work of several writers of the Vietnamese diaspora is either marked by or centers on their experiences or interpretations of the war. The Vietnamese French writer Kim Lefèvre, for example, provides a vivid rendition of war and the destruction of war in her autobiographical novel *Métisse blanche* (*White Métisse*, 1989). Lefèvre was the illegitimate child of a Vietnamese woman and a French officer. *Métisse* relates the difficult years of her childhood and youth in colonial and postcolonial Vietnam before she left for France in 1960 at the age of twenty-five. One of the most dramatic images in *Métisse* is that of the destruction of the town of Tuy Hoa in central Vietnam at the onset of the Indochina War (1946–1954). The Viet Minh set fire to the town as they retreated, and Lefèvre reconstructs a scene of devastation and collective mourning as the townspeople watched their homes burn:

> At the sight of Tuy Hoa burning and from which we could discern the sound of explosions here and there, the women, sitting in scattered groups in the night, beat their heads on the ground and wept at the destruction of the town. . . . In front of us, the fire roared, relentless. . . .
>
> It was my first experience of the irreparable. I will never forget the agonising sight of that funerary wake in front of Tuy Hoa delivered to the destruction of the flames.[3]

In Lefèvre's evocation, it is women who give voice to this collective trauma, and women who later remember and commemorate the past.[4] The townswomen beating their heads on the ground engage in a public act of bereavement, and their pain echoes the damage sustained by their homes and the land.[5] This sight not only left a clear imprint in Lefèvre's memory, it also came to symbolize the devastating effect of war on civilians. Lefèvre and her mother joined the convoy of refugees heading away from the burning town. As Lefèvre writes,

> I have only known war as a civilian, in the company of the sick, the old, women and children. . . . We were afraid, always afraid. Afraid of losing loved ones; afraid of planes, of tanks; afraid of stray bullets. In this confrontation, we were always the hunted, never the hunters.[6]

In this passage, Lefèvre bears witness and presents Tuy Hoa as a traumascape and a site of grieving for its people in wartime.[7]

The concept of Vietnam itself as a vast traumascape appears in a remarkable short story by the writer and translator Phan Huy Duong, entitled "Un squelette d'un milliard de dollars" ("A Billion-Dollar

Skeleton," 1994).[8] "Squelette" is a phantasmagorical tale in which the search of an American billionaire for his missing son—a pilot shot down over North Vietnam in 1972—becomes a metaphor for a country's search for its accumulated war dead. In this story, Vietnam becomes a vast repository of bones crisscrossed by roads and railroad lines, and marked by newly built crematoriums, as people shift through the human remains of thirty years of war in their search for the American's son:

> Day after day, the bones scattered throughout the land of Vietnam headed towards the Centre. Soon the hills became mountains visible from kilometres away. The dense network of rail and freight cars spread rapidly. The four asphalt roads that led to the Centre stretched in all four directions. One could now gain access to the Centre as if through mountain roads, at the bottom of a gorge, between two walls of bones.[9]

Phan Huy Duong appropriates iconographic images of war and genocide in the twentieth century to underline the cumulative effects of decades of war in Vietnam. In his work, "the Vietnam War becomes an amalgam of all wars, and Vietnam itself an extended traumascape."[10] The American does recover the body of his son, but leaves him on foreign soil, alongside the ashes of all the other dead of the war. "Squelette" provides a hallucinatory illustration of individual lives engulfed in a vaster trauma, the sheer scale of losses sustained, and the enduring legacy of war. War, in effect, produces not only external traumascapes in the form of destroyed homes, villages, towns, and landscapes, but also results in internal traumascapes in the form of emotional and psychological scars. I will now explore these traumascapes in the four following narratives.

A LIFE IN FRAGMENTS

The first narrative is that of Kim, born in 1933 in Thanh Hoa, northern Vietnam. She and her family formed part of the mass movement of refugees who fled from the communist North in the wake of the 1954 Geneva Accords. They resettled in Saigon. Kim was imprisoned by authorities in the north because of her Christian faith (although the length of time that she spent in prison is unclear), and the memory of that experience still distresses her more than fifty years after the events that took place. Her life story emerges as a discontinuous, fragmented, and at times confusing narrative that oscillates between the events of

1945, the Indochina War, the Vietnam War, the migration south in 1955, and the escape overseas in 1983. She remembers:

> I was able to have some education until 1945 when I had to discontinue due to the big war [the Indochina War]. We lived in Thanh Hoa but my parents often went to Hanoi on business trips. In 1949, amid the big war, my dad fell ill and passed away when I was only about sixteen or seventeen years old. As a result, I had to take charge of the business for my mum. At that time, trading was quite difficult. Moving around was difficult because Thanh Hoa province was under communist control. Streets were demolished by French air raids. People had to dig into the ground to shelter from the continual air raids.
>
> My parents were in the business of manufacturing fish sauce so they were very wealthy. However, our business was severely affected by the war. Our sole means of transporting goods was by ship. Our ships were destroyed by French planes. It was an extremely tough time for my family. My house escaped damage during air raids because we were in a Christian area. I kept going back and forth between the area dominated by the French on one side and the one dominated by the Viet Cong on the other. It was very tough. We were suspected of being spies and imprisoned by the Viet Cong.
>
> My life was filled with sadness so I don't want to talk about it too much. I was imprisoned for a long time [she paused and became quite distressed]. It was horrible. I don't even want to reveal this to my children. This is a sad story so I don't want to talk about it. . . .
>
> The Viet Cong made up stories to convict people, especially those who were Christian like me. Anyone who moved in and out of the area was suspected of being a spy and was arrested and imprisoned. Until May or July 1954, with the Geneva Agreement, there was a ceasefire. It was not until October of that year that many political prisoners like myself were released. According to that agreement, political prisoners from both sides were released.
>
> There were about three or four women in prison and the rest were all men from the Christian villages. All the village mayors were executed and those who were in trading . . . even a man who was only a blacksmith who knew how to make guns for shooting birds was convicted and executed. These are just some examples that I want to recount to you. I don't wish to even talk about this to my children because it is so sad.
>
> In 1954, I returned, and in 1955, my mother died. When she died, I took all my siblings to South Vietnam. During the nine years that we lived under the Viet Cong regime from 1945 to 1954, they never said

anything that was truthful but there was one time that they said something true and no one would believe them. At that time, there was no
radio or newspapers. We were isolated, and any movement in and out of
the area was forbidden. We were heavily guarded. Then there was the
announcement that anyone who wanted to go to South Vietnam could
apply for a permit to go. No one dared to believe this. We thought that
it was another ploy to arrest us. Only the ones who acted quickly and
applied were granted a permit. All the associated expenses of the trip
like food were covered by international organizations. Yet on the way,
we were asked for money. Whoever could not pay had to go back. We
were driven to Sam Son then we boarded the ship Ba Lan. There was
not enough food on board. There were also demands from the Viet Cong
to pay for the food supplied. There was not enough to eat. I only had a
little bit: I had to save some for the boys [her younger brothers]. The
Viet Cong accompanied us to the estuary of the Saigon river and we
were handed over to the IRC [International Relief Committee]. When
we got there, we were told all sorts of propaganda like all the people
who migrated from the North were restricted to staying there. We would
not be allowed to live with the rest of the community in South Vietnam. If anyone wished to go back they could still do so. The communists
were very persistent with their propaganda. When we came to Saigon, I
remembered it was June 1955.

Her family paid a heavy toll in the war: of her five brothers, four served
in the armed forces of South Vietnam (the fifth was in North Vietnam). Two were killed during the war, the third lost his leg, although
this injury meant that at least he was not sent to re-education in 1975,
and the last died of illness after the end of the war. This is how she
speaks of her dead:

I had five brothers. Two were killed in the conflict; one lost his leg [she
pointed to her left leg]. There was one more who was in the army and he
later died from illness. The fifth one, my eldest one, remained in North
Vietnam. When the Viet Cong tried to capture the local priest, the young
men rallied to protect him. Then the Viet Cong brought in a whole troop
and the area was besieged. There was a big battle. My brother was captured along with some other people. They were sentenced to seventeen
years in prison. He was only released after fifteen years. In 1975, he came
down to South Vietnam and in 1985, he tried to escape by sea and the
whole family died. I had five brothers, two died in battle, one lost his leg,
one was a military man, and one was imprisoned. Now, they are all dead.

War had a direct impact on her family's life: it led to the ruin of her parents' business, the imprisonment of family members, and the death of others, and to their status as refugees in their own land. Northerners who fled south in 1955 had lived for ten years under Ho Chi Minh's regime. Communism did not represent a distant political ideal but a bitterly experienced reality. Kim's family, which had already undergone such major disruption during the war years until 1954, had to rebuild their lives in the south, only to then witness the collapse of South Vietnam two decades later. The story of Kim's elder brother is particularly tragic. He spent fifteen years in North Vietnamese prisons, was separated from his mother and siblings for more than twenty years, and finally came South in 1975, only to die at sea as a boat refugee with his family ten years later.

After the war, Kim was left as sole carer of her five children since her husband was interned in re-education camps. When he escaped from Vietnam in 1982 after his release, the Vietnamese authorities arrested her and confiscated her house. She spent four months in prison. She states of her experiences:

My memory is very sad and unpleasant to recall. I lived through many wars, and witnessed many events. Those impressions are etched indelibly in my mind. I still have memories of my brothers who were like my sons losing their lives in the war. The wounds they sustained were too horrific to speak of. I cannot even open the photo album to look at them. They were like my own children so their deaths were very painful for me. Other than my husband and children, they were a big part of my life. They lived with me when they were very small; I took care of everything for them.

I went on because I had a duty to look after my siblings. If I faltered, who would take care of them? All the things that happened in North Vietnam, the wars, the passing of my mother due to illness, then the imprisonment of my husband. If I did not soldier on who would take care of my children?

Through all the losses and the hardship, I have become stronger, more determined. As a Christian, I have a belief that everything is predetermined, as one would say, if you have some good fortune then you also have some bad luck. If I compare myself to others then I am much luckier than others. I told myself that if my brothers had gotten married and then died, it would have been worse. But my two brothers were single so they left no widows.

Perhaps at different points in our lives, we have to experience hardship and overcome obstacles. I do not say that other people have not experienced hardship but they face different obstacles. During wartime, there were widows with three, five or seven children whose husbands were killed in the war. They must have been devastated. They too experienced turmoil and adversity but their situation was different to mine. No two cases are similar. They too must have had great inner strengths to overcome these obstacles. They too must have been weighed down with duties and responsibilities. I believe that Vietnamese women have great endurance.

In this excerpt, Kim provides a summation of her wartime experiences, responsibilities, cares, and principal losses. She articulates the elements that motivated her to continue to assume her responsibilities toward others and strives to provide an explanation for the events that affected her life and that of her family and country. She positions herself within a wider framework when she compares her experiences to those of her compatriots and other women. In this way, "the traumas of a personal past may be redeemed by joining personal with collective memories."[11] Kim draws comfort from her belief that she is "much luckier" than many others who suffered worse losses in the war. By linking her life story to that of other Vietnamese, she ensures that her experiences become part of a wider collective history of the South Vietnamese in the war.

MEMORIES AND NUMBERS

The second narrative is that of Bon, born in Saigon in 1940. Her narrative moves back and forth between her memory of events in 1945, 1975, postwar Vietnam, and the refugee experience. She remembers a happy and privileged childhood in the village of My Le in southern Vietnam:

I was a very happy child. My father was the richest man in the village, because he owned land and a timber factory. So I was the child of the richest family in the village, with good status. So I was very happy. In the afternoon, we would hang around the field, look at the rice, the buffalos. Our house was built on a riverbank and the two timber factories were on both sides of the river. We got wood from the forest and cut them out, making heaps of money. I had a very happy childhood, and I always want to bring back those good memories. I once went back there to visit my village, just to find out that it has all gone now. My father's

land was taken over by the farmers, and there was nothing left. I could
only visit my parents' graves. The rice fields were still there, but they
were no longer ours.

Bon's narrative sets up a deliberate contrast between her childhood and
the later events that had a negative impact on her family and destroyed
that early happiness. In her reconstruction, her native village signified
security, wealth, and happiness, and she paints the picture of an idyllic
childhood in a house by the river surrounded by rice fields. Her family's displacement from this rural setting denoted a major change in their lives and
was the precursor to a series of losses and tragedies that culminated in the
events of 1975, postwar traumas, and her escape by boat in 1983.

The intrusion of politics, in the form of the Viet Minh, was the catalyst in altering her family's fortunes, although she only understood the
full implications when she grew older. She relates:

> In 1945 when I was five years of age, I witnessed the rise of the Viet
> Minh. My older sister, who was twelve years older than me, was seven-
> teen at the time, the mating age, and she was among them. I only knew
> what she was up to later on. At that time, I did not know anything, I
> just followed her around. The French and the Vietnamese soldiers were
> posted in one area and the Viet Minh in the other. My sister's duty was
> to observe the changes in what was being put on the bamboo poles on
> the soldiers' side. For example, some days they would wash their white
> clothes, some days they would wash other kinds. If something unusual
> happened, like the clothes were taken off, my sister would go and alert
> the Viet Minh and they would run and hide. On one occasion, my sister
> could not inform them on time, the French turned up so suddenly that
> the Viet Minh had no time to run, so they hid in straw stacks. The
> French used their daggers to poke into the straw stack. The men inside
> the straw stack knew that the French were there, so they killed them-
> selves with a grenade. One of them was my parents' nephew. I only saw
> things happening around me, I felt lucky that I was not as old as my sis-
> ter . . . because at that age, around seventeen or eighteen, everyone
> would be after love. They would get together and then they joined the
> Viet Minh, you know. My sister was at that age. She was very passionate
> about it.
>
> I found out later on, because my parents were rich, that two men came
> to our house every few weeks or every month with guns and empty bags.
> They would come at seven or eight o'clock at night, go straight to my
> parents' room and demand things, you know, like a kind of tax. I saw

that, I saw them coming with empty bags and leaving with full bags on their shoulders. After they left, my parents would sit there, in silence. My father loved me very much, as I was their youngest daughter. I would cling to his feet and ask him what had happened. I was seven years of age then. I knew that he was sad, but because he did not tell me any-thing, I could not figure out why he was not happy. I did not understand what was going on in my village at that time.

In 1947, my father closed the two timber factories. He moved to Cho Lon and leased some land from a Chinese man named Hoa. He then moved all of his factories there. I did not know how he did it, but in 1949, when I travelled from the village to Cho Lon, he had finished building them there. My father continued to run his timber factories. I was nine or ten by then so my father wanted me to go to school. But I was so scared of the teacher, I wagged[12] school. I only got to the first grade when I was ten. I wagged school for one year. My father knew nothing about this until I was caught by the police and brought home. My father beat me, enough to make me go to school. I lived in Saigon from the age of ten. I had a rich and happy childhood, but because the Viet Minh took our rice and money, my father had to leave the village. He hated the Viet Minh . . . he did not want to . . . he only wanted to do business, he did not want to get involved in politics.

Bon's narrative relates that her sister joined the Viet Minh out of a heady mixture of romantic and revolutionary ideals, rather than a sense of deep political conviction, and that many other young people of her sister's generation did likewise. Rather less romantic was the tax that the Viet Minh extorted from local villagers and farmers, which in this case led to Bon's parents leaving their village and moving the family to Saigon.

Events took a downward turn after the death of her father in 1964, and she remembers her brother's death in the war:

My family was very poor at that time, because all of us had been relying on my father, and my father had over ten daughters.

My younger brother was shot dead by the Viet Cong. My mother cried a lot, and her sadness took over her life. She got sick and died. What a misery.

He was in the Infantry, and he was sent to Quang Ngai. He failed his high school exams so he was enlisted, you know. He could apply to be exempted as he was the only son in the family, but it was his destiny. The approval came a little late so he went. His Captain said just let him go, and he would then send him home. Then the Captain . . . my brother was killed. He was killed before the Captain arrived. He was

shot dead only two or three days later in Quang Ngai. At that time, I
was married. My husband went there to take my brother's body home.
He was on the plane. . . . My whole family owed him for what he did. . . .
He sat on the plane with all the coffins and the smell. He had to throw
away his uniform when he came back. He was the only one who could
bring the bodies back on the plane, no one else . . . other people could
only ask their superior for an army vehicle if they wanted to take the
bodies back. They would not be able to do it in any other way. That was
why our family owed my husband.

The postwar years for Bon, as for many others, were characterized by
hardship and isolation, as she struggled to care for her family while her
husband spent several years in internment. She continues:

After 1975, my husband was in a re-education camp, and I had to support him. It was awful. I had to go and visit him in Tay Ninh by myself,
with my son Gia, who was only three or four years old at the time. I
would take the bus to Tay Ninh. From there, I would hire a truck with
some other people to get to the camp. I could not sit down in the bus
because the road was very rough. When I gave birth to my son, I had
problems with the sciatic nerve so I could not sit down. I had to squat
kilometre after kilometre. I had to carry ten kilograms of goods and
there was my little boy too. Other people would walk in front of us
while I had to carry some bags with both hands for a short distance
and go back for the rest. And on the way out, I had to carry my son.
When my husband was taken back to the camp, my son would cry
non-stop. Visiting my husband was very hard. They kept moving him
to different camps.
    But escaping from Vietnam was even worse. I tried fourteen times.
We went . . . my husband came home after spending several years in
the re-education camps, and his mother was still alive at the time. He
did not want to leave her. I kept persuading him and he gave in eventually. When my husband agreed to escape with me, I had a lot of students who wanted to escape from Vietnam too. We attempted to
escape several times without success. There were two occasions that I
remember in particular. There was the time I went through Soc Trang
and our boat was shot at, and I was nearly hit. Two or three people on
our boat got killed. My husband, my son and I were sitting next to the
engine. I did not hear anything because the engine was very noisy but
my husband heard the gunshots. He pushed our heads down, but our
son kept lifting his head up. One bullet hit the engine. Somehow, the

captain's wife and my husband's friend were hit. They [the Vietnamese authorities] caught us and brought us in. They stripped us all. We were searched down to our underwear and our shoes. They pulled our boat in, but before they let us come on land, they told us to give them all the gold we had. Gia was only six or seven but he was very smart. I had a few rings left but I did not know where to hide them. Gia told me to hide them under the table's legs, and that he would take them later. The children could run around, but the adults could not. If it weren't for him, I would have lost everything. I was released several days later, because I had a young child with me. I was released, but my husband was not.

Bon's narrative is punctuated by her reiteration of several central elements: that she made fourteen attempts to escape from the country, that she walked thirty kilometers to visit her husband in prison camp, that 120 people were on their boat, that the refugee camp had three lines at immigration, and that she memorized the names of 200 illnesses. The result of her experiences has been a legacy of chronic headaches and insomnia. The word "misery" is a refrain in her account:

My life has been such a misery. When I was at the refugee camp in Singapore . . . you see, there were 120 of us arriving on our boat and there was no. . . . I was like a blind person in a dark world. I could not speak or understand any English. And before I left Vietnam, I tried to learn by heart over 200 names of illnesses. I thought that if I were to fall ill, I would need to describe what my illness was. And I would need to know the names of the food I would want to eat. I also learnt by heart over a hundred irregular verbs, and I read the English grammar book six times.

I have had headaches since 1975, since the communists came. Because I was too poor. And because of the loudspeakers. There was one right where I lived, next to the intersection. And another one was placed outside the house next to mine. Two loudspeakers—one belonged to the Ward, one to the District. The two of them took it in turn to broadcast. They made me crazy. And then my mother was sick, I had to stay awake at night to care for her and I had to work too. I had headaches and I was very tired so I yelled a lot. I taught but my salary was not enough to live on, and I had a husband in the re-education camp to support, too. So I had to do some extra work at home as well. After three or four years of teaching, I realised that I could not just keep lying [she had to teach the state's new version of history]. I resigned. But I still had to bribe them so they would accept my resignation. I was very tired and exhausted. I also had such terrible headaches that I could not bear it. People normally sleep with pillows, but I could not. I had to sleep with my head tilted down. It was strange, but I felt better sleeping that way. Maybe the blood flew better when I lay down that way.

During the first ten years in Australia, I had a lot of dreams about the people in Vietnam. I saw my friends, including those whom I knew in primary school. I saw them, one after the other, and I saw them several times. I even saw myself teaching in my dreams too. Apart from those dreams, I also had nightmares that would wake me up night after night. I saw myself on land and wondering why I was not dead. Those nightmares kept coming back and haunting me. Because I had spent some time at sea trying to escape from Vietnam, when I was at sea, I would only see myself dying. So when I came here, sleeping in a nice and cosy bed, I would wake up from my dreams wondering why I was on land [laughs] I thought I was dead, so I was very scared. I had a nervous breakdown. I had it many times. No wonder a lot of people changed when they came here. Like my sister-in-law who was at sea when it was storming—she said that she wished to die at that time. It was like that.

Bon's description of her condition indicates the classic symptoms of posttraumatic stress syndrome: the reliving of trauma, recurring dreams, headaches, and insomnia. She identifies the specific circumstances that led to these symptoms. Her narrative illustrates a progression from a carefree and blissful childhood in her native village, the intrusion of the Viet Minh and their politics into this remembered idyll, the family's move to Saigon, and then a succession of ruptures: her father's death, her brother's death in the war just after he had enlisted, her mother's breakdown and death, the loss of the South, her husband's imprisonment, and her repeated attempts to leave the country. It is noticeable that her reiteration of numbers relates to postwar events. In a life story marked by displacement and loss, it is not the war itself that caused the greatest trauma but its aftermath: the experience of living under Vietnam's postwar communist regime.

WITNESSES

The last two narratives are those of Hoa, born in My Tho in central Vietnam in 1940, and Lan, born in Hanoi in 1948. Hoa lived for nine years with her mother and brother in Nghe Anh in northern Vietnam.

During that time, her family was split into two, as her father and seven remaining siblings were living in the South. She remembers:

I was number nine in a big family, nine children. My father was a public servant so he moved around and my family have to move with him, but when I was four years old, in 1944, my mother took me and my older brother to Nghe Anh, to look after my grandmother, and a few months later, because of the war, we were stuck in a region controlled by the Viet Minh, and we lost contact with my father and my other siblings in Saigon for nine years, and I grew up there, and during that time, I witnessed so many bad events caused by French airplanes and bombing in my province, mostly in crowded places like schools, markets, or sports grounds, and I witnessed my classmate in Grade 5 being killed by a bomb from a French airplane. He died in front of me. This was in 1952. He was about twelve years old. We had to move to the forest to study at night, because we couldn't afford to lose any more students in the daytime.

My mother had to look after my brother and me, and she also had to look after my grandmother who was really sick. During those years, she was a landlord, and she was a really good landlord. She took care of her employees, and helped the other villagers. She was the richest one in the village, but she was not selfish.

One of my brothers was killed by the French Army. They thought that he was Viet Minh, but in fact he was only sixteen years old, and had not finished secondary school as yet. He was shot with a group including thirty-two other young men in Go Dua [in the district of Thu Duc], and I had another brother who was a pilot in the South Vietnamese Air Force, and he was killed with the whole crew, about eleven soldiers, in 1961 or 1962, he was only twenty-three or twenty-four years old. I was very close to him. We were like twins. I collapsed when I heard the news.

At that time, Mr Nguyen Cao Ky was his direct supervisor, and he tried to use an airplane to look for my brother's body and those of the other soldiers in the forest, but they couldn't find them, because it was an area controlled by Laos. Mr Cao Ky dropped some SOS instruments in case the soldiers were still alive and could signal, but there was no signal. After four days of searching, my brother was declared missing-in-action.

His fiancée waited for him for seven years, and we had to convince her to marry someone else. She's now in California, with her daughter. Her husband died too. She still treats me as a sister-in-law. We are very close.

Hoa's narrative attests to a desire to document the past and bear witness. Her vocabulary underlines this when she says, "he died in front of me." A reference to a later incident in which she saw her neighbors—a woman with her child and servant—killed by a rocket in 1975 uses the same terminology to emphasize the fact that she was there and that she witnessed these deaths. War broke apart her family for nine years and was responsible for the deaths of two brothers.

A refugee at the age of twelve, Hoa relates the story of an extraordinary escape journey in 1953, in which she, her mother, and brother walked for nearly 300 kilometers from Nghe Anh to Hanoi. On the way, they had to hide from French planes as well as Viet Minh troops. The journey took nearly a month. From Hanoi, they were able to fly south to rejoin her father and other siblings in Saigon. She relates:

> I still remember that journey like it was yesterday. One day, my mother took my brother and me out of the house. She lied and said that we were going to my grandparents' for a death anniversary, but after walking about ten kilometres, instead of turning left to my grandparents' house, we continued on ahead, and I reminded her that we'd gone the wrong way, and she then told me the truth, that we had to escape and find a way to be reunited with my father. We walked at night because the French bombed the highways during the daytime. During the day we had to hide in big containers—the ones used for storing rice—because we didn't want the Viet Minh to find out about us. They would have killed us. Our guide was one of my relatives. We got to the border between the region controlled by the Viet Minh and the one controlled by the French, and my mother had an accident on the boat. It was just a short trip on the river but my mother broke her arm, so I had to look after her. Luckily we had relatives in Hanoi. My uncle, *Bac Quat* [Phan Huy Quat] was Minister of Defence at that time, and he looked after my mother and supported us for one month in Hanoi before we went to the South.

Hoa escaped from Vietnam with her husband and children in 1980, and the family resettled in Australia. She returned to Nghe Anh for a brief visit in 2001. This visit triggered painful memories of her childhood and brought up the tragedy of the 1953–1956 Land Reform campaign in North Vietnam in which "landowners" and "rich peasants"—most of whom had only small holdings—were targeted and executed by the Ho Chi Minh regime. Inspired by its Soviet and Chinese antecedents, and intended as a prelude to the collectivisation of agriculture, the Land Reform campaign accounted for, according to the most recent figures from the Vietnamese Institute of Economics, more than 172,000 victims.[13] Hoa relates:

I couldn't find any relative who knew me from before. One person who really upset me was my mother's adopted daughter. She told me that during the Land Reform campaign, they [the communist authorities] forced her to blame my mother, and say that my mother had abused her and treated her like a servant, and not like an adopted daughter, and she told me, "No, I said that Mummy treated me like her own daughter" but she lied. I understand that she was alone and that everybody was so cruel, and under pressure, what else could she say? My mother and I were already in Saigon when they delivered their judgement.

My mother saved money and bought a lot of land for a very cheap price in 1944. She was very good to the peasants. I really admired her. I remember that when the Japanese occupied Vietnam, many villagers died of famine, and my mother used most of the rice reserved for us to give away, and we had to eat potato and sweet potato or barley to survive like the villagers, and when the Viet Minh asked for donations of gold, she didn't have much gold, because she had to save it for our escape, but she still gave them money and some of her wedding jewellery but they still said she was a landlord. Luckily she escaped just one year before that happened.

The last narrative is that of Lan, the youngest of the four women. She was six years old when her family escaped south in 1954, and she lost her mother when she was twelve:

She had an operation. It was partly because of the medical system in the past and partly because of her fate, but it was more the carelessness of the nurses at the time. She was recovering well after the operation, as it was only a tiny lump in her lungs, not tuberculosis. I guess it was a tumour or a type of cancer, but it was only as small as a pea. Her health was good and she could eat and drink like normal. But there was a tube inserted into her lungs to suck the blood out. One night, the tube got loose when she was sleeping. As it was night time, the nurses did not know, and no one came to help put the tube back in. So some air got in and made the blood clot, so . . . she died. She was operated at St Paul's Hospital by Western surgeons and getting special care and treatment because she was a nurse, but things still went wrong. It was her destiny to die then. When she died, we children were still young, and we were taken care of by a nanny.

Our nanny was very special. She used to live in the North, and when the Japanese and then the French fought each other, the Japanese burnt all the rice fields so the French would not have any rice supply. They grew jute instead of rice. About a million people died because there was nothing to eat. Our nanny's first son went with his grandmother to Hanoi when he was eight, and has been missing ever since. Her husband and then her second child, who was only three, died soon after. Before she died, this little girl said, "It would be better if the planes dropped some bombs and killed us all, wouldn't it?" She wanted to be killed by bombs rather than die of starvation. She died of hunger eventually. Our nanny's youngest, who was born in 1945, was the same age as my oldest sister. One day, it was a very cold day, our nanny asked one of her neighbours to take him to the priest in Tri Dung Church, and she never saw him again. She did not have the courage to give him away. That was why she had to ask her neighbour to do so. She hoped it would keep him alive.

Our nanny said that one day, while searching for some leftover potatoes, she saw a boy abandoned by the edge of the field . . . he was naked, crying and calling "Mother!" but no one paid any attention to him. Everyone was hungry, everyone was about to die, so no one wanted to bring him home. He had nothing on, his parents had probably sold his clothes for food, and finally left him there, hoping that he would be picked up by someone. When she went back in the afternoon, the boy had died by the roadside. His body was blackening. There were scenes like that everywhere.

Our nanny then moved to the South. My mother had to work at that time, selling medicine, and my eldest sister was hard to feed and my mother did not have enough milk for her. My mother brought our nanny home as she still had some milk. When my mother died, our nanny took care of the six of us. But our nanny did not have to work, as there was some money left by my mother. She invested the money and used the interest to bring us up until I was old enough to work and take care of my sisters.

Lan's recounting of her nanny's traumatic experiences in the North is detailed and powerful, and all the more striking because she did not witness these events (she was not even born at the time). She is transmitting another's memory. These images were conveyed to her by the woman who cared for her after her mother died and have clearly imprinted themselves in her mind. Ten percent of the population of northern Vietnam died of famine in 1944–1945.[14] Entire families, and

in some case entire villages, disappeared. The repercussions of this collective trauma could be felt for decades afterward. As historian David
Marr writes, "no disaster of this magnitude had afflicted Vietnamese society in living memory. The sounds of lamentation among starving
compatriots, the sight of bodies strewn alongside rural roads and
hedges, or encountered each morning on city sidewalks, continued to
haunt several generations in northern and north-central Vietnam."[15]
In a poem entitled "Famine," the Vietnamese American writer Tran
Thi Nga remembers:

> Worse than the bombs
> was the famine . . .
>
> One day when I opened the gate
> for Father to go out,
> there were corpses collapsed against the wall.
> I fainted.
> Father offered soldiers money to remove the corpses.
> Sometimes they took bodies that were still alive.
> People would call from the carts,
> "Don't take me. Don't take me.
> I'm not dead yet."[16]

Lan pays tribute to another woman's testimony and in doing so adds her
voice to the collective memory of the northern famine.

As for her own memories of the war as a singer, Lan relates:

> I performed in many war zones in Hue, Nha Trang, Cam Ranh, Pleiku,
> Kontum, all of them. It was hard for the soldiers. It was cold in Hue,
> very cold. Storms added to the cold made it unbearable. You could feel
> the cold in your bones. Soldiers had to fight in the cold, down in the
> trenches. There were dead bodies at some of the places where I went to
> sing. Perhaps they did not have enough time to take them away. That is
> why there were only sad songs, as they reflected the social situation at
> the time.
>
> When I was at the nightclubs, I sang with singers like Le Thu, Khanh
> Ly, Thai Thanh. I sometimes sang at Air Force clubs with General Binh
> or Minh [she cannot remember his name]. I mean, I would sing wherever
> they invited me. I felt great sympathy for the soldiers at the front. They
> were posted at out-of-the-way places. So when I sat down and talked to
> them . . . I eased their misery from missing their homes, wives and

children. I made them forget about their life-and-death situation, where their fate was like a bell on a thin thread.

Soldiers had to fight far away from home. They missed their families. They felt lost. And those songs reflected their feelings. They simply depicted the real, long lasting sorrow that people have to bear.

Those losses, I think, are irretrievable. I lost half of my life, my motherland, all the . . . the spiritual things are important, not the material ones. The culture, the things I loved, the childhood memories, the connectedness I had with Vietnam—I lost them all when I left. There have been changes in me, in the people, the environment. How can I ever find again what I have lost? I cried every night when I first came here, particularly the time I spent at Easthill Migrant Hostel, which was surrounded by woodland. I asked myself, where have all the people gone? How come there are no people living in this country? Because I used to live in a crowded, noisy, and animated setting, compared to the empty streets here, I felt really sad. I cried every night, and when my husband noticed it, I had to try not to cry out loud so as not to wake him. For a year, I cried into the pillow, I pressed my mouth against it hard to avoid making any noise. Sometimes when I was out walking, I felt faint and I had to stop. Strange, it was a very strange feeling. And then, I got used to this new environment. I have grown to like the quietness of Australia.

Lan conveys her memories of soldiers on the frontline and the songs that she felt reflected the melancholy mood of the times. She provides a somber assessment of wartime and postwar losses, as well as the ways in which the loss of her country affected her personally. Her perception of her adopted country as empty and isolated reflected the sense of emptiness and initial feelings of alienation that she experienced when she first resettled overseas in 1975. Her narrative reveals, however, that she has now adjusted to her new country and has grown to appreciate what she terms "the quietness of Australia."

MEMORIES OF WAR

These narratives illuminate different facets of war in Vietnam and the consequences of war for civilians—in the form of loss of livelihood, displacement from their homes and native villages, forced migration, imprisonment, and the internment or death of relatives in wartime or after the war. For many South Vietnamese, the postwar years did not represent a period of reconstruction and recovery but rather one of further losses and deprivations. These women's traumas did not end with the war's end. Significantly, their troubles were worsened by the conditions of life in postwar Vietnam, and they led to an even greater loss—the loss of homeland. These four narratives are all marked by personal, familial, and communal losses. The implications of those cumulative losses over the women's lifetimes—through a series of wars and the experience of living in a communist state after 1975—are implicit not only in their memories of past events and the deaths that they witnessed or had to bear, but also in the form of their narratives. As Vieda Skultans writes, "in recounting the past, narrators choose the literary strategies which best convey their experience. Thus meaning is conveyed almost as much by form as it is by content."[17]

The first narrative, Kim's, reflects the narrator's traumatic memory in its shape and structure. Her recounting of events shifts back and forward temporally and between events. She interrupts her reconstruction of past incidents with repeated iterations that she cannot talk of her experiences because the memories are too painful and that she does not even want to tell her children. Her narrative reveals how difficult the act of remembering is for her. Her testimony attests both to the unspeakable nature of past trauma, as well as to her efforts to articulate and convey her experiences to the listener. It reflects a process of moving crabwise toward painful memories of the past, and then shying away from them again, "to sneak up on time" in Günter Grass' words, "in a crabwalk, seeming to go backward but actually scuttling sideways."[18] She cannot bear to speak of past trauma, just as she cannot bear to look at photographs of her dead brothers. Kim's story is full of grief, and it is a story filled with silences and revelations. It includes a conscious effort on her part as narrator to make sense of her life by positioning it within a wider framework and interweaving her experiences with those of other Vietnamese civilians.

The second narrative, Bon's, reveals the narrator's traumatic experience in its language as well as its form. In addition to temporal and episodic shifts in the storyline, one of its most striking features is the repeated reference to numbers—the number of times she tried to escape the country, the number of kilometers she walked to visit her husband in prison, the number of kilograms of supplies she carried, the number of people who were in the boat, the number of words she memorized, and the number of times she read the English grammar book. Her narrative is replete with numbers. In a story of successive losses and cumulative traumas that were then exacerbated by the events of

1975, numbers represent something that is quantifiable and controllable. Although she endured war and the loss of loved ones, it was the stress of living under the postwar regime that significantly traumatized her and affected her health. Trauma "may arise not only from an acute event but also from a persisting social condition."[19] Bon has clearly identified the source of her headaches and insomnia: 1975 and the advent of the communist state. "The most damaging effect of war trauma," writes Daryl Paulson, "is the frequent loss of the feeling that victims are in control of their life."[20] In this context, using numbers is a way for Bon to reclaim a degree of control as a narrator. Numbers provide points of clarity in a narrative characterized by a deluge of information and details. They represent landmarks and identifiers, and they allow her to impose a sense of order over her life story.

As for the last two narratives, those of Hoa and Lan, both provide powerful portrayals of past incidents in which each woman was a witness to war and the destructive consequences of war. For Hoa, it was the memory of separation from her father and other siblings for nine years, witnessing the deaths of civilians in wartime, and making an epic journey on foot with her mother and brother, a journey that she remembers "like it was yesterday." Although the time that she spent in northern Vietnam relates only to a small part of her life in terms of overall years, it looms large in her narrative, just as the memory of her brief return visit to Nghe Anh in 2001, a visit that did not even last a full day, takes precedence over memories of return visits to the south of the country. That childhood experience in the North, and the knowledge that she and her mother and brother were fortunate to escape the atrocities of the Land Reform campaign, coalesce to form the focus of her story. They were formative experiences in her life. The last narrative, that of Lan, relates her memories of South Vietnamese soldiers on the frontline, the dead bodies that she saw, and the wartime songs whose lyrics she believes embodied the fate of soldiers, a fate she describes as "like a bell on a thin thread." Yet one of the most striking and vivid renditions in her narrative is her transmission of a memory that is not hers: her nanny's memory of the northern famine of 1944–1945. The deaths of children during the famine are conveyed with a sense of immediacy, as Lan relates the circumstances in which they disappeared or died, and the words that they uttered. These deaths traumatized Lan's nanny—she lost her three children during this tragedy and spent the rest of her life looking after another family and another woman's children. However, she transmitted this story to her charges, and Lan, in turn, retells it in her life story, proffering in this way yet another facet of civilian life during wartime.

These narratives reveal that while the lives of all these women were affected by war and the postwar period, their means of processing these experiences and conveying their memories remains highly individual. The common threads that bind them are not only women's experience of the destructive nature of war but also the fact that the war led to a scattering of people and lives. It led, in other words, to the diaspora. These women all experienced that scattering or dispersal from their homeland. Their narratives are anchored in an evolving diasporic history. Before they left Vietnam, their lives were lived against a background of war before 1975 and state repression after 1975, and the damage caused was profound. As the narrator in Bao Ninh's *The Sorrow of War* states:

> [E]ach of us had been crushed by war in a different way.
>
> Each of us carried in his heart a separate war which in many ways was totally different, despite our common cause. We had different memories of people we'd known and of the war itself, and we had different destinies in the post-war years . . .
>
> But we also shared a common sorrow, the immense sorrow of war.[21]

While these women are all survivors, and indeed have rebuilt their lives overseas, their stories reveal that each dealt with rupture in a different way. Their narratives illustrate their efforts to provide a shape and structure to their experiences, and a sense of purpose or agency to their lives. Although they all succeed in this to a certain extent, their stories and the narrative devices that they use are indicative of the profound wounds caused by war and the aftermath of war, and the enduring internal traumascapes in these women's lives.

CHAPTER 5

Love across Cultures

In a poem entitled "He covered me with a blanket," the Vietnamese Canadian writer Thuong Vuong-Riddick recalls:

In Montpellier station,
he took all my luggage
on his back,
put his arms around me.
Mother said:
"He is the one for you."[1]

Her words refer not only to a love story across cultures, but also to one that is framed by a story of diaspora and loss. In her bilingual poetry collection *Two Shores/Deux Rives*, Vuong-Riddick remembers and mourns her lost country. She acknowledges the disorienting effects of dislocation and the gift of a love that sheltered her when she was "naked in the world's eyes"[2]—an apt metaphor for a woman bereft of country and compass.

This chapter focuses on the narratives of four Vietnamese women who have intermarried with non-Vietnamese men and made their lives overseas. The contexts for these marriages range from Asia in the 1960s to Australia in the 1990s. The four women are differentiated in terms of generation, class, and level of education, but they all are shaped by the history and legacy of their family and country. Their lives in Vietnam were conducted against a background of political unrest and war, and all have been subjected to displacement or migration, and have experienced profound loss in the shape of the loss of homeland. What do their portrayals of cross-cultural marriage reveal about their relationship with the past and with memory? To what extent does their choice reflect a desire to distance themselves from their past and their history, and to seek a degree of separation from circulating discourses of grief and loss in a Vietnamese environment? Women reflect on the significance of their choices, family responses to their relationship, and the particular challenges and rewards of having a partner from a different cultural background. While they dwell on the interpersonal dimension of their relationship, these women set their experiences within a cultural and familial context. Their narratives reveal that the circumstances surrounding their relationships vary widely and that women have found individual means of negotiating the cultural and social aspects of their marriages. Implicit in this process of negotiation are the women's memories of their Vietnamese past, and their perceptions of Vietnam and what Vietnam signifies in their present lives.

The women's narratives illustrate a significant shift in the representation of cross-cultural marriage for the Vietnamese. Historically, Vietnamese have looked askance at relationships that extend beyond ethnic boundaries, whether between themselves and the Chinese or later the French, the Americans, or the Russians. This hostility is illustrated in Toan Anh's words from 1968:

> Vietnamese girls don't like to marry a man from outside the village, let alone one from a foreign country. Vietnamese from well-behaved families look upon marrying a foreign husband as a bad thing to do, no matter what rank or status the man may have.
>
> When she marries a foreigner, a Vietnamese woman feels ashamed no matter what her social class. . . . The act of taking a Western husband is an act of losing one's origins; the act of going astray by someone who has severed her roots.[3]

These words imply that women are the inheritors and transmitters of Vietnamese culture, and that marriage to a foreigner would impede or destroy this traditional role. As Neil Jamieson underlines, this level of xenophobia was exacerbated in times of colonialism and war.[4] Vietnamese literature dealt in general with the failure of cross-cultural relationships in colonial and postcolonial contexts. Novels such as Truong Dinh Tri and Albert de Teneuille's novel *Bà-Dâm* (*The Frenchwoman*, 1930) and Pham Duy Khiem's *Nam et Sylvie* (*Nam and Sylvie*, 1957) depict failed relationships between Vietnamese men and French women, whether in colonial Indochina in the 1920s, as is the case with *Bà-Dâm*, or in France in the 1930s, as is the case with *Nam et Sylvie*.[5] Published only three years after the demise of French Indochina, *Nam et Sylvie* "illustrates a post-colonial process of mourning—for a lost past and a lost illusion of love."[6] Within these literary frameworks, cross-cultural love cannot overcome the pressures and stresses of colonization.[7]

Relationships between Vietnamese women and European legionnaires in colonial Vietnam are satirized in Vu Trong Phung's *Ky Nghe Lay Tay* (*The Industry of Marrying Europeans*, 1934).[8] The author's mockery, as his translator Thuy Tranviet notes, is directed not only at these women and their "industry" but also at Vietnamese customs and traditions, and the institution of marriage.[9] As the narrator remarks to a legionnaire in conversation:

> In my country since the beginning of time, all marriages are business transactions. As you probably already know, the majority of people in my country still follow the old customs. There aren't many people who are able to marry the ones they love. It never happens in my society that a young couple is able to discuss their affairs freely with one another.[10]

The Vietnamese French writer Kim Lefèvre chronicles her mother's story in her autobiographical novel *Métisse blanche* (*White Métisse*, 1989). Lefèvre's mother fell in love with a French officer and defied the conventions of her time by living with him until she became pregnant (at which point he left her). It was the 1930s. She was ostracized by her family and community for her behavior, and this rejection was extended to her Eurasian daughter. Lefèvre writes:

> Everything about me was deeply offensive to my relatives: my Eurasian looks, my character which they found unpredictable and difficult to understand—in short, everything about me was un-Vietnamese. My French blood was blamed for all that was bad in me. This prevented them from showing me any affection. I understood this, I even approved of it. I too hated the blood that ran through my veins. When I was a little girl, I used to dream of providential accidents that would empty me of all this accursed blood, and leave me purely Vietnamese, at peace with my surroundings and myself. For I loved this land, with its rice fields, its green bamboo hedges, the ponds where I used to splash with other children my age.
>
> I have no memories of my early childhood, apart from the sensation of being everywhere displaced and a stranger. I suffered greatly as a result of this. I did not see it as an injustice but as an existential flaw.[11]

The experience of Lefèvre's mother illustrates the negative perception of cross-cultural relationships asserted in Toan Anh's words. While Lefèvre's writing reveals the unhappy fate of many Eurasian children and their mothers during colonial times, the travails of Amerasian children and their mothers in postwar Vietnam are powerfully conveyed in oral histories and memoirs such as Kien Nguyen's *The Unwanted* (2001).[12] Both Lefèvre and Nguyen were marginalized by their society and culture and had to bear the stigma of their mixed blood against a background of Vietnamese nationalism and xenophobia.[13] Both eventually left Vietnam and made new lives overseas.

Postwar Vietnamese society and the relationships between Vietnamese and Russians are the subject of Duyên Anh's 1983 novel *Mot Nguoi Nga o Saigon* (*A Russian in Saigon*). A well-known writer in South Vietnam before 1975, Duyên Anh was imprisoned for six years by the communist regime, during which time he was incarcerated in three separate prisons and two re-education camps.[14] Freed through the efforts of PEN Club and Amnesty International in 1981, he escaped by boat in 1983, and wrote *Mot Nguoi Nga o Saigon* in the refugee camp of Pulau Bidong in Malaysia.[15] His novel, which was published in France as *Un Russe à Saigon* in 1986, concerns an ultimately tragic love story between a Soviet engineer and a South Vietnamese woman in 1980.[16] As the novel relates, Vietnam and the Soviet Union may have been socialist friends but theirs was "a friendship between peoples, not between individuals."[17]

Not all exogamous relationships, however, are delineated in such a negative light in Vietnamese literary culture. Ly Thu Ho's novel *Au Milieu du carrefour* (*In the Middle of the Crossroads*, 1969) features the story of Xinh, a young Vietnamese woman who falls in love with John, an American soldier, during the Vietnam War. Their courtship is portrayed as an attraction of opposites and differs considerably from earlier literary renditions of doomed love affairs between Vietnamese men and French women. After John is badly wounded in an engagement, Xinh proposes marriage to him and both eventually leave Vietnam.[18] Ly Thu Ho's novel is contemporaneous with Toan An's work but depicts a radically different approach to cross-cultural love. But then Ly Thu Ho was a female writer and had spent a considerable part of her life overseas. Her work displays an open-minded attitude toward cross-cultural relationships,[19] an attitude that is reflected in recent autobiographical narratives and memoirs by Vietnamese women of the diaspora.[20] I will now explore cross-cultural love through the lens of the four following narratives.

COSMOPOLITAN LIVES

The first narrative is that of Kieu, born in Phnom Penh, Cambodia, in 1942, the daughter and granddaughter of Vietnamese administrators who served in Cambodia during colonial times. Kieu remembers a vibrant and cosmopolitan upbringing in Phnom Penh in the 1940s and 1950s. As she relates:

> My paternal grandfather was sent to Cambodia to work in the Post Office for the French colonial administration and as a result my father was born there. My father worked in the Treasury. When Cambodia became independent in 1954, he was transferred to the Royal Cambodian Public Service. He remained there until his retirement as *Inspecteur de Trésorerie.* Father and mother had five children. I was the only girl. We had a happy childhood and went to the only French *lycée* (high school) in Phnom Penh, Lycée Descartes. It was a selective co-ed and multiracial school. There were Cambodians of course, as well as Vietnamese, Chinese, Indian, French, English and American students. Right from a young age, we were placed in this very cosmopolitan environment and I took it for granted but now, in retrospect, it was something unique. To foster integration, we were forbidden to speak our mother tongue while inside the lycée. Needless to say, we all learnt French very quickly! I formed lasting friendships there. It was only in the later years, during the Vietnam War, that latent nationalistic tensions came to the surface.

Kieu met her husband in Phnom Penh in 1967. After obtaining a law degree in Phnom Penh, she went to France and completed her postgraduate degree at the *Institut d'Etudes Politiques* (Institute of Political Science), better known as "Sciences-Po." She obtained a job with UTA, a French airline, and it was while she was waiting for a new exit visa from Cambodia that she met Claude through some mutual friends. She remembers:

> He was an Australian diplomat of French origin. At first, I didn't want to marry him, I was still hoping to get my visa and go back to Paris but this took a few months, and by then I'd learned to know Claude better. He was bicultural, like me. I found that he was a bit like my father, he was very kind and very honest so I said yes, and wrote a letter to the director of UTA to explain the situation. We were married in December 1967 and had a big party at the Royal Cambodian Yacht Club with a multinational crowd of relatives and friends.

She states that the fact that Claude was not Vietnamese was not an issue for her family. The first cross-cultural marriage had taken place thirty years earlier in the previous generation, when one of her aunts had married a French administrator. She ascribes her affinity with Claude to their joint experience of biculturality:

> White people who marry Asians do so because they are attracted to that culture. Claude is halfway Vietnamese and I'm halfway French, so we understand each other. He knew what marriage to a Vietnamese girl would entail. He knew that when you marry into a Vietnamese family you have to accept the whole family.

Kieu's narrative is marked by a vocabulary that underlines her awareness of her multicultural childhood and upbringing. The words "bicultural," "multicultural," "multiracial," and "cosmopolitan" feature repeatedly in her account. They highlight her exposure to different cultures and countries, and her willingness to adjust her life to these varied contexts. Her life story is structured around an overarching theme of the positive blending of cultures. Her narrative of cross-cultural love illustrates a confluence of cosmopolitanism and class. Her memory of growing up in Phnom Penh, her education in Cambodia and in France, her marriage, and her later work and life, all reflect this multiplicity of experiences, peoples, and cultures.

Kieu's marriage to Claude led to life in Australia, the Congo (where they went in 1969 and worked for two years as teachers), Vietnam, Indonesia, and France. They were in Saigon from 1972 until 1975. Kieu's assertion of Claude's biculturality, and his understanding and acceptance of the consequences of marriage into a Vietnamese family, is borne out by events that occurred in 1975. Kieu and Claude took over the care of three Cambodian children—the children of a Vietnamese mother (Kieu's youngest aunt on her mother's side) and a Cambodian father. Kieu relates:

> Lycée Descartes was partially destroyed in the bombing, so my aunty, the one who had married a high-ranking Cambodian (her husband was Chief of Air Cambodge), said: "Look, the kids are twelve, ten and eight and there's no school for them so either they could go to Lycée Marie Curie in Saigon or I'll have to send them to France to boarding school." I told her: "Don't be silly, they are too young to go to boarding school. Send them to me." When the situation in Vietnam deteriorated and in Cambodia it was even worse, my aunty rang me and said: "I can't come

and see the children now. I'll try to." I didn't pay much attention to events because by that stage I had four kids with me [Kieu's and Claude's daughter was born in Saigon]. When Claude told me in early April, "You have to expect to be evacuated," I rang her and said to her to come grab the kids and go to France, and she said, "We'll try. If you have to evacuate, please take the kids with you and I'll try to rejoin you." I said, "No problem." I never thought it [the Khmer Rouge genocide] would happen. I know the reason she didn't try was because her husband was [Norodom] Sihanouk's[21] cousin and nobody thought that the Khmer Rouge would trick Sihanouk, imprison him and kill his subjects. Nobody knew, so they stayed behind. When the time for the evacuation came I had to grab the three kids with me and fly to Bangkok. From there, we were airlifted with all the orphans to Australia.

They [her aunt and uncle] were killed, you know. The French embassy remained there for a while and some of the French people that we knew said that they thought—they were not quite sure—that they saw my aunty and her husband being wrist-bound and marched to the stadium. The prisoners passed in front of the embassy. You know that the first few days the Khmer Rouge had a big pogrom, a big purge so they marched everybody to the stadium and clobbered them. I knew they had died, because when I married Claude, every time my family wanted to reach me, they would write a letter to us care of the Department of Foreign Affairs, but since the liberation of Cambodia they've never written any letter, so we knew they were dead.

This episode of Kieu's and Claude's married life saw them witness the collapse of two countries to communist regimes, the rupture of a transnational family, the disappearance of family members, and a personal and familial legacy of loss in the form of the three Cambodian children whose guardians they became. Even in this instance of lives intersected with war and traumatic loss, Kieu's narrative stresses the positive aspects of biculturality. The family's traits of cultural openness were instrumental in saving her brother's life. She recounts:

He was the Chief Medical Officer in the province of Vinh Binh, and when Saigon surrendered on the 31st of April, he went into the military hospital and said "I'm the Chief Medical Officer. We will all fight, we will not surrender." They fought for two days and they killed a lot of communists, and when they ran out of ammunition, he had to surrender and my father was there staying with him, so they condemned him to death for resisting. Vinh Binh was a South Vietnamese province full of

Cambodians because it used to be part of Cambodian territory. My brother could speak Cambodian, so he helped a lot of the monks in the pagoda when they were sick, and when people were sick he treated them for free. So as soon as he was sentenced to death, all the monks rallied, and the Cambodian population rallied for a big demonstration for my brother. The communists had just conquered the South and had enough problems on their hands. They didn't want to further antagonize the population and after that big rally, they commuted his sentence to hard labour for life.

Being Buddhist I could see that what goes around comes around. All those years my brother was Chief Medical Officer he did everything for the poor, for the Cambodians, many of whom were downtrodden. Cambodians were often seen as second-class citizens, but he didn't see them as such because we were Cambodian-born. They repaid him by saving his life.

Her brother's familiarity with Cambodian language and culture, and his care for the welfare of Cambodians in the province, contributed to saving him from a communist firing squad.[22] For Kieu's family, biculturality proved not only to be a desirable characteristic, but also a matter of life or death.

The second narrative, that of Lan, also reflects on a positive intersection of cosmopolitanism and class between a Vietnamese woman and her Western partner. Lan was born in Go Cong, southern Vietnam, in 1944. Her father was a politician and her parents separated when she was very young. She states that she was largely brought up by her paternal aunt. Lan joined the South Vietnamese Foreign Service in 1968 after completing a university degree in Da Lat. Few women were in her position. She remembers only ten women who ranked as Foreign Service officers (as opposed to those who worked in support roles). She recollects:

After two years in Saigon with the Foreign Service, I was posted to London. I covered London, The Hague and Vienna. So it was very interesting and I was absolutely in my element, loved every moment of it. To start with, you're Third Secretary and then I went up to Second Secretary and then I met Michael and that was the end of my career. [laughs]

Lan assisted a friend with an exhibition of furniture from Vietnam and this is how she remembers her meeting with Michael:

We invited all the people in charge of organising furniture at the various department stores to come to the exhibition and Michael came along, looked around and said: "Are they for sale now?" I said: "Yes, and I can take further orders, advance orders." And then he bought the whole lot [laughs], even before we had any canapés or anything. So that's how it started. And I looked at him and said to myself: "This fellow is quite nice and quite handsome but probably happily married with two children, with a country house somewhere, and a London pad. In which case, it was best to keep away. Anyway let's see what he is going to do, whether he succumbs to the charm. Is he going to make a pass?" He didn't for two weeks and then the beginning of the third week I received a little note with a bunch of flowers saying thank you very much for your help, would you care to have dinner? [laughs] I said all right, so that's how it started and then we got married in '73.

In marrying an Englishman, Lan had to resign from her position. She states that it was regulations at the time: Foreign Service officers who married non-Vietnamese had to resign. She was then reemployed as a locally engaged staff. When I asked her whether the same rules applied to male employees, her response was:

I think so. At the London Embassy there was a man, he was a Foreign Service Officer, he married a French lady and he had to resign. When I arrived, he was working as a local employee. Yes, it applies to both, because you have to ask for permission to have a foreign spouse and normally it would not be granted.

Because she knew the regulations at the time, she did not ask for permission to marry Michael. Neither did she seek her father's permission:

By that time, I was totally emancipated, I said: "Sure, you are my father and I respect you but it has nothing to do with you." As for my aunt I did write to her. I said: "Look! We are in love and he is a good person and I think that I can have a life with him." My aunty had a typical Vietnamese reaction and wrote me a long letter: "Oh you know, there are so many Vietnamese young men who would not dream of even asking for your hand but I have lots of them ready. If you just let me know, I will find you one. You don't need to marry anybody non-Vietnamese." And she added, *"Ta ve ta tam ao ta, du trong du duc ao nha van hon,"* that means that we'd rather go back to our pond and swim in it even if the pond is troubled and murky, it's still our own pond, you know, my daughter." That's what she wrote to me. I said: "Well, I've been swimming in a big swimming pool Mum." [laughs] So she came to my wedding in London, and of course, she loves Michael, Michael loves her, there's no problem.

Lan and her husband moved to Australia within a few years of their marriage, and their daughter was born in Melbourne. As a migrant and the wife of a successful English businessman, she was spared much of the hardship and dislocation experienced by Vietnamese refugees in the 1970s and 1980s. She ascribes the success of her cross-cultural marriage to two factors: first, a cosmopolitan education; and, second, geographic distance from her Vietnamese relatives. She specifies:

> I was brought up with the French influence. The Anglo-Saxon influence is slightly different and that's the only thing that I find sometimes could have been better, had I had some Anglo-Saxon influence or on the other hand had I married a Frenchman. But I never had any qualms about marrying out of the family, out of the country, out of the citizenship or anything. For me what matters is that the person is a good person. And also I consider that if you are good with each other, it doesn't matter what country you are from, you can still make a good marriage. However, if two people are not compatible it doesn't matter whether you're born in the same village, you still can't have a good marriage. Michael's side of the family is very Anglo-Saxon, they all keep to themselves. That's the good thing about the Anglo-Saxons, they don't interfere, you know, that's wonderful. The Vietnamese always say: "The English are so cold, you know, so keep away," but in a way it's very good because they never interfere. If you select somebody, that's your life, they leave you alone. That's one thing I didn't have when I was growing up. You know how it is in a large Vietnamese family, you have aunties and uncles who always let you know their opinion even when you don't ask for it. I found that there was a lot of interference when I was young. And I said to myself: "When I grow up, I would never interfere like that because it makes things more difficult. There are too many cooks in the kitchen."

Lan's narrative is structured around the theme of independence. She was a well-educated and successful public servant in a male-dominated field. She was living an independent life overseas, and made her choice of partner without needing the approval of her immediate or extended family. She evinces a clear appreciation of the freedom afforded by her removal from an extended kinship network in Vietnam. The fashioning of a life away from Vietnam and from her family, however, was not without cost. She admits to "a visceral longing for a Vietnamese environment" during her first year in London, but avers that her sense of emotional attachment to Vietnam is "long gone." Her marriage to an Englishman displays the conjunction of education, career interests, and class that Kieu's story reveals. The only drawback to the relationship that she acknowledges is the cultural gap between the French influence in her life and her husband's Anglo-Saxon background, but she also stresses that this latter aspect enables her to enjoy a marriage free of what she terms "interference" from relatives (his as well as hers).

POSTWAR LIVES

The third narrative, Tuyet's, differs considerably from Kieu's and Lan's. Born in 1956 in Saigon, Tuyet experienced great hardship and privation in Vietnam after 1975, and she married later in life. She introduces herself in the following terms:

> I am the wife of a veteran. I'm fifty years old. I was born in Saigon, South Vietnam. My parents had to escape the communists in 1954, they ran from the North to the South. They settled down in South Vietnam, and after nearly two years I was born. I was the first child to be born there. And my father settled down very quickly because he had a good education and worked for the government. And my mum, she ran a small business and looked after us. My family had seven children, two boys and five girls, so it was a big family and it was very hard for our parents to look after us. My parents' intention was to invest all their money in the children's education. My elder sister won a Colombo scholarship to Australia in, I think it was in 1970 or 1972. Growing up, I was very good because I wanted to follow my sister's example. I studied very hard, I wanted to go overseas, but I was unlucky. In 1975 I hadn't finished high school yet when the communists came. I didn't want to escape because I was frightened, I was too young and had never left the house on my own. In 1975, my family lost everything.

This downturn in her family's fortunes, their eviction from their home, and the harassment and discrimination that she was subjected to because her brother and uncles had served in the Republic of Vietnam Armed Forces, are subject matters that still distress her. Her narrative shifts back and forth between her individual experiences and those of her family. The loss of South Vietnam was particularly difficult for her father because he had already been a refugee once before in his life, when he escaped from North to South Vietnam in 1954. He had worked hard to shape a new life for himself and his family in the South only to lose everything again in 1975. This time, however, he was too old to rebuild his life. Tuyet's life in postwar Vietnam became a relentless struggle to obtain education and employment. She underwent several interrogations at the hands of Vietnamese authorities, and as a schoolteacher, she was pressured to join the Communist Party and follow state directives relating to children's education.

She met her Australian husband through a friend. It was a cross-border relationship that was initiated by an exchange of letters and evolved through correspondence. Terry was a veteran of the Vietnam War and had met a Vietnamese girl during the war; however, because he was married with children at the time, they had become only friends. After his divorce in Australia in the 1980s, he sought to find her. He failed in this. Instead, Tuyet's friend introduced him to Tuyet, and the two began corresponding at the end of 1991. Tuyet recollects:

> My husband was Vice-President of the Vietnam Veterans' Association in Australia. My friend told him: "Maybe you need to meet Tuyet," and from the letters my husband wanted to know some of the truth about what had happened in Vietnam. I have good English and we wrote letters to each other and after that he liked me and said: "I want to marry you. Maybe you can help me a lot in my job," and he loved the way I talked to him. After that I had to struggle to get all the documents ready. After we were married, we signed all the documents with the government in 1992.

Terry's service in the Vietnam War was the factor that drew them toward each other. Tuyet refers to common elements in their postwar lives:

> At that time I was thirty-six, I had struggled hard in my life and I was old enough to know where I wanted to go. I knew how to be independent. I thought: "If I can survive the communists, why can't I survive in Australia? I can survive anywhere, and that's it." When you become the wife of a veteran, you have to share everything with them, you have to understand that. Some people who have married Vietnamese, American or Australian veterans, divorce easily. But because of what I lived through, I have flashbacks of the war, a lot of flashbacks of what the communists made me suffer, and my husband gets flashbacks a lot because he served on the frontline.

She provides advice to the wives of war veterans and relates how hard it can be to live with a Vietnam veteran. Marriage, however, also led in her case to the unexpected happiness of a child:

> In my life in Vietnam, I never thought I'd have a child because life for me was very hard, and I didn't want my child to grow up and have a hard life like mine. I said enough is enough, I didn't want another person to be unhappy like me. I now try to help my husband and to look after my daughter, because she is my future. She's eleven now.

Tuyet's narrative is marked by grief and by the personal and familial aspects of loss. She positions herself as the "wife of a veteran" from the beginning of her narrative. Marriage to an Australian Vietnam veteran has provided her with a new identity and a new life after the years of adversity and privation in postwar Vietnamese society. She discourses on her family history, and the ways in which the events of 1975 affected her life, before engaging in observations of the challenges of marriage to a war veteran. Her own experience of war and of the travails of life in the aftermath of war have sensitized her to the experiences of her husband and other veterans of the Vietnam War, a war that proved to be the connecting factor that led to their meeting and marrying and the mutual understanding and support that they provide each other.

CROSS-CULTURAL ROMANCE

The last narrative I will refer to here is that of Hanh, and hers is an unusual story of cross-cultural romance in contemporary Australia. It is unusual because her husband is Egyptian.[23] Like her, he was a migrant and they met while they were in English class. Hanh remembers a slowly burgeoning romance and a partner who had to woo not only her but her family as well, since the latter initially disapproved of the relationship. He did so with patience and tact, and their marriage is a testament to the sturdiness of that love and that relationship.

Hanh was twenty-five years old when she migrated to Australia with her parents in 1992. The family had been sponsored by one of Hanh's older sisters, who had escaped from Vietnam by boat in 1984. Hanh relates:

> Sammy was better in English than I was. We were in the same class for one term; because he was better, he was promoted to a higher class.

Sammy had to go to another school but he did not want to. After some time at the other school he returned to our school pretending that the level at that school was too high for him. He asked to be in the same class with me. We became friends but my family did not agree. We were five daughters in the family, three of us married foreigners.

When Sammy and I began to know each other, my father had already passed away so there was only my mother. My mother did not like Sammy at first because she could not communicate with him. Then she discovered that she had cancer and she had to go to the hospital every day. All of us were busy studying or working and none of us could stay home with her. At that time Sammy was working the afternoon shift and he lived in a flat close to my home. He came to my house every day because my mother had to go to the Peter McCallum Hospital that specialised in the treatment of cancer. The treatment lasted two to three hours, sometimes more, but Sammy was always there to drive my mother to and from the hospital.

We were engaged for almost a year. We could accomplish it thanks to Sammy's patience; he loved me and he did not flinch from any hardship to please me. At that time he worked the evening shift; in the morning he took me to school, because I only went to work some time after our wedding. Then he drove my mother to the hospital; at noon, he had to take my mother shopping because my sister-in-law had given birth to her child and my mother cared for her. In the afternoon he went to fetch me from school before going to work. He was the chauffeur of our family.

Hanh was thirty years old when they married. She and her husband are not only from different cultural backgrounds but also of different religion, and her account is leavened with humor when she speaks of the ways in which they have handled this issue within the family:

Sammy is Christian. All my sisters married Christians and became Christian. When it was my turn, my mother asked me keep the faith of our ancestors; we had to agree that we would each keep our own faith. We did not celebrate our wedding in the church. Sammy was placed in a very awkward situation but since he loved me very much he had to comply. Before I gave birth to our children, his mother came to visit; he told me that in his country they do not know about Buddha, so, if his mother asked about the picture of Buddha I had to tell her that it was the picture of my "smiling grandparent." He said that if I loved him I had to say so because the faith of his mother is very strong. If she ever knew that he had not married according to the rites of his religion she would be sad until she died. When she came, he introduced my "grandparent" and my mother to her and he told her that I had converted to his religion.

Hanh ascribes the success of her marriage to her husband's easy temperament and flexibility in adapting to life in a Vietnamese household. She points to similarities between their two cultures:

> There are many similar points between the two cultures: for example, in Vietnam we have a high regard for teachers. It is the same in Egypt: over there, people respect their parents and elderly people exactly like us. Sammy said he loves me because of the way I love people in my family.

The one handicap that she acknowledges is that of language, and that is a source of some pain for her. English is a second language for her (as it is for her husband), and she believes that she will never be able to fully express herself, her thoughts or her feelings, because she does not have access to that vocabulary:

> Sometimes you can't express all that you feel deep down. Many times, I've wanted to use sweeter or more romantic words to express my love for him, but I could only express myself in Vietnamese. I did not know the equivalent words in English. I think that if he were Vietnamese, we would be much happier. I told him that if he were Vietnamese, he would understand me better and love me more.

Hanh's narrative is framed and buttressed by the multicultural context of contemporary Australia. Her experience of migration and displacement took place with her family, and her romance with Sammy is positioned within this setting. Her mother and her sisters in particular expressed clear resistance to her relationship initially. They believed that she and Sammy would never be happy because they would never overcome the language barrier. Although Hanh's narrative does convey her concerns relating to language, it also reveals her ability to negotiate these family pressures and balance them with her own needs. Sammy's patience and persistence, and their love, sufficed to overcome differences in race, culture, and even religion.

MARRIAGE ACROSS CULTURES

Although these narratives may reflect the gendered nature of transnational marriage-scapes, in which marriage migrants are largely women,[24] they reveal the highly individual choices these women have made and the different contexts of their marriages. Writing on the subject of cross-cultural marriage, William Klausner notes that

> Few would deny that communicating, sharing and understanding in a marriage is difficult enough even among those with similar cultural backgrounds. How much more difficult it is when, as in the case of East and West, the husband and wife come from different religious, philosophical, linguistic and historical traditions with all the baggage of quite marked dissimilarities in values, attitudes, perspectives and customs. But therein lies the challenge . . .
>
> While accommodation, adaptation, conciliation and compromise are dual responsibilities in any marriage, they are especially crucial in a cross-cultural one. And the burden of such responsibilities will naturally tend to fall more on the one foreign to the environment in which the couple is living.[25]

These four narratives illustrate the evolution of cross-cultural relationships for Vietnamese women. Their memories, even in lives that have been marked by war and loss, are of largely positive and transformative relationships. These women have taken different paths from that of most of their contemporaries by choosing a partner from another cultural background. If this choice was easier for some than for others—marriages indicative of a confluence of cosmopolitanism and class appear to have been the least problematic—it still represents an unusual option, and is a clear indicator of women's agency. "Memories," as Stephen Rose notes, "are living processes, which become transformed, imbued with new meanings, each time we recall them."[26] These women's narratives not only illustrate their perception and experience of cross-cultural marriage, but also justify their decision to engage in one. Arranged marriages in Vietnam were common forty years ago and "remain common, although they are more common in villages than in urban areas."[27] Women were prepared to resist cultural stereotypes and not only choose foreign partners but also do so in cross-cultural contexts. As Rosemary Breger and Rosanna Hill suggest,

> Living in a mixed marriage can be an intimate performance of juggling identities and the ideologies associated with them, a dance sometimes threatening to perform as well as to behold. It is sometimes enriching, but always calls into question deeply held assumptions about the nature of one's own identities, and those of one's reference groups.[28]

These narratives reveal that women were able to successfully negotiate and reconfigure cultural identities, practices, and lifestyle. For three of the women, Kieu, Lan, and Hanh, their reconstruction of marriage follows romantic plots of initial resistance or obstruction (either in the form of their own inhibitions or resistance from their immediate family), followed by resolution, and the evaluation of their marriage as a successful confluence of cultures and expectations. For the most grief-filled narrative, that of Tuyet, marriage brings not only companionship and joy, but also an accepted and shared burden of posttraumatic stress disorder.

In the first two narratives explored, Kieu's and Lan's, marriage to Westerners appears to be a logical consequence of the women's education and career choices. Their narratives reveal "cartographies . . . or sites of desire"[29] in which each partner is attracted to the culture of the other. These marriage-scapes, suggests Nicole Constable, "are formed by confluences of culture, border crossings, exchanges, and fluid terrain, rather than simple unidirectional flows of power or desire. [They] both reflect and are propelled by fantasies and imaginings about gender, sexuality, tradition, and modernity."[30] Both women identify and articulate the multicultural influences in their lives that have contributed to the enduring nature of their marriages.

On another level, however, their stories reveal underlying factors that may explain their impetus to marry outside their country and culture. As a second-generation Cambodian-born Vietnamese, and a French-educated member of the elite, Kieu formed part of a minority in her society and culture. Her narrative reveals that she is aware of how unusual her multicultural upbringing was. She was, in many ways, an anomaly. This freedom from cultural confines meant that she was less likely to be bound by the traditional expectations of marriage for Vietnamese or Cambodian women of her generation. She was therefore at greater liberty to form an attraction for a man outside these cultural confines. As a French-born Australian diplomat working in Asia, her husband Claude, like her, was also in many ways an anomaly. Their marriage seems to reflect an acknowledgment of this common feature in their backgrounds.

Lan's narrative, on the other hand, evinces a clear imperative to distance herself from her Vietnamese family and culture. Her life story reveals a family history of unhappy marriages and ruptured relationships, and the intrusion of Vietnamese politics into this history. Rather than remaining within this context, Lan opted for life with a partner on another continent. By this means, she was able to separate herself geographically, socially, and emotionally from her relatives in Vietnam and the constraints, pressures, and obligations of kinship. Her marriage attests to a yearning for space and freedom, and a degree of distance from her Vietnamese past.

Unlike Kieu's and Lan's narratives, Tuyet's narrative details the lasting negative impact of the postwar years on her life and family. It chronicles the failures of her early hopes, from her dreams of following in her sister's footsteps and studying overseas, to her efforts to forge a teaching career in the postwar years. Hers is a trauma narrative, in which her memory of the collective tragedy of the South includes personal tragedies in the form of her father's mental breakdown and her younger sister's suicide in 1994. Although she married an Australian and remade a life for herself away from her homeland, her marriage to a Vietnam veteran means that she is never far removed from her past and from traumatic memories of Vietnam. Both she and her husband carry psychological injuries as a result of the Vietnam War and its aftermath. Her narrative is suffused with a sense of loss, and it reveals the traumatic intrusion of memories of the past in the present—hers of state repression after 1975, his of war from a soldier's perspective. Instead of seeking to distance herself from that past, Tuyet in fact embraces it, and uses that knowledge to help herself and others. She acknowledges that her husband's ill health in his later years represents yet another postscript to the Vietnam War, the war that was the cause of much mutual suffering but that ultimately led them toward each other.

For Hanh, the youngest of the four, marriage reflects a process of acculturation in the aftermath of dislocation. She made an unexpected match and one that was purely made possible by migration—hers from Vietnam with her family, and his from Egypt on his own. Both found love, unexpectedly, as migrants in a strange land. Their meeting in an English class (one of the first points of contact in the experience of migrants) and their romance reveal a gradual opening up of perspectives, concessions, and acceptance on the part of her family. Hanh's insistence on keeping her Buddhist faith, maintaining a Vietnamese home, and remaining close to her family indicate the continuing importance of Vietnamese culture for her.

The following words by Lan encapsulate the principal concerns surrounding the issue of cross-cultural marriage:

Well, I think that a marriage between two people of the same cultural background would work, I wouldn't say would work better than if it were between two people from a different cultural background. In every marriage, you understand, both parties have got to work at it, and in a marriage with two cultures, both parties will probably be working harder because there's some unwritten rule that you don't know and therefore you have to learn and things like that. But the success rate of marriages between two cultures compared to the success rate of marriages of one culture cannot be compared because how many marriages of one culture are just marriages in name? There's no relationship behind that name, behind that façade of marriage. While with two cultures, marriage with two cultures, marriage of two cultures, it has to be a real marriage because otherwise both parties would just move on, isn't it right? And I know of many couples of the same culture, Vietnamese-Vietnamese, who just stay married because they have to stay married, and that's not a marriage. So therefore if a marriage works, and if you're conscious that you want to make it work, it will work independently of whether it's two persons from two different cultures, that's how I see it. Because the basis of a successful marriage, a successful relationship is the same, exactly the same, and that is: firstly, there's got to be love; secondly, you've got to have understanding; and thirdly, you've got to have forgiveness. Those three elements exist in any culture. If you can't find those three elements and mix them well, then the elixir is not drinkable. You see? Right? [laughs]

In their study *Intermarriage*, Janet Penny and Siew-Ean Khoo write that

Popular perceptions associate intermarriage with the assimilation of migrants, that is, it is supposed to enhance the migrant's chances of becoming part of the established community. In turn, many ethnic communities see intermarriage as a threat to the cohesion and strength of the community group. Both these views are oversimplifications.[31]

Their observations are borne out by the varied and enriching experiences of the four women whose narratives are explored here. Contrary to historical expectations, these women have successfully overridden the traditional Vietnamese cultural hostility toward exogamous relationships. Framed as they are by the women's communal experience of loss at a number of different levels, their relationships are positively formulated as both enabled by and enabling cultural adaptability and a broadening of perspectives. Within the context of their marriages, women have shaped their own vision of Vietnam and what Vietnam means, and how much of that past to bring into their relationship. While their narratives of cross-cultural marriage remain a minority voice in the Vietnamese diaspora, it is one that will surely evolve and expand in the coming years.[32]

CHAPTER 6

Return Journeys

Return journeys to the homeland may be imbued with a multitude of meanings for travelers, but for Vietnamese refugees and migrants, it is a journey that is often emotional and fraught. As Andrew Lam has remarked:

> We return in order to take leave . . .
> And some return only in their mind.[1]

The majority of those whom Robert Templer refers to as "the melancholy tribe"[2] left their country under conditions of great stress and hardship in the postwar years, and the memory of that departure remains engraved in their minds. Even those who left Vietnam in more orderly fashion as sponsored migrants in the 1980s and 1990s have memories of failed escape attempts, internment, or divided families. Under these conditions, the return to Vietnam is not a decision taken lightly. An increasing number of overseas Vietnamese, however, have opted to return to their former country, whether for short or extended stays.[3] In this chapter, I will explore the narratives of six women and the significance of return journeys for them. Four of the women have made the return trip to Vietnam, but two have chosen not to, and their narratives will reveal why.[4] I will examine how women have managed and negotiated this return, how they remember the past, and what function memory serves in the context of return narratives.

While the timing and circumstances of the women's return journeys may vary, their stories contain recurring narrative elements: their overwhelming emotion on first seeing their country again; heightened levels of anxiety, apprehension and anticipation; and, inevitably, the traumatic reliving of their initial departure. Their reconnection with a place that had once been familiar is characterized by ambiguity, as they detail the changes that they observe and struggle to adjust to the gap between their memories and the reality. Return narratives share a sense of grief and loss, as well as the regret engendered by lives lived away from kin. The return marks not only an opportunity to reunite with family and loved ones but a journey toward a remembered place, whether the family home, the native village, or the town or city in which women had lived prior to their exodus from Vietnam. The narratives of those who were either children when they left or who were too young to remember the original departure, on the other hand, reveal yet another dimension. Their accounts illustrate the extent to which their parents' memories and their parents' trauma have colored their perception of Vietnam and of the return journey. Overall, the women's narratives reveal two central factors: first, the predominance of family as the motivation for the journey home; and second, the women's acknowledgment that their lives now lie in their new country and that the Vietnam they remember is truly lost to them.

In *Return Migration*, Russell King writes that "when migrants are asked to indicate their reasons for return in questionnaire and interview surveys, most studies report the predominance of non-economic factors. The most frequently mentioned motives are family ties and the desire to rejoin kin and old friends."[5] This reflects the experience of the women in these narratives. Their return journeys were largely undertaken for family reasons. and for two of them, it was the only motivator that was strong enough for them to overcome their initial reluctance to travel and their considerable apprehensions about the possible consequences of such a journey in terms of their personal safety.[6] "Imagining the return," suggest Ellen Oxfeld and Lynellyn Long, "is often an emotionally charged experience, becoming more so as it is imminent. In order to return, people analyze the potential consequences (such as degree of danger, financial viability, and reception) and confront strong emotion."[7] The return of refugees is particularly problematic since their memories of their homeland are often associated with high levels of trauma. As Oxfeld and Long note, "returns require managing one's own expectations. Both returnees and 'homelands' are altered during the time apart and the return itself forces further alterations."[8] Of the six women whose narratives are explored here, five were refugees in the 1970s and 1980s. The sixth left Vietnam as a sponsored migrant in

1984 after making two failed escape attempts in the 1970s. Their return journeys span two decades, with the earliest taking place in 1989, and the latest in 2006. All were short-term journeys. Their narratives highlight the impact of the first return journey in particular, and the disjuncture between past memory and contemporary experience.

The malaise that early returns engendered in women reflects that portrayed in Vietnamese literary accounts of return journeys in the first half of the twentieth century. In the works of Vietnamese francophone writers, these journeys are largely undertaken by men and involve protagonists who become alienated from their country and culture after their years of study in metropolitan France. Novels such as Pham Van Ky's Frères de sang (Blood Brothers, 1947) and Cung Giu Nguyen's Le Fils de la baleine (The Whale's Son, 1956) depict central characters who return to Vietnam only to find themselves literally and figuratively adrift, at home neither in their country nor overseas. As cultural and linguistic hybrids, these men have become strangers in their own land.[9] Their conflicted emotions and reactions to their homecoming are specific to the migrant experience and resurface in the accounts of Vietnamese returnees fifty years later. In his memoir Saigon to San Diego, for example, Trinh Do relates his return to Vietnam in 1995, seventeen years after he had escaped from the country. Both his parents died at sea in 1982. Do writes,

> On my return, I found some old friends, including Trang, who still lived in the city. The reunions brought me many bittersweet realizations, including the dawning understanding that I had changed so much in the years living outside Vietnam. While I shared a past with my old friends, we had nothing in common in the present and the future. When I left Vung Tau, I felt like a foreigner in my own homeland.[10]

While the return journeys of male protagonists have been depicted in Vietnamese francophone novels, because it was young men who went overseas to study in the 1920s and 1930s, those of Vietnamese women who left to study in the 1950s and 1960s for the most part have not been recorded or fictionalized in Vietnamese literary culture. Kim Lefèvre's Retour à la saison des pluies (Return to the Rainy Season, 1990) is a notable exception, in that it focuses on her return to the country of her birth after a gap of thirty years. Hers is a bittersweet journey, since Vietnam was the site of the rejection and grief she experienced growing up as an illegitimate Eurasian child in the 1930s and 1940s.

She chronicles the fact that it was the publication of her earlier auto-biographical novel *Métisse blanche* (*White Métisse*, 1989) that led her to renew her ties with her aged mother in Vietnam. She writes:

> Everything changed with the publication of the book. By writing it, I had set in motion, without being aware of it, a time machine to the past. And the light-years that I had wanted to throw between Vietnam and myself, between my childhood and myself, like a great space of oblivion, were all at once abolished.
>
> The armour that I had forged, year after year, behind which I shut away an acute sensitivity to all that had to do with the past, cracked silently.[11]

In *Retour*, Lefèvre not only relates her return journey and her reunion with her mother and half-sisters, she also fills in the lacunae in her earlier life story.[12] As Jack Yeager observes, "the narrator, her mother and sisters, weave their stories together, moving towards the goal of recording and thus rescuing the past."[13] Lefèvre's return journey therefore enables her not only to reconnect with her family and her past, but also to reconstruct that past in her writing, and she is conscious of the fragility of this process:

> The past endures in the receptacle of my memory. There, it lives in the secret of my memory, always as coloured, as rich in emotions. But, like those prehistoric caves where rock art fades when the light of the present is introduced, so is my past dissolving. The movement and the noise of everyday life have taken it away. And I cannot resurrect it in any other way except on the paper in which I write.[14]

The memory of the past, and its transitory nature, color the narratives of the women explored here, as they reflect on the significance of the return journey and convey what Vietnam means to them now, after more than twenty years of establishing new lives overseas. For most, the return journey is an intensely emotional experience that enables women to reassess and modify their conception of home and homeland. As Hue-Tam Ho Tai suggests,

> Exiles provide, mostly from afar, a truly contrapuntal voice to the official discourse . . . [T]he past is a familiar place and a familiar time; it is the present that is strange. Where they reside does not quite feel like home,

but their homeland is now out of bounds. What happens when their own narratives of the past and those circulating in the homeland collide, or when their memories are set side by side with present realities is worth further analysis.[15]

With pasts disrupted by war, political upheaval, and dislocation, Vietnamese refugees have trouble dissociating themselves from pervasive memories of their home country and often dream obsessively of home. As Mandy Thomas notes, these dreams are characteristic of displaced people and play an important role in counteracting their sense of displacement as well as reconnecting them to their former lives.[16] These dreams are accompanied by acute homesickness.[17] Although the intensity of this feeling may fade with the passage of years, home and the preoccupation with homeland continue to assume a disproportionate importance in the Vietnamese diasporic imaginary. As Michael Seidel reminds us, "the memory of home becomes paramount in narratives where home itself is but a memory."[18]

The strong attachment of the Vietnamese to kin and land is manifest in the extensive flow of money and goods from the diaspora to Vietnam, a flow that, as Thomas notes, "illuminates the extension of the Vietnamese family beyond the boundaries of a single nation."[19] Although these women's narratives illustrate their continued attachment to relatives in Vietnam, they also demonstrate that their lives are now based overseas. Even if women had been unsure of where "home" truly was before their return journeys, the trip to their former homeland was to affirm their place in the diaspora and their adopted land as "home."

FIRST RETURNS

The first narrative is that of Vinh, born in Quang Nam, central Vietnam, in 1942. A pharmacist in Da Nang before 1975, she remembers fleeing to Saigon with her two children just a few days before Da Nang fell to communist forces. Her husband had stayed behind with her parents and for a while she had no news of them. Her husband had an engineering degree from Australia and was imprisoned for two years in a re-education camp. She was not allowed to visit him during his internment. After his release, he had to report to the police every two weeks and their home was subjected to regular midnight raids by authorities. They tried to escape the country in 1978 and then again in

1979. Her husband finally escaped successfully as a land refugee in 1980 and sponsored her and their daughters to Australia in 1984. The traumatic nature of her experiences manifested itself in her depressed state during her first few months in Australia, and in recurring dreams of her homeland and of those she had left behind. Vinh made her first return trip in 1989, only five years after leaving the country. It was at a time when, as she notes, few refugees had yet made the return trip home. It was a journey filled with anxiety, but one that she undertook to be reunited with her mother and sisters. She highlights her reception at Tan Son Nhat Airport:

> I can't tell you clearly how I felt by the time the plane landed. It was a mix of emotions: happiness, anxiety and sadness. I had to fill in forms stating how much money and gold I'd brought into the country and lodge them. After about fifteen minutes, a customs officer called out my name and said, "Follow me." I was the only one he took to his office. I started shaking. The airport was hot and dirty, but his office was air conditioned and very modern. He asked me to sit down. He asked me how much gold I'd brought over. I said twelve taels.[20] He said that I was supposed to pay $800 in tax. I said, "Yes, I know." I was wearing a gold necklace and ring and he said, "Just declare your necklace and ring. I'll take your form and destroy it. Just declare these two items and I'll forget about the other items on your list." I thought "Oh my God, they're taking all my gold and how can I give it to all those people?" I said, "No, no, this is from my relatives. They gave it to me to give to their families. You can't take this from me!" He said, "No, no, I'm not taking it from you, just do like I said, just fill in the form and declare the money, the necklace and ring. Just do it!" I was so scared. I did it. He said, "You normally have to pay $800 for that amount of gold. Now you only have to pay $400 and I'll take you out of the airport." I said, "Are you serious? How about later on when I leave the airport?" He said, "It's just a form so it won't matter." I had no choice. I was still shaking, but he didn't take the gold from me, he didn't ask me to show him the gold, he just asked me to pay the $400 and then he let me go. I was shaking as I paid him the money. He took me out of the airport. And in the taxi home [to her mother's house] I was still shaking.

Her narrative underlines her increasing agitation and is structured around a rapid succession of interrogative and exclamatory sentences that convey the tempo of feelings and events. The reiterated phrase "I was shaking" reveals the level of her distress and the physiological reaction that she could not seem to control. The first roil of emotions that her return engendered was overtaken by this later reaction. In the process of retelling this episode in her life story, her voice became quieter and at times almost inaudible, as if her throat was constricting. I had to lean forward to hear her words. Her experience of official corruption parallels that of many other returnees, and this was a memory that had clearly marked her. The fact that she made it through airport customs was a palpable relief. She states, "I was so happy, because I was so worried that something was going to happen to me. I still had to report to the police station and bribe them with money, cigarettes and clothes, otherwise they could have made trouble anytime." She was able to visit her mother for four weeks and subsequently made several return trips to Vietnam.

The second narrative is that of Thi. Born in 1965 in Saigon, she made a failed escape attempt as a twelve-year-old in 1977, as a result of which she was imprisoned by the Vietnamese authorities, interrogated, and placed in solitary confinement for three days.[21] She was released from prison two weeks later and was able to rejoin her family in Saigon. This experience, however, scarred her emotionally and psychologically.[22] She finally escaped by boat as an unaccompanied minor when she was thirteen, but the refugees were only rescued after a harrowing month at sea and the death of a woman on board. Thi then spent more than two years alone in a refugee camp in Thailand. Already traumatized by her first escape attempt and incarceration, this later experience and her isolation in the refugee camp led to depression and attempted suicide. She was eventually reunited with family members in Australia in 1981. Her decision to return to Vietnam in 1990 was therefore a particularly fraught one, but she did so to attend her father's funeral and support her eldest sister, the sister who had brought her up and whom she called "mother." She remembers:

> When I decided to go, I was really scared. I contacted the Australian Embassy to see whether they would help me if anything happened to me in Vietnam. I had been told that if you were born in Vietnam then you were Vietnamese, and not Australian. It didn't matter if you were the citizen of another country. I had to go through with it, because I loved my father.
>
> I had to stay a few days in Malaysia. I remember that when I went to the airport to get on the plane to Vietnam I was so scared. I didn't really know what was going to happen in an hour's time—it only takes about an hour from Malaysia to Vietnam. I didn't know what to think, what to

do. If they asked me questions about my escape, what could I say? I didn't really know the correct answer. When we landed in Vietnam, I saw two policemen holding shotguns, and I remember that I was shocked and said to myself, "Should I go out or should I just sit here and fly back to Malaysia?" But everyone had to get out, you had no choice.

I didn't really know what was going to happen next. I tried to fill in the Vietnamese form at first. I hadn't written Vietnamese for so long, I didn't know all the spelling and accents, and I found it hard to find words in my head and complete the form. When I got to Customs they looked at the form and said, "You haven't filled this, you haven't filled that. Go out there and fill it in again and then come back." The queue was out the door. Why didn't they help me or tell me what I'd done wrong? I wanted to cry, I only came back because of my father. This time I thought, "I don't care, I'll just use the English form." So I filled out the English form and went to a different table. The guy looked at me and said "Can you speak Vietnamese?" and I said "I can" and he said "Do you know how to read and write in Vietnamese?" and I said "I know some, you know, and I don't know certain words so that's why I filled out the English form" and he just smiled at me and let me through. Then I got out. The last time I saw my family, I was so young, it had been eleven, twelve years and I'd changed a lot, and when I saw them, I nearly cried because they didn't recognize me and I thought they weren't welcoming me back. I went past my sister and she just ignored me, so I turned back and said, "Can't you recognize me?" and she screamed, "You've changed! I couldn't recognize you!" I guess they still thought of me as the baby in the family.

This excerpt deals with several elements. First the overwhelming apprehension she felt even while she was making arrangements to travel, and her last-minute indecision and panic when the plane landed in Vietnam and she thought seriously about not getting off. She then had to deal with Customs and the unfamiliarity of Vietnamese forms—delays and aggravations that international travelers are accustomed to. For her, however, this stress was magnified because she had left the country illegally and had experienced internment at the hands of Vietnamese authorities. Her repeated references to her father underline the fact that he was the only denominator powerful enough to make her undertake this journey. She states that she fell ill after a week in Vietnam and had to be hospitalized—an experience she describes as "bad, really bad." She wanted to return to Australia at that point, but ultimately she spent two months with her family. Like Vinh, she remembers regular inspections and interrogations by the Vietnamese police during her stay.

For Thi and Vinh, the return journey was a fraught experience, from the moment of its conception to that of its realization. Both women were marked by their background as escapees or failed escapees and had understandable fears relating to their return to their former country. It was the strength of family loyalty, and the love for, or memory of kin that finally brought them back. Both have since made several return trips to Vietnam, but these later journeys have not overlaid the memory of that first and most difficult journey home or the powerful emotions and apprehensions associated with it.

LATER RETURNS

For women who made later returns in the last decade of the twentieth century or the first decade of the twenty-first century, and as more and more overseas Vietnamese traveled to Vietnam, the return is less associated with fears of being arrested or subjected to harassment by the local authorities. However, it can be no less painful an experience for that.

Tien was born in 1950 in Saigon. She was studying for a postgraduate degree in legislation and working as a teacher to supplement her family's income when South Vietnam fell in 1975. A Vietnamese Chinese, she became a refugee following the regime's discriminatory measures against the Chinese community. The compulsory registration of Chinese citizenship in 1976–1977 was followed by the closure of private businesses and the forced relocations of tens of thousands of ethnic Chinese to the New Economic Zones.[23] As a high school teacher, Tien witnessed students denouncing their parents in public. She objected to what she termed the "brainwashing" of children. She made several failed attempts to leave Vietnam before finally succeeding in 1979. Her boat was fourteen meters long and held 136 people. Three days into the voyage, they were rescued by an American petrol tanker just as a storm came up and their boat was about to sink.[24] She made two return trips to Vietnam: the first in 1994 and the second in 2005. The first return brought in its wake memories of her departure, and the second underscored her feelings of loss. She relates:

> I returned for the first time in 1994, fifteen years after I left the country. The purpose of my return was to attend the wedding of my second

youngest brother, the only one who wasn't married at the time. It was a very emotional trip because it was the first time after fifteen years. From the airplane, I looked down and I could see the city, the Saigon river, and I couldn't stop crying. The river reminded me of the sea and the time that I left the country [crying]. It was such a dangerous journey and I didn't know whether I'd survive. I've always longed to see the place that I thought I'd never see again. I thought I'd already lost my country. I thought I'd lost it forever.

The first time, I traveled alone back to Vietnam. My children were very small and I didn't know what conditions were like and I didn't think it was safe to bring them—I was worried about hygiene and medical care—so I didn't bring them with me.

Saigon, before it fell, was beautiful. The streets were still quite quiet and tree-lined, and I could go on bicycle rides along the river. But when I went back there were so many people, so many cars. The second time around in Saigon, I felt like a stranger. I won't ever live in Saigon, it's now lost to me. The things that I most longed to see, I couldn't find them anymore. All the memories, the street corners, the schools, I couldn't find them anymore. I've lost the city that I loved.

Tien's narrative has an elegiac and nostalgic dimension. Her repeated assertions that she can no longer find what she is seeking reflect the experience of many other diasporic Vietnamese. Her words underline the feelings of bereavement that the return journey engendered. The city and country that she once knew had altered beyond recognition. Her memory of Saigon may bear the patina of melancholy reminiscence, but it corresponds to the portrayal of the wartime city provided by Susan Terry, an Australian nurse who worked in South Vietnam in 1964–1965 and published a book of her experiences the following year.[25] Terry describes Saigon in the following terms:

Saigon we found to be a beautiful city, though we could imagine it to have been more beautiful still before so many restrictions had closed over it. Tree-lined streets, very tall shady trees, many parks at the corners, many gardens; lovely buildings, charming homes and stately French architecture give that city an air of graciousness and dignity. (It is sad that because the government has more pressing problems so many have fallen into disrepair.)[26]

Terry notes the large numbers of soldiers in the city and increasing troop movements, midnight curfews, the nightly sound of artillery fire

around the city's outskirts, signs of extreme poverty, and Saigon's beg-
gars, but these observations do not detract from her assessment of the
city's fading attractions. Tien's recollections of the level of traffic in
the city before 1975 are also borne out by the fact that although more
than 700 taxi drivers were registered by 1968 (and taxicabs were for
the most part French-made Renault compacts), private vehicles were
still comparatively rare.[27] Urban traffic consisted largely of bicycles and
increasing numbers of Honda motorcycles.[28] On the other hand, the
constant noise of street vendors began early in the morning and lasted
well into the night.[29]

Throughout the length of the war, Saigon and other southern urban
centers witnessed successive waves of refugees, most notably the massive
influx of refugees from North Vietnam in 1954–1955. For many Saigonese, however, war became a backdrop to busy lives. Tien's nostalgia is for
the Saigon of her past, a city that she could navigate easily and confi-
dently, and in which streets and buildings were familiar. This nostalgia
not only reflects a longing for a younger self, but also provides a commen-
tary on how drastically life altered for Tien after the end of the war. It
may signify, as Thomas notes, "a yearning for the promise of democracy,
freedom and capitalism that the South brought in the 1950s and 1960s."[30]
The fall of Saigon in 1975 marked a traumatic turn of events for Tien as
an individual, a Vietnamese Chinese, and a southerner. The postwar years
represented a time of instability and anguish, while the Saigon of the new
millennium appears in the guise of a polluted, overcrowded, and alien
cityscape. Saigon "before the fall" is therefore remembered as quiet and
beautiful in contrast. As Nicola King suggests, "there are moments when
memory seems to return us to a past unchanged by the passing of time;
such memories tend to be suffused with a sense of loss, the nostalgia out of
which they may be at least in part created."[31]

Another narrative, that of Diem, differs considerably from Tien's. It
is lighter in tone. Born in Ba Tri in 1975 and a child refugee in 1979,
Diem states that she has no memories of Vietnam at that time. Her
parents were from a rural background and were farmers. They left the
country after experiencing harassment at the hands of Vietnamese
authorities and losing their farm. The regime began collectivizing agriculture in early 1978.[32] Diem's earliest memories are of the refugee
camp in the Philippines where her family awaited resettlement overseas. She returned to Vietnam for the first time in 2003, and she did so
for a holiday. She and her older sister traveled with their partners.

Diem's reunion with her extended family in Ba Tri led to some unexpected insights into her family story and its place in the wider narrative of the diaspora. She became conscious of the grief experienced not only by those who had left (her parents) but also by those who had been left behind (her grandparents, aunts, and uncles). Her discovery of the strength of interlocking family relationships in her native village—her aunts and uncles all lived in the same street—made her realize the scale of what her parents had lost when they left their country and escaped with their seven children.

Growing up in Australia, Diem remembers that most of the Vietnamese children she went to school with came from what she terms "broken families"—in other words, families in which either the mother or father and some children were still in Vietnam. Her visit to Vietnam allowed her not only to get acquainted with her parents' siblings and their children, but also to acknowledge her family's legacy of loss. Like many others in the postwar years, her parents made the decision to escape in secret. They simply disappeared one night. Considering the high fatality rate of escapees and the possible repercussions for family members left behind, their relatives had to bear their concerns in private. As Diem relates:

> One of the things I wanted to experience was to see my relatives. Going South, we went to the place where my parents grew up. It was far south 'cause we were in Saigon, we had to take a long bus ride and then we had to go on the ferry. It took hours to get there. We went to visit my grandmother in the house that my mother grew up in, and across the street lives my father's sister and her family and then there's about five other siblings who live in houses right next to each other so the whole street is pretty much full of close relatives. It's such a large and close-knit family, it's amazing, 'cause I guess that sense of family is not something that we get in Australia 'cause we don't have family here, but over there, my mother has nine or ten siblings. One of them owns a glass shop in the town and others are farmers, and they do all sorts of stuff. And so we'd just walk down the street and through people's backyards and went into all these houses you know, and they're all family, so it was really cool, and I got a real impression of what my parents had left behind when they came to Australia, and how hard it must have been.
>
> When my parents left they didn't actually tell anybody that they were leaving, they just disappeared one night, and so it was really hard for my relatives. My parents said, well, they couldn't tell anyone, they didn't want anyone to get into trouble if they were found out. I think that it was

really tough for their family when they just disappeared. They didn't know what was going on, they didn't even have a chance to say goodbye.

Her return narrative begins as an untroubled account of a holiday and then reveals successive layers of family history, as well as a greater insight into the sorrows experienced by her parents' generation. Her journey and her exposure to her wider family also enabled her to discern missing elements in her own life: the support and closeness that an extended kinship network can provide.

NO RETURNS

This chapter would not be complete without discussing the reasons for which women chose not to return to Vietnam, even thirty years after the end of the war. While some of the reasons given for this may be anticipated, such as the refugees' experience of state repression, imprisonment, harassment, or escape in postwar Vietnam, others are less predictable, especially on the part of the younger generation.

Ngoc was born in Saigon in 1969 and left the country as a child refugee with her parents and siblings in 1979. Their boat was twelve metres long and held 140 people. There was no compass on board. They were rescued after a few days at sea by the crew of an American petrol tanker but only because her father spoke English and was able to plead their case with the captain of the tanker. She gives the following reasons for not returning to Vietnam:

> Even though I have been here since 1980, I have no yearning to return to Vietnam at all. I have no close connection with Vietnam. My first love was in Australia, and all the sweet memories I have are all here, so I have never thought of going back to Vietnam even though my grandfather and grandmother only recently passed away, but even before that I had no inclination to go back because I left the country as a refugee and it was a very treacherous journey and I felt that by going back I'd be betraying all the people who have lost their lives and all the soldiers who have risked their life to defend our country, so that's why I haven't returned.
>
> I remember all the struggles we had after 1975. It was a very hard time. We couldn't afford to have rice everyday to eat, we had to use cheaper substitutes, not *bo-bo*[33] but some type of bean, and I remember that we had finely minced peanuts and sesame seeds with lots of salt to eat with rice when we couldn't have real food. We used whatever

substitute we could have. My grandfather and uncle had to go to the re-
education camps because they were both highly ranked soldiers. My
grandfather was a colonel. They had to do hard labour in the camps and
had very little food and my mum had to go to North Vietnam to support
them. They were only released after ten years, after we had all left as refugees. My grandfather was too old to be any danger to the government
and my uncle had been badly injured after an accident. I think they
would not have been released had this not happened, because they [the
government] wanted to destroy people's spirit. That's why I don't want
to go back, under that same regime.

It took a long time for my parents to plan our escape, I think it took a
few years, it seemed like ages, and we had to keep that information secret. I remember getting very agitated because the plan took a long time
to eventuate. It was a long time before we actually made the final journey. When we left, I was worried about being starved to death, of not
having enough food or water, but obviously my parents were a lot more
worried, about the pirates, the weather conditions, and things like that.
When we left the country, it was July, it was the roughest time of year
for the sea, it was a really rough journey.

Her narrative contains a clear summary of her principal reasons for refusing to return, and then elaborates in more detail on these reasons. The
central theme here is that of loyalty. She is loyal to the memory of those
who died in the exodus and of those who died defending the South. She
remembers her grandfather's and uncle's ordeal, and the hardships experienced by her mother and family. Her family's journey by boat, and the
high levels of stress and anxiety associated with the planning of their
escape as well as the actual escape, left an indelible mark on her childhood. She links her reluctance to return to her sense of belonging to a
new land, and the fact that what she terms her "sweet memories" are
bound up with the country of resettlement rather than that of her birth.

Another young woman whose memory is compelling is Thy, who was
one year old when her family escaped from Vietnam by boat in 1979.[34]
For her, Vietnam is an imaginary place shaped by the stories of others and
by old pictures, news footage and documentaries of the Vietnam War. Her
imaginary return to Vietnam took the form of travel to another Southeast
Asian country, Indonesia, where she went on vacation in 2005. She says:

I don't remember Vietnam at all. I don't have a personal image of Vietnam or a personal recollection of anything that ever happened to me in
Vietnam. The only ties that I have with Vietnam are my parents, and

the stories they told, not that they told me stories, but the stories that I would overhear. My parents spoke about boats, and *ma* (ghosts). My mother would talk about *ma* stories in Vietnam. My dad used to talk a lot about the war. He spoke of it with pride because I think it was a time in his life when he had purpose, he was worth something, his life had value. He was wounded several times, he still has the bullet scars. I think that the war was something really big in his life, so big that he can't share it with his kids.

When I went to Bali, I thought, this is how Vietnam would be like—the scenery, the trees, the sky, the sea, the smells and the air. The image that I have of Vietnam is of the sky being not the blue-blue that we have here, but a blue-purple, like in the seventies, maybe because there were so many images of Vietnam in the seventies, because of the Vietnam War, and maybe the resolution that they had on the TV programs gave it that grade and colour. In my head, the sky is purply-blue, and the sea is not crystal blue but more kind of like a green-blue, and the grass is that avo-cado-mix green, you know. The colours are different and strange. And going back to Bali, when I looked at it, it was quite different, it was a tropical place, it wasn't home—like a gum tree is home, you know. When I stepped off the plane in Bali I thought, "I can't breathe because of the heat, this is not good for me," the air was too sickly, and it bothered me a bit. I think also that I'm not a good traveller, I don't like travelling, I love Melbourne, I don't think I'll ever move anywhere else.

Like Ngoc, she is sensitive to the experiences of the generation before her. Her narrative is composed of a palimpsest of images, impressions, and memories, many of which are not her own. Vietnam consists of fragments of her parents' memory, stories that she gleaned from over-heard conversations, and the vivid imprint of photographs and televi-sion footage of the war. Her reconstruction contains several strands that interweave her parents' experience of war, trauma, and dislocation, with their imperfect transmission of this experience to their children, and her own frustrated efforts to obtain more information. Her visual "memory" of Vietnam is extraordinarily rich and multihued because it speaks of a potent and imaginative interpretation of family history.

JOURNEYS "HOME"

These narratives reveal that women's perception of Vietnam and of their former home is principally driven by their emotional attachment to family. It is this desire to reconnect with loved ones that provides the impetus and motivation for the journey "home." Vietnam means above all, family. Women stressed that they felt no sense of yearning for the place itself, but only returned for the sake of family, whether mother, father, or sibling. Their stories reveal, however, how strongly women reacted to the physical sight of their native land, and to familiar landscapes. The narratives chronicle women's difficult and constantly evolving negotiation of past and present. Their perceptions of Vietnam shift and alter as they lay their personal recollections and expectations alongside their experience of the return journey. For those who left Vietnam as adults, this journey is marked by a recognition of loss and of missed years that could have been spent close to kin. Vinh has made several return trips, the latest in 2006, but these have lost much of their attraction since her mother died in 2002. She reveals:

> Now that she is no longer there, I think about her whenever I travel. I still feel very sad and the reason for that is that I wished I could have stayed with her for the last few years of her life. I will always feel sad about that.

Women's memories of the past and of pre-1975 Saigon are valuable, not so much because of the images that they convey—important as they are in themselves as perceptions of a vanished time—but for what they reveal about the ways in which the events of April 1975 and postwar communism affected the women's lives. Vietnam was at war for thirty years. Women had relatives who served in the armed forces, and they lived with curfews, the sight of soldiers in the streets, and the sound of helicopters, planes, gunfire, and bombardments. Even the Saigonese, who felt particularly sheltered throughout the duration of most of the war, were subjected to terrorist attacks and rocket fire. War was such a constant in these women's lives, however, that it ceased to feature uppermost in their minds. They were concerned with their education, their work, and their families, and they made plans for their futures. This part of their life is remembered as a time of stability and hope. As Nicola King suggests, "we long for a time when we didn't know what was going to happen next—or, conversely, to relive the past with the foreknowledge we then lacked."[35] The communist takeover in 1975 destroyed these women's hopes and plans. Their memories of the South not only are colored by nostalgia, but also provide a sharp contrast with their experience of destabilization, detention, and discrimination, whether on political or ethnic grounds, in the postwar years. Tien's vivid memories of Saigon before 1975 are evocative precisely because they are such a powerful reverse reflection of the sense of distress and alienation that she experienced after 1975.

Memory serves three different functions here. The first is to remember and commemorate a country that ceased to exist in 1975. This entails recreations of past homes, villages, towns, and cities, many of which have changed profoundly. Women describe social and familial networks that were disrupted by the collapse of the South and its aftermath. The second is to justify the women's decision to join the exodus from their country (or for those who left as children, to justify their parents' decision to do so). All the women left their homeland under difficult conditions. Whatever form it took, their departure signified their rejection of Vietnam's postwar regime. The level of state repression after 1975, and the erosion of much of southern society, served only to underline how much better life seemed before 1975. The third is to anchor the women firmly in their new lives and their adopted homes. Their narratives signify a resistance to Vietnam in the present. As Marianne Hirsch and Leo Spitzer note, "a past reconstructed through the animating vision of nostalgia can serve as a creative inspiration and possible emulation within the present."[36] The women's nostalgia for and remembrance of the past highlight their past trauma as well as the fact that they have constructed new lives and new identities elsewhere. Vinh asserts:

> I now feel more familiar with Australia than Vietnam. When I go back to Australia, I feel it is my home, but when I go back to Vietnam, I feel like a visitor. Of course the memories are still there, but I don't want to go past my old house in Saigon or my house in Da Nang because that would bring back a lot of memories I don't want to remember because it makes me so sad.

Returnees, write Oxfeld and Long, "reconstruct their homelands both figuratively and in practice."[37] Women remember their former homeland but affirm their attachment to their new country, even if this affirmation is laced with heartache. As Tien says,

> Australia is definitely home for me. I feel this even more deeply since my second trip to Vietnam. I've lived longer in Australia now than in Vietnam and my children were born here. Vietnam is my first home, but it is out of reach. I love it deeply. It represents my memories, my

childhood, the place in which I was brought up and educated, and I'm still grateful to it. But I knew in my heart that Australia was my home, I already knew that.

The narratives of the older generation are colored by grief and longing, since their memories encompass formative parts of their lives—child-hood, youth, and adulthood—and therefore a correspondingly deeper sense of loss. The memories of younger women, on the other hand, take a different shape by failing to reveal a similar nostalgic yearning for Vietnam. For them, images of early happiness are largely overlaid by the difficulties and tensions of the postwar years, and the memory of the exodus. Even those who have no personal memory of Vietnam remain responsive to the experience of their parents, and the collective experience of the diaspora.

The narratives of Ngoc and Thy are the most unexpectedly poign-ant. Their consciousness of Vietnam and what Vietnam signifies are shaped by their parents' stories and experiences. As narrators, they inscribe themselves and their stories into a wider collective framework of loss. In this way, they remember those who have gone before them. Ngoc was ten years old when she became a refugee. Although her fam-ily survived the sea journey, she is marked by the memory of that voy-age. Her reluctance to return is not only shaped by her awareness of the sacrifices made by so many soldiers for the preservation of South Vietnam, but by her recollection of postwar privations and injustices, and the knowledge that many were less fortunate than her family. She does not discount ever going back and imagines that she will do so one day for the sake of her children, so that they can "discover their roots." Her reflections include a hypothetical return narrative detailing the potential dangers of such a journey: "What if we couldn't leave?" She articulates a sentiment expressed by many others, that if she went back to Vietnam it would be as a foreigner:

> I feel that some day I will have to bring my children back to Vietnam to their roots to know their ancestors, and for them to get a feel of the country where their parents were brought up. I think it would be essen-tial for me to do that, but I'm very reluctant to do any such thing at this stage, because I have very strong feelings about going back and I've heard all these horrible stories about all the bribery that you need to do at the airport, and the corruption that's rife in Vietnam. Frankly I'm very anxious, I feel like I'd be a foreigner going back to my own country.

Thy, for her part, has no memory of either Vietnam or the exodus, but she bears the imprint of the previous generation's trauma. The kaleidoscope of visual and sensory impressions that she has of Vietnam represents what Hirsch and Spitzer, writing about the children of Jewish Holocaust survivors, refer to as a "postmemory, a secondary, belated memory mediated by stories, images and behaviours among which [they] grew up, but which never added up to a complete or linear tale."[38] Thy is conscious of this postmemory and feels the lack of a "complete tale" acutely. As she says:

> I think that parents should be encouraged to talk about their story and their history, 'cause for children, it's their only connection to Vietnam, it's through their stories. And if they're not sharing them, then their children are basically cut off. If you don't share stories of what happened in Vietnam, then, you know, you've lost it. You can't expect your child to understand. And if you don't have a history, if you don't know your history, you can't know yourself. In terms of cultural identity, I think a lot of us [second generation] are lost, because we lack that history, because the first generation has not shared that story with us. And because the second generation hasn't asked the first generation to share that story.

Her narrative illustrates the difficulty of transmitting traumatic history across the generations. She mourns the fact that much of this history is lost to her and to other members of the second generation. Her mother died of leukemia when she was seventeen. It is perhaps for this reason that she is particularly conscious of the lost histories of the first generation. Like the narratives of post-Holocaust generations, hers "speaks about what is not known by one generation and what has not been said by another."[39] Diagnosed with depression when she was twenty, she reflects:

> My mother would say, you know, that when she was pregnant with me, she was really sad so that's why I'm sad. And my dad fought in the war, and he was in hiding a lot, because people were trying to find him to lock him up in re-education camp, and so it was not a good time. And I think in his head, he has never let go of Vietnam. I grew up with stories about Vietnam. I shared in my parents' struggles, you know. I shared in that story. I remember hearing someone talking about the Jewish community and the children of Holocaust survivors, and about the high number of the second generation having depression, and that was the first time I thought, "Oh, maybe that's what happened to me."

Thy's narrative reveals not only the partial and truncated stories of her parents, but also her frustration that it is a story that she will never truly know. The secondary trauma that she is subjected to is compounded by her grief at her mother's premature death and the difficulty of communicating with her father. The silence between the generations is too great, and it is one that she is unlikely to bridge. Vietnam remains an imaginary site associated with a pain-filled past: her parents, the war, and the exodus. It represents a geographic space that she is reluctant to revisit. Even though it took many years for her to feel "at home" in her new homeland, since, like the children of other refugees, she "inherited [her] parents' knowledge of the fragility of place, their suspicion of the notion of home,"[40] her affirmation of Australia as her new "home" is a tribute to her parents, a means of justifying their decision to leave Vietnam, and of thanking them for the sacrifices they made.

In the final analysis, these women's return journeys, whether real or imagined, were undertaken, in Andrew Lam's words, "in order to take leave."[41] The return brings with it a double realization: the fact that they have truly lost the country they remember and that their lives now lie elsewhere. Their narratives explore plural truths, a mixture of experience, history, and perceptions.[42] They record an elusive history, in which "memory acquires a central importance for the preservation of authenticity and truth as well as a peculiar poignancy."[43] They chronicle the mourning and adjustments of the Vietnamese diaspora over time, and the shifts in understanding and allegiance that women bring to their experience of migration and resettlement.

CONCLUSION

I belong to a country
you cannot look for
on maps, in books, movies.
—Thuong Vuong-Riddick[1]

Memory is indeed another country. The memories of Vietnamese women are of another country, but in a metaphorical sense, they are also in themselves a country to explore. "Memories," write Robert Perks and Alistair Thomson, "are living histories."[2] In remembering and storying their lives, Vietnamese women create and produce memory-scapes peopled with a diverse array of characters and unforgettable images of Vietnam—its people, its landscapes, its villages, towns, and cities, its wartime tragedies, and its postwar losses. While women may mourn a country lost and loved ones lost—a brother killed in war, a sister drowned at sea, a mother dead through illness—their memories and their stories allow them to live on. Like a paneled screen slowly unfolding, the places of the past, the faces of people they once knew, remembered conversations, and scenes of private and public signifi-cance gradually emerge. Some of these impressions are faint and distant and may be difficult to discern, while others stand out clearly and sharply in the foreground. Superimposed on these images of the past like lines of calligraphy are the women's own thoughts, dreams, inter-pretations, and desires. "Human rememberings, whether individual or collective," writes Inga Clendinnen, "are not inert archives. They are factories of dreams, hopes, illusions."[3] The women's narratives reveal perceptions of the past that are continually evolving and altering.

Their stories sometimes uncover unexpected details and furtive glimpses of people and events on the periphery of their lives. Their narratives are dominated, however, by the memory of formative central events—wartime losses, the collapse of their country in 1975 and its consequences, their experience of state repression in the postwar years, and the circumstances in which they left their country.

Women carried their family legacy of stories into their lives as refugees or migrants. Their narratives reveal that one of the greatest impositions of life under the postwar regime was the sense of oppression and isolation that it engendered. People kept silent about postwar privations and injustices. They were afraid of being denounced to the police or coming to the attention of Vietnamese authorities if they spoke out. The level of trauma experienced was made worse because people could not confide in each other or support each other at a communal level. As one noted, who could she talk to? What could she say? Who could she trust? Women struggled alone to care for children or aged parents while their fathers, brothers, or husbands were interned in remote prison camps. Some themselves suffered internment. They strove to reshape their lives, and made their escape plans in secret. Their experiences exacted a heavy emotional toll. As Laurence Kirmayer notes, "a private space of trauma places the victim in a predicament, since the validation of suffering depends on recovering enough memory to make it real for others."[4] With no public space in which to speak their stories, the grief of the postwar years lay like a heavy weight over their lives, and it was a burden that they could not share with others until they were able to leave their country and construct a new life elsewhere.

Migration and resettlement did not in themselves, however, resolve the issue of enabling women to speak their stories. In the aftermath of a war remembered as an "unpopular" war, there was little interest in knowing or understanding the stories of Vietnamese refugees. The plight of the boat people did receive international recognition, but few were willing to explore the reasons why the Vietnamese were leaving their homeland in such unprecedented numbers. Vietnam was predominantly remembered as a war, while the "mourning of Vietnamese refugees and exiles," in Suzette Min's words, was "dealt with infrequently or surreptitiously."[5] The experiences of Vietnamese refugees reflected in many ways those of East European refugees after the Second World War, many of whom were confronted with a similar lack of understanding on the part of their host communities as to their reasons for escaping communism.[6] It took the Vietnamese American writer Yung Krall ten years, for example, to find a publisher for her memoir *A Thousand Tears Falling*.[7] She remembers that editors responded positively to the book, but advised her that it would not sell because Americans wanted to forget about Vietnam.[8] When her book was finally published in 1995, it was nominated for the Georgia Writers' Non-Fiction Author of the Year Award.[9]

The experience of displacement and of migration to another country carried its own heavy burdens. Women had to reinvent themselves and reconstruct their lives. Their energies went toward learning another language and adapting to another culture, and working long hours to support their families as well as relatives left behind in Vietnam. This left them little time for reflection or contemplation. Three decades after the end of the war, however, the time is now constitutive for Vietnamese refugees and migrants to speak of their experiences and their past, and to create a public space for their stories. As Kirmayer writes,

> Trauma shared by a whole community creates a potential public space for retelling. If a community agrees traumatic events occurred and weaves this fact into its identity, then collective memory survives and individual memory can find a place (albeit transformed) within that landscape.[10]

The role and the importance of women in this context are to be noted. Women are traditionally perceived to be the keepers and transmitters of culture.[11] In this case, they are custodians of the suppressed and silenced histories of the Vietnamese diaspora. Their stories reflect changing cultures and histories and provide counterstories to national narratives circulating in their native country. As Selma Leydesdorff, Luisa Passerini, and Paul Thomson note:

> Memories supportive of the maintenance of existing power structures are usually assured a wider social space and easier transmission. But memories of subordinate groups can also show striking resilience, and they can be transmitted, as women's memories often must be, from the interstices of society, from the boundaries between the public and the private.[12]

The narratives of Vietnamese women may be redolent of sorrow and loss, but they also reveal that women have been able to transmute their grief into the storying of new lives. Their memories are part of an evolving diasporic archive. Vijay Mishra suggests that "for diasporas, facing up to their own ghosts, their own traumas, their own memories is a necessary ethical condition."[13] Vietnamese women have done more than face up to their own ghosts and traumas. By speaking their stories, they have provided their own "living histories," and in doing so enabled the people and the country they have loved and lost to live on in their memories, in the words they utter, and in the pages of this book.

NOTES

PREFACE

1. John C. Schafer, *Vietnamese Perspectives on the War in Vietnam: Annotated Bibliography of Works in English* (New Haven, CT: Yale University Council on Southeast Asian Studies, 1996), 1, http://www.yale.edu/seas/bibliography/home.html.

2. Vietnamese women from Melbourne, Sydney, Brisbane, Canberra, and Adelaide, and one respondent from the United States participated in this project.

3. I conducted interviews with women in Melbourne, Sydney, and Canberra.

INTRODUCTION

1. Barbara Tran, *In the Mynah Bird's Own Words* (Dorset: Tupelo Press, 2002), 4.

2. "Viet Minh" is a condensation of "Viet Nam Cach Mang Dong Minh" (Alliance of Vietnamese Revolutionaries).

3. See Nguyen Trieu Dan, *A Vietnamese Family Chronicle: Twelve Generations on the Banks of the Hat River* (Jefferson: McFarland and Company, 1991), 161–168. The brothers were Nguyen Tue and Nguyen Huyen, and they were both awarded the doctorate third class.

4. The older brother, Nguyen Tue, became a minister of the Mac Dynasty and is recorded in the *History of Dai Viet* as "Hung An ba Nguyen Tue" (Nguyen Tue, Count of Hung An). Nguyen, *Vietnamese Family Chronicle*, 167–168.

5. Upper echelons of the administration.

6. François Guillemot writes that up to 50,000 Vietnamese may have died between 1945 and 1947. He notes that although violence did occur on both sides of politics, it was much more systematic on the part of the Viet Minh. See François Guillemot, "Au cœur de la fracture vietnamienne: L'élimination de l'opposition nationaliste et anticolonialiste dans le Nord du Vietnam (1945-1946)," in *Naissance d'un Etat-Parti: Le Viêt Nam depuis 1945/The Birth of a Party-State: Vietnam since 1945*, ed. Christopher E. Goscha and Benoît De Tréglodé, 208-209 (Paris: Les Indes Savantes, 2004).

7. In the *Twenty-Five Year Century*, for example, former South Vietnamese General Lam Quang Thi writes that the majority of officers and troops of the Marine Division were northerners. Lam Quang Thi, *The Twenty-Five Year Century: A South Vietnamese General Remembers the Indochina War to the Fall of Saigon* (Denton: University of North Texas Press, 2001), 370.

8. Before 1975, "the number of Vietnamese students, scholars, revolutionaries and labourers who went into forced or voluntary exile had represented only a small minority of the country's population, and their experiences had not made a significant impact on national life or consciousness." Nathalie Huynh Chau Nguyen, *Voyage of Hope: Vietnamese Australian Women's Narratives* (Altona: Common Ground Publishing, 2005), 1.

9. "The most conservative estimates suggest a 10 per cent attrition rate, or 100,000 deaths, but other estimates put the figure much higher, at 50 to 90 per cent." Nguyen, *Voyage of Hope*, 16; see also W. Courtland Robinson, *Terms of Refuge: The Indochinese Exodus and the International Response* (London: Zed Books, 1998), 59; Linda Hitchcox, *Vietnamese Refugees in Southeast Asian Camps* (Basingstoke: Macmillan in association with St Antony's College, Oxford, 1990), 85.

10. Roya Hakakian, *Journey from the Land of No* (Sydney: Bantam, 2004), 14.

11. As Selma Leydesdorff, Graham Dawson, Natasha Burchardt, and T. G. Ashplant write, "[R]ecent research suggests that trauma is contagious, transmissible from survivors to their listeners and witnesses; and, both within families and by means of wider, collective processes, to subsequent generations." Selma Leydesdorff, Graham Dawson, Natasha Burchardt, and T. G. Ashplant, "Introduction: Trauma and Life Stories," in *Trauma and Life Stories: International Perspectives*, ed. Kim Lacey Rogers, Selma Leydesdorff and Graham Dawson, 17 (London: Routledge, 1999).

12. My book *Voyage of Hope* was the first to focus on the experiences and narratives of overseas Vietnamese women.

13. Barbara Tran, Monique T. D. Truong, and Luu Truong Khoi, "A Note to the Reader," in *Watermark: Vietnamese American Poetry and Prose*, ed. Barbara Tran, Monique T. D. Truong, and Luu Truong Khoi, 224 (New York: Asian American Writers' Workshop, 1997).

14. Huynh Sanh Thong, "Live by Water, Die from Water," in *Watermark*, vi.

15. Huynh Sanh Thong, "Live by Water," in *Watermark*, vii.

16. Nguyen, *Voyage of Hope*, 17.

17. Oscar Wilde, *De Profundis*, 43rd ed. (London: Methuen & Co., 1925), 16.

18. David Gross, *Lost Time: On Remembering and Forgetting in Late Modern Culture* (Amherst: University of Massachusetts Press, 2000), 3.

19. See Katharine Hodgkin and Susannah Radstone, eds., *Contested Pasts: The Politics of Memory* (London: Routledge, 2003); Catherine Kohler Riessman, *Narrative Methods for the Human Sciences* (Thousand Oaks, CA: Sage Publications, Inc., 2008); Robert Perks and Alistair Thomson, eds., *The Oral History Reader*, 2nd ed. (London: Routledge, 2006); Paul Antze and Michael Lambek, eds., *Tense Past: Cultural Essays in Trauma and Memory* (London: Routledge, 1996).

20. Inga Clendinnen, "The History Question: Who Owns the Past," *Quarterly Essay* 23 (2006): 38.

21. Nicola King, *Memory, Narrative, Identity: Remembering the Self* (Edinburgh: Edinburgh University Press, 2000), 175.

22. Robert Perks and Alistair Thomson, "Introduction," in *The Oral History Reader*, 3.

23. Janet Carsten, "Introduction: Ghosts of Memory," in *Ghosts of Memory: Essays on Remembrance and Relatedness*, ed. Janet Carsten, 16 (Malden, MA: Blackwell Publishing, 2007).

24. Personal Narratives Group, "Truths," in *Interpreting Women's Lives: Feminist Theory and Personal Narratives*, ed. Personal Narratives Group, 262 (Bloomington: Indiana University Press, 1989).

25. Catherine Kohler Riessman, *Narrative Methods for the Human Sciences* (Thousand Oaks, CA: Sage Publications, Inc., 2008), 8.

26. Riessman, *Narrative Methods*, 12–13.

27. Riessman, *Narrative Methods*, 12–13.

28. Susan E. Bell, "Narratives and Lives: Women's Health Politics and the Diagnosis of Cancer for DES Daughters," *Narrative Inquiry* 9, no. 2 (1999): 348.

29. Judith Lewis Herman, *Trauma and Recovery* (New York: Basic Books, 1992), 181.

30. Robert Perks and Alistair Thomson, "Advocacy and Empowerment: Introduction," in *The Oral History Reader*, 449.

31. The term "traumascape" is drawn from Maria Tumarkin's *Traumascapes: The Power and Fate of Places transformed by Tragedy* (Melbourne: Melbourne University Press, 2005).

32. Elie Wiesel, *Ethics and Memory* (Berlin: Walter de Gruyter, 1997), 13, 15.

33. As Sherna Berger Gluck and Daphne Patai note, "women's experiences [are] inherently valuable and [need] to be recorded." Sherna Berger Gluck and Daphne Patai, "Introduction," in *Women's Words: The Feminist Practice of Oral History*, ed. Sherna Berger Gluck and Daphne Patai, 1 (New York: Routledge, 1991).

34. Vietnamese women are often perceived as submissive, subservient, and "silent." See Mandy Thomas, *Dreams in the Shadows: Vietnamese-Australian Lives in Transition* (St. Leonards: Allen & Unwin, 1999), 170–171.

CHAPTER 1

1. Janet Carsten, "Introduction: Ghosts of Memory," in *Ghosts of Memory: Essays on Remembrance and Relatedness*, ed. Janet Carsten, 19 (Oxford: Blackwell Publishing, 2007).

2. "Viet Cong" is a condensation of "Viet Nam Cong Sang" (Vietnamese Communists).

3. Andrew Lam, *Perfume Dreams: Reflections on the Vietnamese Diaspora* (Berkeley, CA: Heyday Books, 2005), 1.

4. Inga Clendinnen, *Reading the Holocaust* (Melbourne: Text Publishing, 1998), 194.

5. Tessa Morris-Suzuki, untitled poem in *Peeling Apples* (Canberra: Pandanus Books, 2005), 47. She writes, "This poem is dedicated to the memory of the 353 people who drowned when the boat known as 'SIEV-X' sank in waters between Indonesia and Australia on 19 October 2001."

6. *The Upanishads*, Swami Nikhilananda, trans. (New York: Harper, 1949–1959), 4:326. The words are from the dialogue between Narada and Sanatkumara: "I am one afflicted with sorrow. Do you, venerable Sir, help me to cross over to the other side of sorrow."

7. Lam, *Perfume Dreams*, 2.

8. Hoang is the interviewee's middle name, and is used with her permission.

9. Guenter Lewy, *America in Vietnam* (New York: Oxford University Press, 1978), 273. Lewy writes, "The exercise of violence by the VC

[Viet Cong]/NVA [North Vietnamese Army] was methodical. The primary instrument of repression—the communist term for eliminating, neutralizing, punishing and reforming enemies—was the VC Security Service, a highly professional organization operating in all parts of South Vietnam and an organic part of the DRV [Democratic Republic of Vietnam] Ministry of Public Security . . . Statistics for the years 1968-72 indicate that about 80 percent of the terrorist victims were ordinary civilians and only about 20 percent were government officials, policemen, members of the self-defense forces or pacification cadres."

10. Anthony James Joes, *The War for South Viet Nam, 1954-1975*, rev. ed. (Westport, CT: Praeger, 2001), 139. Joes writes, "The North had a superiority of 2.2 to 1 in heavy artillery, and 20 to 1 in overall personnel. Besieged Ban Me Thuot would at one time have been supplied by air, but the rise in oil prices and the cutback in U.S. aid now made this impossible, while the Communist ring around the city made reinforcement by truck exceptionally difficult. On March 11, 1975, Ban Me Thuot fell. This disaster was to change the whole war and indeed seal the destiny of South Viet Nam."

11. Nathalie Huynh Chau Nguyen, *Voyage of Hope: Vietnamese Australian Women's Narratives* (Altona: Common Ground Publishing, 2005), 122. In *The Long Journey*, Nancy Viviani writes, "[M]any of the former Vietnamese professional class remain highly dissatisfied, since their deskilling has been accompanied by loss of status, not only in the ethnic but in the broader community, and by loss of relative income" Nancy Viviani, *The Long Journey: Vietnamese Migration and Settlement in Australia*, (Carlton: Melbourne University Press, 1984), 221.

12. This saying is well known in Vietnamese refugee and migrant circles. Another variation is: "In those days, if street lights could have walked, they would also have wanted to leave Vietnam." See Nguyen, *Voyage of Hope*, 115.

13. Vieda Skultans, *The Testimony of Lives: Narrative and Memory in Post-Soviet Latvia* (London: Routledge, 1998), 28. Skultans writes, "The role of memory has certain similarities in all totalitarian societies where the state has claimed a monopoly of truth (Passerini 1987). Under such conditions, individual lives bear witness against the state."

14. See Jacqueline Desbarats, "Human Rights: Two Steps Forward, One Step Backward?" in *Vietnam Today: Assessing the New Trends*, ed. Thai Quang Trung, 48–53 (New York: Crane Russak, A Member of the Taylor & Francis Group, 1990).

15. "More than a million people were placed in 're-education camps.' Many died while tens of thousands were to languish in detention until the

late 1980s." United Nations High Commissioner for Refugees, *The State of the World's Refugees: Fifty Years of Humanitarian Action* (Oxford: Oxford University Press, 2000), 82.

16. Desbarats, "Human Rights," 63. See also Nguyen Van Canh, *Vietnam Under Communism, 1975–1982* (Stanford: Hoover Institution, 1982), 123–128.

17. Desbarats, "Human Rights," 60.

18. James M. Freeman and Nguyen Dinh Huu, *Voices from the Camps: Vietnamese Children Seeking Asylum* (Seattle: University of Washington Press, 2003), 7.

19. Linda Hitchcox, *Vietnamese Refugees in Southeast Asian Camps* (Basingstoke: Macmillan in association with St. Antony's College, Oxford, 1990), 37.

20. See Desbarats, "Human Rights," 48–49. For the treatment of Amerasians, see Kieu-Linh Caroline Valverde, "From Dust to Gold: The Vietnamese Amerasian Experience," in *Racially Mixed People in America*, ed. P. P. Maria Root, 144–161 (Newbury Park: Sage Publications, 1992); Steven DeBonis *Children of the Enemy: Oral Histories of Vietnamese Amerasians and Their Mothers* (Jefferson, NC: McFarland & Company, 1995); Robert S. McKelvey, *The Dust of Life: America's Children Abandoned in Vietnam* (Seattle: University of Washington Press, 1999); and Nathalie Huynh Chau Nguyen, "Eurasian/Amerasian Perspectives: Kim Lefèvre's *Métisse blanche* (*White Métisse*) and Kien Nguyen's *The Unwanted*," *Asian Studies Review* 29, no. 2 (2005): 117.

21. W. Courtland Robinson, *Terms of Refuge: The Indochinese Exodus and the International Response* (London: Zed Books, 1998), 50; see also Bruce Grant, *The Boat People: An "Age" Investigation* (Ringwood: Penguin Books, 1979), 216–217.

22. Freeman and Nguyen, *Voices from the Camps*, 7.

23. David Gross, *Lost Time: On Remembering and Forgetting in Late Modern Culture* (Amherst: University of Massachusetts Press, 2000), 140.

24. Toni Morrison, *Sula* (London: Pan Books, 1991), 174.

25. Desbarats, "Human Rights," 50–51; Nguyen Van Canh, *Vietnam Under Communism*, 146–150. See also Nguyen Hung Quoc, "Vietnamese Communist Literature (1975–1990)," in *Vietnamese Studies in a Multicultural World*, ed. Nguyen Xuan Thu, 120–124 (Melbourne: Vietnamese Language & Culture Publications, 1994).

26. Desbarats, "Human Rights," 50.

27. Nguyen Van Canh quoting Radio Hanoi on May 16 and May 20, 1981. Nguyen Van Canh, *Vietnam Under Communism*, 149.

28. The interviewee is Ngoc, born in 1969 in Saigon. She escaped from Vietnam by boat with her parents and siblings in 1979.

29. Lewis P. Hinchman and Sandra K. Hinchman, "Introduction" in *Memory, Identity, Community: The Idea of Narrative in the Human Sciences*, ed. Lewis P. Hinchman and Sandra K. Hinchman, xiv (Albany: State University of New York Press, 1997).

CHAPTER 2

1. Robert Sanders, *Sibling Relationships: Theory and Issues for Practice* (Basingstoke: Palgrave Macmillan, 2004), 2.

2. Katharine Hodgkin and Susannah Radstone, "Introduction: Contested Pasts," in *Contested Pasts: The Politics of Memory*, eds. Katharine Hodgkin and Susannah Radstone, 1 (London: Routledge, 2003).

3. Monica McGoldrick, "Sisters," in *Women in Families: A Framework for Family Therapy*, eds. Monica McGoldrick, Carol M. Anderson, and Froma Walsh, 246 (New York: W.W. Norton & Company, Inc., 1989).

4. See Marcia Millman, *The Perfect Sister: What Draws Us Together, What Drives Us Apart* (Orlando: Harcourt, Inc., 2004), xiii, and McGoldrick, "Sisters," 257.

5. Millman, *The Perfect Sister*, xiii.

6. Hodgkin and Radstone, "Introduction," 1.

7. David W. Haines, *The Limits of Kinship: South Vietnamese Households, 1954–1975* (DeKalb: Southeast Asia Publications, Center for Southeast Asian Studies, Northern Illinois University, 2006), 188–189.

8. Haines, *Limits of Kinship*, 189.

9. James M. Freeman, *Hearts of Sorrow: Vietnamese-American Lives* (Stanford, CA: Stanford University Press, 1989), 11.

10. See Pham Duy Khiem, *Légendes des terres sereines* (Paris: Mercure de France, 1951), 177–187.

11. Neil L. Jamieson, *Understanding Vietnam* (Berkeley: University of California Press, 1995), 8.

12. For a detailed analysis of Kieu, see Nathalie Huynh Chau Nguyen, *Vietnamese Voices: Gender and Cultural Identity in the Vietnamese Francophone Novel* (DeKalb: Southeast Asia Publications, Center for Southeast Asian Studies, Northern Illinois University, 2003), 12–23.

13. Nguyen Du, *The Tale of Kieu: A Bilingual Edition*, trans. Huynh Sanh Thong (New Haven, CT: Yale University Press, 1983), 157–158.

14. Nguyen Du, *The Tale of Kieu*, 167.

15. Helen Garner, "A Scrapbook, An Album," in *Sisters*, ed. Drusilla Modjeska, 79 (Sydney: Angus & Robertson, 1993).

16. The issue of contrasting memories between siblings is a sensitive one, and a subject that I found particularly difficult to write about. Both sisters had entrusted me with their stories and their memories, and I wanted to do justice to both. I had already conducted two interviews with Anh in 2005 and she was familiar with my work (her narrative features in my book *Voyage of Hope*). She had touched on her memories of her brother Kiet and her sisters Nga and Suong in her interviews, and I had hoped to hear more about the siblings. When I approached her again in 2006 and asked for a further interview, she agreed. Her sister Suong also agreed to be interviewed. I asked both sisters before their interviews whether they would be willing to speak of the loss of their brother and sister, a topic that I knew would be painful for them, and both said yes. Each knew that I was interviewing the other. Both were generous with their time and their reflections. I did not query the different interpretations of the past offered by the sisters during these interviews but have sought, instead, to interpret them in turn in my work.

17. Hodgkin and Radstone, "Introduction," 4.

18. Hodgkin and Radstone, "Introduction," 16.

19. Maria Tumarkin, *Traumascapes: The Power and Fate of Places transformed by Tragedy* (Melbourne: Melbourne University Press, 2005), 73.

20. See, for example, the story of Dzung in Nguyen, *Voyage of Hope: Vietnamese Australian Women's Narratives* (Altona: [0]Common Ground Publishing, 2005), 31. Dzung lost two sisters and a brother at sea in 1978, but she still says "we don't know yet" in relation to the fate of her siblings.

21. Ruth Wajnryb, *The Silence: How Tragedy Shapes Talk* (Crows Nest: Allen & Unwin, 2001), 30.

22. Wajnryb, *The Silence*, 19.

23. Patricia Foster, *Sister to Sister: Women Write about the Unbreakable Bond* (New York: Doubleday, 1995), 15.

24. Wajnryb, *The Silence*, 223.

25. See, for example, Cam Nguyen, "East, West, and Vietnamese Women," *The Journal of Vietnamese Studies* 5 (1992): 46.

26. Andrew Lam, *Perfume Dreams: Reflections on the Vietnamese Diaspora* (Berkeley, CA: Heyday Books, 2005), 9–10.

27. Vieda Skultans, *The Testimony of Lives: Narrative and Memory in Post-Soviet Latvia* (London: Routledge, 1998), 47. Skultans is quoting Colin Davis, "Understanding the Concentration Camps: Elie Wiesel's *La Nuit* and Jorge Semprun's *Quel Beau Dimanche!*" *Australian Journal of French Studies* 28, no. 3 (1991): 302.

28. Luisa Passerini, "Memories between Silence and Oblivion," in *Contested Pasts: The Politics of Memory,* ed. Katharine Hodgkin and Susannah Radstone, 247 (London: Routledge, 2003).

29. Wajnryb, *The Silence,* 51.

30. Passerini, "Memories," 238.

31. Joan Laird, "Women and Stories: Restorying Women's Self-constructions," in *Women in Families: A Framework for Family Therapy,* ed. Monica McGoldrick, Carol M. Anderson, and Froma Walsh, 432 (New York: W. W. Norton & Company, Inc., 1989).

32. Nancy Boyd Webb, "The Impact of Traumatic Stress and Loss on Children and Families," in *Mass Trauma and Violence: Helping Families and Children Cope,* ed. Nancy Boyd Webb, 19 (New York: The Guilford Press, 2004).

33. Laird, "Women and Stories," 435.

34. Millman, *The Perfect Sister,* xiii.

35. Drusilla Modjeska, "Introduction," in *Sisters,* xiii and ix.

CHAPTER 3

1. The Three Obediences were to father, husband, and son, and the Four Virtues were Right Occupation, Right Speech, Right Appearance, and Right Conduct. See, for example, Cam Nguyen, "East, West, and Vietnamese Women," *Journal of Vietnamese Studies* 5 (1992): 46.

2. Jeffrey Grey, "Review of Lam Quang Thi, *The Twenty-Five Year Century: A South Vietnamese General Remembers the Indochina War to the Fall of Saigon.* Denton: University of North Texas Press, 2001." *H-War, H-Net Reviews in the Humanities and Social Sciences* (April 2004), http://www.h-net.org/reviews/showrev.php?id=9193.

3. Dong Van Khuyen, *The RVNAF* (Washington, DC: U.S. Center of Military History, 1980), vi.

4. See Robert K. Brigham, *ARVN: Life and Death in the South Vietnamese Army* (Lawrence: University Press of Kansas, 2006), 112–118.

5. Brigham, *ARVN,* 113.

6. See Karen Gottschang Turner, *Even the Women Must Fight: Memories of War from North Vietnam* (New York: John Wiley and Sons, 1998).

7. See Sandra C. Taylor, *Vietnamese Women at War: Fighting for Ho Chi Minh and the Revolution* (Lawrence: University Press of Kansas, 1999).

8. Dang Thuy Tram's wartime diary also presents a North Vietnamese perspective of the war. See Dang Thuy Tram, *Last Night I Dreamed of Peace: The Diary of Dang Thuy Tram,* trans. Andrew X. Pham (New York: Harmony Books, 2007).

9. Heonik Kwok, *Ghosts of War in Vietnam* (Cambridge, MA: Cambridge University Press, 2008), 48.

10. As Ilya V. Gaiduk writes, "Although the Democratic Republic of Vietnam was supported throughout the war by its powerful allies, the USSR and the People's Republic of China, these supporters have virtually escaped the attention of historians of the conflict in Indochina." Ilya V. Gaiduk, *The Soviet Union and the Vietnam War* (Chicago: Ivan R. Dee, 1996), xi. See Chen Jian, "China and the First Indo-China War 1950-54," *China Quarterly* 133 (1993): 85–110; Chen Jian, "China's Involvement in the Vietnam War, 1964-1969," *China Quarterly* 142 (1995): 356–387; and Qiang Zhai, *China and the Vietnam Wars*, 1950-1975 (Chapel Hill: University of North Carolina Press, 2000). Qiang Zhai's book relates that China sent more than 320,000 troops to North Vietnam between 1965 and 1968, including "ground-to-air missile, antiaircraft artillery, railroad, engineering, minesweeping, and logistic units" (135). These "enabled the PAVN to send large numbers of troops to South Vietnam for the fighting" (135). While the American presence in South Vietnam has been well documented, the histories of Soviet and Chinese servicemen of the Vietnam War still need to be fully examined.

11. Turner writes that the war service of North Vietnamese women was undertaken at great personal cost: "Many women . . . lost their sexual health after years in the jungles, returning to their villages barren, unmarriageable, condemned to life on the margins in a society that values family above all else. Stress, back-breaking labor, malnutrition, contact with death and blood had eventually robbed these young girls of the very future they sought to defend when they left their home in the first place." Turner, *Even the Women Must Fight*, 4.

12. Hue-Tam Ho Tai, "Faces of Remembrance and Forgetting," in *The Country of Memory: Remaking the Past in Late Socialist Vietnam*, ed. Hue-Tam Ho Tai, 182 (Berkeley: University of California Press, 2001).

13. Tai, "Faces of Remembrance," 191.

14. This situation may gradually change in Vietnam. Heonik Kwon notes that "[a]s Vietnam is opening up its doors to the economic and cultural influences from the formerly opposite side of the bipolar world order, the meaning of the country's recent war, which was one of the most formative events and violent manifestations of this order, is also opening up to new interpretations." Heonik Kwok, *Ghosts of War in Vietnam* (Cambridge, MA: Cambridge University Press, 2008), 1.

15. *Dac San Cuu Nu Quan Nhan QLVNCH: Ky Niem Ngay Hoi Ngo NQN 12 Thang 8 Nam 2001* (Magazine of the Servicewomen of the

Republic of Vietnam Armed Forces: Special Bulletin of the Reunion of Servicewomen on August 12, 2001).

16. Phung Thi Hanh, "South Vietnam's Women in Uniform" (Saigon: The Vietnam Council on Foreign Relations, c. 1970). I am grateful to Mary McLain Saffell from the Vietnam Center and Archive at Texas Tech University for informing me about this article on South Vietnamese service-women. The Vietnam Center and Archive has two versions of the same article, one published by the Vietnam Council on Foreign Relations, illus-trated with photographs, and undated, and the other published by the Vietnam Feature Service, without photographs, and dated April 1970.

17. See Ho Thi Ve, "Nu Quan Nhan (Servicewomen)," in *Dac San Cuu Nu Quan Nhan QLVNCH: Ky Niem Ngay Hoi Ngo NQN 12 Thang 8 Nam 2001* (Magazine of the Servicewomen of the Republic of Vietnam Armed Forces: Special Bulletin of the Reunion of Servicewomen on August 12, 2001), 7 and 18. Translation by Phuong Mai Ung.

18. Ho, "Nu Quan Nhan," 7.

19. Ho, "Nu Quan Nhan," 13.

20. Phung, "Women in Uniform," 5.

21. Phung, "Women in Uniform," 5.

22. Ho, "Nu Quan Nhan," 13.

23. Ho, "Nu Quan Nhan," 14.

24. Ho, "Nu Quan Nhan," 14.

25. Phung, "Women in Uniform," 7. Phung adds, "The tour of duty is three years for enlisted personnel and four years for officers. Most women finish their tours. According to Colonel Huong, only one percent quit to marry or have children. After two years of service, WAFCs are permitted to marry and may stay in the corps after they have children if they wish." Phung, "Women in Uniform," 7.

26. Ho, "Nu Quan Nhan," 15.

27. Phung, "Women in Uniform," 5.

28. Dong, *RVNAF*, 208. The figures appear in Table 20, RVNAF School Enrollments for 1970.

29. Ho, "Nu Quan Nhan," 16.

30. Ho, "Nu Quan Nhan," 17–18. In Dong's *RVNAF*, Table 19, ARVN Personnel Trained in U.S. Army Service Schools and Installations 1955-1970, lists a total of 5,442 Vietnamese personnel trained in the United States between 1955 and 1962, and yearly figures from 1963 until 1970, with the highest being 1599 in 1970. See Dong, *RVNAF*, 206.

31. "The Women's Army Corps School was founded at Fort McClellan on September 25, 1952. Approximately two years later, official ceremonies

were conducted to establish the post as the first permanent home of the U.S. Women's Army Corps Center. Fort McClellan remained its home until the Corps was disestablished and its flag retired in 1977." See http://www.mcclellan.army.mil/Info.asp?article_id=2. See also Interview with Ann B. Smith, June 23, 2004, Ann B. Smith Collection, The Vietnam Archive, Texas Tech University. In 1970, Smith spent a year as senior advisor to the Vietnamese WAFC.

32. Ho, "Nu Quan Nhan," 18.

33. Phung, "Women in Uniform," 5.

34. Phung, "Women in Uniform," 7.

35. This, in combination with the fact that South Vietnamese servicewomen served in far fewer numbers than their North Vietnamese counterparts, may account for their lack of visibility. Turner refers to "sixty thousand women" in the North Vietnamese Army, and a total of 1.5 million, including women in the militia and local forces. Turner, *Even the Women*, 21. With respect to women in the militia and local forces, overall numbers were comparable between North and South Vietnam, since South Vietnam had more than 1 million women in the PSDF. Phung writes that "870,000 women are in PSDF support roles and 130,000 are in the combat forces defending hamlets and urban neighbourhoods. Combat volunteers, male and female, complete a 60-hour course of instruction directed by the Ministry of Interior. ARVN regulars, Regional or Popular Forces militia, and Revolutionary Development cadres train them in weapons, military tactics, and political indoctrination. Classes are held wherever there is space—pagodas, schools, or open fields. In Saigon, 1,265 women have volunteered as combat troops. Their training, one day a week for eight weeks, is held at the Quang Trung Military Training Center, 15 kilometres west of Saigon." Phung, "Women in Uniform," 17.

36. Phung, "Women in Uniform," p. 7.

37. General mobilization was decreed on June 19, 1968. Dong, *RVNAF*, 17.

38. See Yung Krall, A *Thousand Tears Falling: The True Story of a Vietnamese Family Torn Apart by War, Communism, and the CIA*, Atlanta: Longstreet Press, 1995.

39. Author's interview with Yung Krall in Atlanta, Georgia, on November 27, 2000.

40. Krall, *Thousand Tears*, 170.

41. Dang Kim Hoa, "Toi vao linh" (I joined the army), *Dac San Cuu Nu Quan Nhan QLVNCH: Ky Niem Hoi Ngo NQN Ky IV 25-26 Thang 8 Nam*

2007 Tai Nam California (Magazine of the Servicewomen of the Republic of Vietnam Armed Forces: Special Bulletin to commemorate the Fourth Reunion of Servicewomen on August 25–26, 2007, Southern California), 12–13. Translation by Ngoc Bui.

42. Gerard J. DeGroot, "Introduction to Part 1: Arms and the Woman," in *A Soldier and a Woman: Sexual Integration in the Military,* ed. Gerard J. DeGroot and Corinna Penistonj-Bird, 6 (Harlow: Longman, 2000).

43. Thuy refers to a higher number of required jumps than Dong in RVNAF, although Dong is referring to the Paratrooper's Course in the 1960s, and training periods may have been shortened. "The program of instruction was four weeks and required two practice jumps. Upon graduation, paratroopers were entitled to a monthly air duty allowance whether or not they were assigned to an airborne unit providing that they made four jumps each year under the sponsorship of the Airborne Training Center." Dong, *RVNAF,* 185.

44. Quy also referred briefly to Madame Nhu in her narrative: "Madame Nhu ordered for the abolition of enlisted female personnel in all fields except for the army medical corps and social service. She was only in an advisory role but she misused her power. She did not hold any official title in the army. She was only the President's sister-in-law. She established the Female Republican group, but these were not female army personnel. When she left, the group ceased to exist. Her daughter, Thuy Le Dinh Ngo was in that group."

45. Ho writes that of the WAFC in 1965: "the war was escalating and there was a need for more fighting troops; the policy to recruit women to replace male soldiers in the rear was considered by the Ministry of Defence. The establishment of the WAFC as an integral part of the armed forces was carried out, with the WAFC accounting for less than 1% of the strength of non-combatant soldiers." Ho, "Nu Quan Nhan," 13.

46. "The first instructor's course was conducted in 1962 by the Thu Duc Infantry School for the purpose of training its own instructors. It was subsequently made an official course by the Central Training Command with a six-week program of instruction. The course was given both at the Thu Duc Infantry School and the Quang Trung Training Center." Dong, *RVNAF,* 184.

47. As Dong notes, "career army personnel with 15 years of service or more were entitled to discharge with prorated retirement benefits." Dong, *RVNAF,* 61.

48. Penny Summerfield, *Reconstructing Women's Wartime Lives: Discourse and Subjectivity in Oral Histories of the Second World War* (Manchester: Manchester University Press, 1998), 3.

49. Phung, "Women in Uniform," 9.

50. Neil L. Jamieson, *Understanding Vietnam* (Berkeley: University of California Press, 1995), 295–296.

51. Nguyen Van Canh, *Vietnam under Communism, 1975-1982* (Stanford, CA: Hoover Institution Press, 1983), 190–191.

52. Nguyen Van Canh, *Vietnam under Communism*, 192.

53. Tiziano Terzani as quoted in Nguyen Van Canh, *Vietnam under Communism*, 192. Nguyen writes that Terzani was in Saigon at the time, and was "at first favorably disposed towards the regime." Nguyen Van Canh, *Vietnam under Communism*, 192, 197.

54. See Jacqueline Desbarats, "Human Rights: Two Steps Forward One Step Backward?" in *Vietnam Today: Assessing New Trends*, ed. Thai Quang Trung, 54–55 (New York: Crane Russak, A Member of the Taylor & Francis Group, 1990).

55. See Nguyen Van Canh, *Vietnam under Communism*, 188; Nghia M. Vo, *The Bamboo Gulag: Political Imprisonment in Communist Vietnam* (Jefferson, NC: McFarland & Company, 2004), 59. Nghia Vo writes that "Son Ha reported that in 1954, after the communists' take over of North Vietnam, seven northern doctors who had served with the French legionary forces were sent to reeducation for two years. They were allowed to return home and practice for one year; afterwards they were sent back to reeducation camps for seven more years. Five out of the seven, who had forgotten everything about their profession by the time they were released, had to work as laborers on collective farms. The two remaining worked as orderlies in hospitals. They eventually became nurses and were allowed to practice medicine six years after their release." Vo, *Bamboo Gulag*, 59.

56. Nguyen Van Canh, *Vietnam under Communism*, 188.

57. Nguyen Van Canh, *Vietnam under Communism*, 198–199. Camp sizes varied and Nguyen details those. He also provides a map and list of prisons and re-education camps in Vietnam by province.

58. Vo, *Bamboo Gulag*, 60.

59. Vo, *Bamboo Gulag*, 86–88.

60. Jacqueline Desbarats wrote in 1990: "The practice of illegal arrest and detention is still common in the SRV [Socialist Republic of Vietnam], and includes cases of temporary detention exceeding the limits set by the law. In particular, there is much evidence of arbitrary arrest, and detention without trial in re-education camps and prisons. Arrests, which were particularly common in the post liberation period, have continued, though with decreasing frequency, over the past decade. In December 1985, for instance, the police security forces in the province of Long An 'searched

and interrogated 180,000 families, arresting a total of 6,100 people who were then sent to concentration camps for re-education.'" Desbarats, "Human Rights," 54.

61. Kien Nguyen, *The Unwanted* (Sydney: Pan Macmillan, 2001), 245–249.

62. Nguyen, *Unwanted*, 245.

63. Nguyen, *Unwanted*, 249.

64. See for example, Lucien Trong, *Enfer rouge mon amour* (Paris: Editions du Seuil, 1980), and Tran Tri Vu, *Lost Years: My 1,632 Days in Vietnamese Reeducation Camps* (Berkeley: Institute of East Asian Studies, University of California, 1988).

65. Jean Libby, "Preface," in *Hoa Lo/Hanoi Hilton Stories*, ed. Nguyen Chi Thien, xi (New Haven, CT: Yale University Southeast Asia Studies, 2007).

66. Nguyen Chi Thien, *Hoa Lo*, 9–13.

67. Nguyen Chi Thien, *Hoa Lo*, 10.

68. Libby, "Preface," xiii.

69. Nguyen Chi Thien, *Flowers from Hell* (Hoa Dia-Nguc), trans. and ed. Huynh Sanh Thong (New Haven, CT: Council of Southeast Asia Studies, Yale Center for International and Area Studies, 1984).

70. A recent memoir entitled *Doa Hong Gai* (Thorny Roses) by Nguyen Thanh Nga, for example, describes the author's ten years of internment in re-education camps in Vietnam. However, it is only available in Vietnamese, which largely limits its readership to the Vietnamese diaspora.

71. W. Courtland Robinson notes that, "a 1985 UNHCR study revealed that 65 per cent of those apprehended by the authorities were imprisoned and of those 86 per cent were detained less than a year and 30 per cent less than a month." W. Courtland Robinson, *Terms of Refuge: The Indochinese Exodus and The International Response* (London: Zed Books, 1998), 179–180.

72. The Vietnam Center and Archives' Families of Vietnamese Political Prisoners Association (FVPPA) Collection has the records of more than 12,000 former political prisoners. Ann Mallett, project archivist, advises that the collection contains records of women who served as doctors and nurses in the RVNAF, but that no information is as yet available on how many of the 12,000 are women (private correspondence April 18, 2008). The Vietnam Center and Archive is located at Texas Tech University, Lubbock, Texas. See http://www.vietnam.ttu.edu/vietnamarchive/fvppa/index.htm. See also Linda Trinh Vo, "Managing Survival: Economic Realities for Vietnamese American Women," in *Asian/Pacific Islander American Women*, ed. Shirley Hune and Gail M. Nomura, 243 (New York: New

York University Press, 2003). Vo refers briefly to South Vietnamese military women and to their imprisonment in postwar Vietnam.

73. Vo, *Bamboo Gulag*, 65.

74. Summerfield, *Reconstructing Women's Wartime Lives*, 2.

75. Phung, "Women in Uniform," 7.

76. Dong, *RVNAF*, 274-275.

77. Dong, *RVNAF*, 275.

78. DeGroot, "Introduction to Part 1: Arms and the Woman," 6, 16.

79. Inga Clendinnen, "The History Question," *Quarterly Essay* 23 (2006): 39.

80. Ho, "Nu Quan Nhan," 13.

81. Summerfield, *Reconstructing Women's Wartime Lives*, 28.

82. Nguyen Thi Hanh Nhon, "Thu Moi Hop Mat Nu Quan Nhan Hai Ngoai" (Letter of Invitation to a Meeting of Overseas Servicewomen), *Dac San Cuu Nu Quan Nhan QLVNCH: Ky Niem Ngay Hoi Ngo NQN 12 Thang 8 Nam 2001* (Magazine of the Servicewomen of the Republic of Vietnam Armed Forces: Special Bulletin of the Reunion of Servicewomen on August 12, 2001), 5. Translation by Phuong Mai Ung.

83. Nguyen Thi Hanh Nhon, "Phat bieu cua Dai dien Ban To Chuc Hoi Ngo Nu Quan Nhan Hai Ngoai Ky IV" (Speech of the WAFC Committee Representative delivered at the Fourth Overseas Reunion), *Dac San Cuu Nu Quan Nhan QLVNCH: Ky Niem Hoi Ngo NQN Ky IV 25-26 Thang 8 Nam 2007 Tai Nam California* (Magazine of the Servicewomen of the Republic of Vietnam Armed Forces: Special Bulletin to commemorate the Fourth Reunion of Servicewomen on August 25–26, 2007, Southern California), 5. Translation by Ngoc Bui.

CHAPTER 4

1. The wars after 1945 are referred to as the Indochina War (1946–1954) and the Vietnam War (1959–1975), the First and Second Indochina Wars, or the French War and the American War. Because Vietnam was in a nearly continuous state of war for three decades, the Vietnam War is also referred to as covering the entire 1945–1975 period.

2. Michael Humphrey, The *Politics of Atrocity and Reconciliation: From Terror to Trauma* (London: Routledge, 2000), 52.

3. Kim Lefèvre, *Métisse blanche* (Paris: Bernard Barrault, 1989), 132–133. Author's translation.

4. Nathalie Huynh Chau Nguyen, "Landscapes of War: Traumascapes in the Works of Kim Lefèvre and Phan Huy Duong" in *Land and Landscape*

in *Francographic Literature: Remapping Uncertain Territories*, ed. Magali Compan and Katarzyna Pieprzak, 96 (Newcastle: Cambridge Scholars Publishing, 2007).

5. Nguyen, "Landscapes of War," 94–95.

6. Lefèvre, *Métisse*, 129. Author's translation.

7. Nguyen, "Landscapes of War," 96. The term "traumascape" is adopted from Maria Tumarkin's *Traumascapes: The Power and Fate of Places Transformed by Tragedy* (Carlton: Melbourne University Press, 2005).

8. The story features in Phan Huy Duong's collection *Un Amour métèque* (A Foreign Love). See Phan Huy Duong, *Un Amour métèque: nouvelles* (Paris: L'Harmattan, 1994).

9. Phan Huy Duong, *Un Amour*, 18. Author's translation.

10. Nguyen, "Landscapes of War," 89.

11. Vieda Skultans, *The Testimony of Lives: Narrative and Memory in Post-Soviet Latvia* (London: Routledge, 1998), 47.

12. Australian slang for truancy.

13. Dang Phong, ed., *Lich Su Kinh Te Viet Nam, 1945–2000* (Vietnamese Economic History, 1945–2000), vol. 2: 1955–1975 (Hanoi: Social Sciences Publishing House, 2005), 85. I am grateful to Nguyen Ngoc Phach and Phuong Mai Ung for the Vietnamese translation.

14. David Marr ascribes several different reasons for the famine: falling rice output over the previous two decades while the population expanded; the fact that some rice land was converted to the use of such crops as castor oil seed and jute in 1941–1944; and drought, insect infestations, and typhoons in 1944. French and Japanese officials were aware of the famine and could have organized for the transfer of rice from southern Vietnam (where large surpluses had accumulated) but prioritized military logistics over the transport of rice to starving civilians. See David G. Marr, *Vietnam 1945: The Quest for Power* (Berkeley: University of California Press, 1995), 96–107.

15. Marr, *Vietnam 1945*, 105.

16. Tran Thi Nga, "Famine," in *Shallow Graves: Two Women in Vietnam*, ed. Wendy Wilder Larsen and Tran Thi Nga, 156–157 (New York: Random House, 1986).

17. Skultans, *The Testimony of Lives*, xii.

18. Günter Grass, *Crabwalk*, trans. Krishna Winston (London: Faber and Faber, 2003), 3.

19. Selma Leydesdorff, Graham Dawson, Natasha Burchardt, and T. G. Ashplant, "Introduction: Trauma and Life Stories," in *Trauma and Life Stories: International Perspectives*, ed. Kim Lacy Rogers, Selma Leydesdorff and

Graham Dawson, 2 (London: Routledge, 1999). The authors are referring to the work of Kai T. Erikson.

20. Daryl S. Paulson, "War and Refugee Suffering," in *The Psychological Impact of War Trauma on Civilians: An International Perspective*, ed. Stanley Krippner and Teresa M. McIntyre, 117 (Westport, CT: Praeger, 2003).

21. Bao Ninh, *The Sorrow of War*, English version by Frank Palmos (London: Secker and Warburg, 1993), 216.

CHAPTER 5

1. Thuong Vuong-Riddick, *Two Shores/Deux Rives* (Vancouver: Ronsdale Press, 1995), 158.

2. Vuong-Riddick, *Two Shores*, 158.

3. Neil L. Jamieson, *Understanding Vietnam* (Berkeley: University of California Press, 1995), 339–340.

4. Jamieson, *Understanding Vietnam*, 339.

5. See Nathalie Huynh Chau Nguyen, *Vietnamese Voices: Gender and Cultural Identity in the Vietnamese Francophone Novel* (DeKalb: Southeast Asia Publications, Center for Southeast Asian Studies, Northern Illinois University, 2003), 104–129.

6. Nguyen, *Vietnamese Voices*, 123.

7. Nguyen, *Vietnamese Voices*, 129.

8. See Vu Trong Phung, *The Industry of Marrying Vietnamese*, trans. Thuy Tranviet (Ithaca, NY: Southeast Asia Program Publications, Cornell University, 2006).

9. Thuy Tranviet, "Introduction," in Vu, *The Industry*, 14.

10. Vu, *The Industry*, 56.

11. Kim Lefèvre, *Métisse blanche* (Paris: Bernard Barrault, 1989), 14–15. Author's translation.

12. See Steven DeBonis, *Children of the Enemy: Oral Histories of Vietnamese Amerasians and Their Mothers* (Jefferson, NC: McFarland & Company, 1995); Robert McKelvey, *The Dust of Life: America's Children Abandoned in Vietnam* (Seattle: University of Washington Press, 1999); Kien Nguyen, *The Unwanted* (Sydney: Macmillan, 2001); Nathalie Huynh Chau Nguyen, "Eurasian/Amerasian Perspectives: Kim Lefèvre's *Métisse blanche* White Métisse and Kien Nguyen's *The Unwanted*," *Asian Studies Review* 29, no. 2 (2005): 107–122; and Kieu-Linh Caroline Valverde, "From Dust to Gold: The Vietnamese Amerasian Experience," in *Racially Mixed People in America*, ed. P. P. Maria Root, 144–161 (Newbury Park, CA: Sage Publications, 1992), 144–161.

13. Nguyen, "Eurasian/Amerasian Perspectives," 107.

14. Ghislain Ripault, "Pour présenter Duyên Anh," in *Un Russe à Saigon*, ed. Duyên Anh, trans. Jean Maïs and Ghislain Ripault, 13–14 (Paris: Pierre Belfond, 1986).

15. Ripault, "Duyên Anh," 14–15.

16. Duyên Anh, *Un Russe à Saigon*, trans. Jean Maïs and Ghislain Ripault (Paris: Pierre Belfond, 1986).

17. Duyên Anh, *Un Russe à Saigon*, 142. Author's translation.

18. Ly Thu Ho, *Au milieu du carrefour* (Paris: Editions Peyronnet, 1969), 119.

19. See Nguyen, *Vietnamese Voices*, 58–64.

20. See, for example, Yung Krall, *A Thousand Tears Falling: The True Story of a Vietnamese Family Torn Apart by War, Communism, and the CIA* (Atlanta: Longstreet Press, 1995). Krall fell in love with an American navy pilot during the war and they were married in the United States in 1968. He was instrumental in ensuring that her family would be safely evacuated from Vietnam in April 1975.

21. Norodom Sihanouk was King of Cambodia between 1941 and 1955, and between 1993 and 2004.

22. Kieu's brother survived hard labor in a camp close to the Chinese border (largely because he was a skilled surgeon and the camp commander made use of his services) and was released after six years, after repeated bribes on the part of his family.

23. A recent article by Siew-Ean Khoo, Bob Birrell, and Genevieve Heard reveals for example that second-generation Vietnamese in Australia do not have spouses of Middle Eastern ancestry. See Table 4: Second-Generation Partnered Men and Women Who Have a Spouse of a Different Ancestry, Percentage Distribution by Spouse's Ancestry, 2006, in Siew-Ean Khoo, Bob Birrell, and Genevieve Heard, "Intermarriage by Birthplace and Ancestry in Australia," *People and Place* 17, no. 1 (2009): 22.

24. Nicole Constable, "Introduction: Cross-Border Marriages, Gendered Mobility, and Global Hypergamy," in *Cross-Border Marriages: Gender and Mobility in Transnational Asia*, ed. Nicole Constable, 4 (Philadelphia: University of Pennsylvania Press, 2005).

25. William J. Klausner, "Valuing Cross-Cultural Marriage," *The Nation*, June 24 2004, 12A.

26. Stephen Rose, *The Making of Memory* (London: Bantam Books, 1993), 2.

27. Hung Cam Thai, "Clashing Dreams in the Vietnamese Diaspora: Highly Educated Overseas Brides and Low-Wage U.S. Husbands," in *Cross-Border Marriages: Gender and Mobility in Transnational Asia*, ed. Nicole Constable, 152 (Philadelphia: University of Pennsylvania Press, 2005).

28. Rosemary Breger and Rosanna Hill, "Introducing Mixed Marriages," in Cross-*Cultural Marriage: Identity and Choice*, ed. Rosemary Breger and Rosanna Hill, 28 (Oxford: Berg, 1998).

29. Constable, "Introduction," 7. Constable is citing Gregory M. Pflugfelder, *Cartographies of Desire: Male-Male Sexuality in Japanese Discourse, 1600–1950* (Berkeley: University of California Press, 1999), and Lenore Manderson and Margaret Jolly, eds., *Sites of Desire/Economies of Pleasure: Sexualities in Asia and the Pacific* (Chicago: University of Chicago Press, 1997).

30. Constable, "Introduction," 7.

31. Janet Penny and Siew-Ean Khoo, *Intermarriage: A Study of Migration and Integration* (Canberra: Bureau of Immigration, Multicultural and Population Research, 1996), 209.

32. Siew-Ean Khoo, Bob Birrell, and Genevieve Heard write that the rate of intermarriage in the Vietnamese community in Australia (based on the 2006 Australian Census) is very low for the first generation and still relatively low for the second generation. Vietnamese women of the first generation, however, have a higher rate of intermarriage than Vietnamese men. See Khoo, Birrell, and Heard, "Intermarriage by Birthplace and Ancestry in Australia," 15–28.

In *Intermarriage*, Penny and Khoo note that "[a]s nearly a sixth of all couple families in Australia are married to people born in other countries, the intermarriages we have described illustrate an important influence in Australian life. Statistically at least, intermarried couples occupy a midpoint between the traditions of many of the migrant societies and the modern trends in family life seen in Australia as a whole, as illustrated by the divorce rate. Overall, the divorce rate of birthplace intermarriages is lower than for Australian couples generally, but higher than the rate for in-married couples born overseas. What these unions contribute then, is actually a combination of value systems that work better in the present climate to preserve intact families than if there were no intermarriages. Statistically at least, intermarried couples have contributed to family stability in Australia." Penny and Khoo, *Intermarriage*, 201.

CHAPTER 6

1. Andrew Lam, *Perfume Dreams: Reflections on the Vietnamese Diaspora* (Berkeley, CA: Heyday Books, 2005), 115.

2. Robert Templer, *Shadows and Wind: A View of Modern Vietnam* (London: Abacus, 1999), 309.

3. According to the Vietnamese government, the number of overseas Vietnamese traveling annually to Vietnam rose from 8,000 in 1986 to approximately 250,000 by the end of the 1990s. In 2004, it reached 400,000 (Ministry of Foreign Affairs, 2005). Annual remittances from the diaspora to Vietnam are estimated at US$3 billion, "roughly equivalent to 10 per cent of Vietnam's gross domestic product and constituting a major source of foreign exchange" Ashley Carruthers, "Saigon from the Diaspora," *Singapore Journal of Topical Geography* 29 (2008): 71.

4. Of the forty-two women who were interviewed for this book, the majority—thirty-one—have made return trips to Vietnam, and most have done so more than once.

5. Russell King, "Generalizations from the History of Return Migration," in *Return Migration: Journey of Hope or Despair?* ed. Bimal Ghosh, 17 (Geneva: International Organization for Migration and the United Nations, 2000).

6. Overseas Vietnamese may return for a wide variety of reasons aside from reconnecting with family members. These range from establishing businesses to seeking spouses—see Hung Cam Thai, *For Better or for Worse: Vietnamese International Marriages in the New Global Economy* (New Brunswick, NJ: Rutgers University Press, 2008)—or affordable medical procedures. The women in this study, however, overwhelmingly cited family as the reason for their return.

7. Ellen Oxfeld and Lynellyn D. Long, "Introduction," in *Coming Home? Refugees, Migrants, and Those Who Stayed Behind*, ed. Lynellyn D. Long and Ellen Oxfeld, 7 (Philadelphia: University of Pennsylvania Press, 2004).

8. Oxfeld and Long, "Introduction," 15.

9. Nathalie Huynh Chau Nguyen, *Vietnamese Voices: Gender and Cultural Identity in the Vietnamese Francophone Novel* (DeKalb: Southeast Asia Publications, Center for Southeast Asian Studies, Northern Illinois University, 2003), 173–174.

10. Trinh Do, *Saigon to San Diego: Memoir of a Boy Who Escaped from Communist Vietnam* (Jefferson, NC: McFarland, 2004), 226.

11. Kim Lefèvre, *Retour à la saison des pluies* (Paris: Bernard Barrault, 1990), 18. Author's translation.

12. Nathalie Huynh Chau Nguyen, "Writing and Memory in Kim Lefèvre's Autobiographical Narratives," *Intersections: Gender, History and Culture in the Asian Context* 5 (2001), paragraph 11, http://wwwsshe.murdoch.edu.au/intersections/issue5/nathalie.html moved in April 2008 to http://intersections.anu.edu.au/issue5/nathalie.html.

13. Jack A. Yeager, "Kim Lefèvre's *Retour à la saison des pluies*: Rediscovering the Landscapes of Childhood," *L'Esprit Créateur* 33, no. 2 (1993): 54.

14. Lefèvre, *Retour*, 220–221.

15. Hue-Tam Ho Tai, "Afterword: Commemoration and Community," in *The Country of Memory: Remaking the Past in Late Socialist Vietnam*, ed. Hue-Tam Ho Tai, 229 (Berkeley: University of California Press, 2001).

16. Mandy Thomas, *Dreams in the Shadows: Vietnamese-Australian Lives in Transition* (St. Leonards: Allen & Unwin, 1999), 177.

17. Thomas, *Dreams in the Shadows*, 177.

18. Michael Seidel, *Exile and the Narrative Imagination* (New Haven, CT: Yale University Press, 1986), 11.

19. Thomas, *Dreams in the Shadows*, 189.

20. A unit of weight used in eastern Asia.

21. Vietnamese authorities did not appear to have a consistent policy toward escapees. If caught, some were fined, but others were imprisoned for any length of time between a few weeks to more than a year, and this included women and children. W. Courtland Robinson notes that, "a 1985 UNHCR study revealed that 65 per cent of those apprehended by the authorities were imprisoned and of those 86 per cent were detained less than a year and 30 per cent less than a month." W. Courtland Robinson, *Terms of Refuge: The Indochinese Exodus and The International Response* (London: Zed Books, 1998), 179–180.

In his memoir *The Unwanted* (2001), Kien Nguyen writes of a failed escape attempt he made as a thirteen year old in 1981, for which he was interned in "Re-education Camp No PK 34," reserved for "boat criminals" (245). He spent two months there doing hard labor before his mother was able to bribe camp authorities for his release, and notes that this was "a specific camp for women and children." Kien Nguyen, *The Unwanted* (Sydney: Macmillan, 2001), 249.

22. Thi's experiences as an unaccompanied minor are explored in detail in the chapter on "Refugee Children" in Nathalie Huynh Chau Nguyen, *Voyage of Hope: Vietnamese Australian Women's Narratives* (Altona: Common Ground Publishing, 2005), 49–73.

23. The forced closure of Southern businesses affected the Chinese community particularly badly. Robinson writes, "On 24 March 1978 the government radio station announced: 'The policy of terminating all bourgeois tradesmen's business will be carried out in a uniform manner throughout [Ho Chi Minh City] and all southern provinces, regardless of nationality or religion.' In fact, the hammer came down first and hardest in Cholon, the Chinatown of Ho Chi Minh City and 'a strong capitalist heart beating inside the Socialist body of Vietnam.' The same day, 30,000 youth volunteers accompanied by soldiers conducted a house-to-house search,

confiscating hidden gold bars and dollar bills, inventorying property for state appropriation, and closing businesses. By mid-June, the authorities had relocated nearly 16,000 people to three NEZs [New Economic Zones] outside the city." Robinson, *Terms of Refuge*, 29.

24. Tien's account of her escape by sea is depicted in Nguyen, *Voyage of Hope*, 25–26.

25. Susan Terry was part of an Australian medical team consisting of eight surgeons, four anaesthetists, four physicians, two radiographers, and five nursing staff from the Royal Melbourne Hospital who were assigned to Long Xuyen Hospital in An Giang, South Vietnam, between October 1964 and November 1965. She worked as Ward Sister. Her book *House of Love: Life in a Vietnamese Hospital,* was published in 1966. "House of Love" is the literal translation of the Vietnamese term for hospital: *nha* (house) *thuong* (to love). See Susan Terry, *House of Love: Life in a Vietnamese Hospital* (London: World Books, 1966).

26. Terry, *House of Love*, 7.

27. Stewart Lone writes that "the total number of imported cars registered between January and May 1967 was just 1,587." Stewart Lone, "Remembering Life in Urban South Vietnam, circa 1965-1975," in *Daily Lives of Civilians in Wartime Asia: From the Taiping Rebellion to the Vietnam War*, ed. Stewart Lone, 221 (Westport, CT: Greenwood Press, 2007).

28. Lone, "Remembering Life," 222.

29. Lone, "Remembering Life," 221.

30. Thomas, *Dreams in the Shadows*, 185.

31. Nicola King, *Memory, Narrative, Identity: Remembering the Self* (Edinburgh: Edinburgh University Press, 2000), 2.

32. Linda Hitchcox, *Vietnamese Refugees in Southeast Asian Camps* (Basingstoke: Macmillan in association with St. Antony's College, Oxford, 1990), 40–44.

33. *Bo-bo* is a type of grain that Vietnamese ate in the postwar years. It features in other refugee accounts. Here is one: "I tried to cut down on my family's expenses. At that time the government sold *bo-bo* grains and noodles to the people. *Bo-bo* was a very hard grain and only used to feed horses in other countries. I had to use a lot of fuel to cook it, however eating this type of grain made us feel full for a long time. To save money, I bought green and red beans and cooked them together with the *bo-bo* or noodles and we ate them with salt or salted sesame. I divided this food equally into five bowls so that the youngest child would have as much to eat as the oldest." Nguyen, *Voyage of Hope*, 113.

34. Thy's narrative features in Nguyen, *Voyage of Hope*, 13–14, 142–145.

35. King, *Memory*, 2.

36. Marianne Hirsch and Leo Spitzer, "'We Would Never Have Come Without You': Generations of Nostalgia," in *Contested Pasts: The Politics of Memory*, eds. Katharine Hodgkin and Susannah Radstone, 83 (London: Routledge, 2003).

37. Oxfeld and Long, "Introduction," 13.

38. Hirsch and Spitzer, "We Would Never Have Come Without You," 85.

39. Ruth Wajnryb, *The Silence: How Tragedy Shapes Talk* (Crows Nest: Allen & Unwin, 2001), 27.

40. Hirsch and Spitzer, "We Would Never Have Come Without You," 93.

41. Lam, *Perfume Dreams*, 115.

42. Personal Narratives Group, "Truths," in *Interpreting Women's Lives: Feminist Theory and Personal Narratives*, ed. Personal Narratives Group, 262 (Bloomington: Indiana University Press, 1989).

43. Vieda Skultans, *The Testimony of Lives: Narrative and Memory in Post-Soviet Latvia* (London: Routledge, 199), 28.

CONCLUSION

1. Thuong Vuong-Riddick, *Two Shores/Deux Rives* (Vancouver: Ronsdale Press, 1995), n.p.

2. Robert Perks and Alistair Thomson, "Introduction to Second Edition," in *The Oral History Reader*, 2nd ed., ed. Robert Perks and Alistair Thomson, ix (London: Routledge, 2006).

3. Inga Clendinnen, *Reading the Holocaust* (Melbourne: Text Publishing, 1998), 206.

4. Laurence J. Kirmayer, "Landscapes of Memory: Trauma, Narrative, and Dissociation," in *Tense Past: Cultural Essays in Trauma and Memory*, ed. Paul Antze and Michael Lambek, 190 (New York: Routledge, 1996).

5. Suzette Min, "Remains to Be Seen: Reading the Works of Dean Sameshima and Khanh Vo," in *Loss: The Politics of Mourning*, ed. David L. Eng and David Kazanjian, 245 (Berkeley: University of California Press, 2003).

6. Vieda Skultans, a child refugee from Latvia who moved to Britain in 1948, remembers the hostility that was directed toward East European refugees and writes, "the East Europeans might have seen themselves as political refugees but their host country saw them as economic migrants." Vieda Skultans, "Narratives of Displacement and Identity," in *Narrative Research in Health and Illness*, ed. Brian Hurwitz, Trisha Greenhalgh, and Vieda Skultans, 294 (Malden, MA: Blackwell Publishing, 2004). Many

Vietnamese refugees were similarly labelled "economic migrants," especially in the 1980s.

7. Author's interview with Yung Krall in Atlanta, Georgia, on November 27, 2000. Krall's book was published in 1995. See Yung Krall, *A Thousand Tears Falling: The True Story of a Vietnamese Family Torn Apart by War, Communism, and the CIA* (Atlanta: Longstreet Press, 1995).

8. Author's interview with Yung Krall in Atlanta, Georgia, on November 27, 2000.

9. Letter to Yung Krall from Betty Anderson and Virginia Davis, Co-Chairmen, 1995 Georgia Author of the Year Awards Committee, dated February 14, 1996.

10. Kirmayer, "Landscapes of Memory," 189–190.

11. Kumari Jayawardena, *Feminism and Nationalism in the Third World* (London: Zed Books, 1986), 257.

12. Selma Leydesdorff, Luisa Passerini, and Paul Thompson, "Introduction," in *Gender and Memory*, ed. Selma Leydesdorff, Luisa Passerini, and Paul Thompson, 8 (New Brunswick, NJ: Transaction Publishers, 2006).

13. Vijay Mishra, *The Literature of the Indian Diaspora: Theorizing the Diasporic Imaginary* (London: Routledge, 2007), 16.

BIBLIOGRAPHY

Bao Ninh. *The Sorrow of War*. English version by Frank Palmos. London: Secker and Warburg, 1993.

Bell, Susan E. "Narratives and Lives: Women's Health Politics and the Diagnosis of Cancer for DES Daughters." *Narrative Inquiry* 9, no. 2 (1999): 347–389.

Breger, Rosemary, and Rosanna Hill. "Introducing Mixed Marriages." In *Cross-Cultural Marriage: Identity and Choice*, ed. Rosemary Breger and Rosanna Hill, 1–31. Oxford: Berg, 1998.

Brigham, Robert K. *ARVN: Life and Death in the South Vietnamese Army*. Lawrence: University Press of Kansas, 2006.

Carruthers, Ashley. "Saigon from the Diaspora." *Singapore Journal of Topical Geography* 29 (2008): 68–86.

Carsten, Janet. "Introduction: Ghosts of Memory." In *Ghosts of Memory: Essays on Remembrance and Relatedness*, ed. Janet Carsten, 1–35. Malden, MA: Blackwell Publishing, 2007.

Chen Jian. "China and the First Indo-China War, 1950–54." *The China Quarterly* 133 (1993): 85–110.

———. "China's Involvement in the Vietnam War, 1964–69." *The China Quarterly* 142 (1995): 356–387.

Clendinnen, Inga. "The History Question: Who Owns the Past?" *Quarterly Essay* 23 (2006): 1–72.

———. *Reading the Holocaust*. Melbourne: Text Publishing, 1998.

Constable, Nicole. "Introduction: Cross-Border Marriages, Gendered Mobility, and Global Hypergamy." In *Cross-Border Marriages: Gender and Mobility in Transnational Asia*, ed. Nicole Constable, 1–16. Philadelphia: University of Pennsylvania Press, 2005.

Cung Giu Nguyen. *Le Fils de la baleine*. Sherbrooke, Québec: Editions Naaman, 1978. Paris: Fayard, 1956.

Dang Kim Hoa. "Toi vao linh" (I joined the army). *Dac San Cuu Nu Quan Nhan QLVNCH: Ky Niem Hoi Ngo NQN Ky IV 25-26 Thang 8 Nam 2007 Tai Nam California* (Magazine of the Servicewomen of the Republic of Vietnam Armed Forces. Special Bulletin to commemorate the Fourth Reunion of Servicewomen on August 25–26, 2007, Southern California): 12–13.

Dang Phong, ed. *Lich Su Kinh Te Viet Nam, 1945–2000* (Vietnamese Economic History, 1945–2000). Vol II: 1955–1975. Hanoi: Social Sciences Publishing House, 2005.

Dang Thuy Tram. *Last Night I Dreamed of Peace: The Diary of Dang Thuy Tram*, trans. Andrew X. Pham. New York: Harmony Books, 2007.

Davis, Colin. "Understanding the Concentration Camps: Elie Wiesel's *La Nuit* and Jorge Semprun's *Quel Beau Dimanche!*" *Australian Journal of French Studies* 28, no. 3 (1991): 291–303.

DeBonis, Steven. *Children of the Enemy: Oral Histories of Vietnamese Amerasians and Their Mothers*. Jefferson, NC: McFarland & Company, 1995.

DeGroot, Gerard J. "Introduction to Part 1: Arms and the Woman." In *A Soldier and a Woman: Sexual Integration in the Military*, ed. Gerard J. DeGroot and Corinna Peniston-Bird, 3–17. Harlow, UK: Longman, an Imprint of Pearson Education, 2000.

Desbarats, Jacqueline. "Human Rights: Two Steps Forward, One Step Backward?" In *Vietnam Today: Assessing the New Trends*, ed. Thai Quang Trung, 47–66. New York: Crane Russak, A Member of the Taylor & Francis Group, 1990.

Do, Trinh. *Saigon to San Diego: Memoir of a Boy Who Escaped from Communist Vietnam*. Jefferson, NC: McFarland & Company, 2004.

Dong Van Khuyen. *The RVNAF*. Washington, DC: U.S. Army Center of Military History, 1980.

Duyên Anh. *Un Russe à Saigon*, trans. Jean Mais and Ghislain Ripault. Paris: Pierre Belfond, 1986.

Eng, David L., and David Kazanjian, eds. *Loss: The Politics of Mourning*. Berkeley: University of California Press, 2003.

Foster, Patricia, ed. *Sister to Sister: Women Write about the Unbreakable Bond*. New York: Doubleday, 1995.

Freeman, James M. *Hearts of Sorrow: Vietnamese-American Lives*. Stanford, CA: Stanford University Press, 1989.

Freeman, James M., and Nguyen Dinh Huu. *Voices from the Camps: Vietnamese Children Seeking Asylum*. Seattle: University of Washington Press, 2003.

Gaiduk, Ilya V. *The Soviet Union and the Vietnam War*. Chicago, IL: Ivan R. Dee, 1996.

Garner, Helen. "A Scrapbook, An Album." In *Sisters*, ed. Drusilla Modjeska, 77–110. Sydney: Angus & Robertson, 1993.

Gluck, Sherna Berger, and Daphne Patai. "Introduction." In *Women's Words: The Feminist Practice of Oral History*, ed. Sherna Berger Gluck and Daphne Patai, 1–5. New York: Routledge, 1991.

Grant, Bruce. *The Boat People: An "Age" Investigation*. Ringwood, Australia: Penguin Books, 1979.

Grass, Günter. *Crabwalk*, trans. Krishna Winston. London: Faber and Faber, 2003.

Grey, Jeffrey. "Review of Lam Quang Thi, The Twenty-Five Year Century: A South Vietnamese General Remembers the Indochina War to the Fall of Saigon." *H-War, H-Net Reviews in the Humanities and Social Sciences* (2004): 1–2, http://www.h-net.org/reviews/showrev.php?id=9193.

Gross, David. *Lost Time: On Remembering and Forgetting in Late Modern Culture*. Amherst: University of Massachusetts Press, 2000.

Guillemot, François. "Au cœur de la fracture vietnamienne: L'élimination de l'opposition nationaliste et anticolonialiste dans le Nord du Vietnam (1945–1946)." In *Naissance d'un Etat-Parti: Le Viêt Nam depuis 1945*, ed. Christopher E. Goscha and Benoît De Tréglodé, 175–216. Paris: Les Indes Savantes, 2004.

Haines, David W. *The Limits of Kinship: South Vietnamese Households, 1954–1975*. DeKalb: Southeast Asia Publications, Center for Southeast Asian Studies, Northern Illinois University, 2006.

Hakakian, Roya. *Journey from the Land of No*. Sydney: Bantam, 2004.

Herman, Judith Lewis. *Trauma and Recovery*. New York: BasicBooks, 1992.

Hinchman, Lewis P., and Sandra K. Hinchman. "Introduction." In *Memory, Identity, Community: The Idea of Narrative in the Human Sciences*, ed. Lewis P. Hinchman and Sandra K. Hinchman, xiii–xxxii. Albany: State University of New York Press, 1997.

Hirsch, Marianne, and Leo Spitzer. "'We Would Never Have Come Without You': Generations of Nostalgia." In *Contested Pasts: The Politics of Memory*, ed. Katharine Hodgkin and Susannah Radstone, 79–95. London: Routledge, 2003.

Hitchcox, Linda. *Vietnamese Refugees in Southeast Asian Camps*. Basingstoke: Macmillan in association with St Antony's College, Oxford, 1990.

Ho Thi Ve. "Nu Quan Nhan" (Servicewomen). *Dac San Cuu Nu Quan Nhan QLVNCH: Ky Niem Ngay Hoi Ngo NQN 12 Thang 8 Nam 2001* (Magazine of the Servicewomen of the Republic of Vietnam

Armed Forces: Special Bulletin of the Reunion of Servicewomen on August 12, 2001): 7–18.

Hodgkin, Katharine, and Susannah Radstone. "Introduction: Contested Pasts." In *Contested Pasts: The Politics of Memory*, ed. Katharine Hodgkin and Susannah Radstone, 1–21. London: Routledge, 2003.

Humphrey, Michael. *The Politics of Atrocity and Reconciliation: From Terror to Trauma*. London: Routledge, 2000.

Hurwitz, Brian, Trisha Greenhalgh, and Vieda Skultans, eds. *Narrative Research in Health and Illness*. Malden, MA: Blackwell Publishing, 2004.

Huynh Sanh Thong. From "Live by Water, Die from Water." In *Watermark: Vietnamese American Poetry and Prose*, ed. Barbara Tran, Monique T. D. Truong, and Luu Truong Khoi, vi–vii. New York: Asian American Writers' Workshop, 1998.

Jamieson, Neil L. *Understanding Vietnam*. Berkeley: University of California Press, 1995.

Jayawardena, Kumari. *Feminism and Nationalism in the Third World*. London: Zed Books, 1986.

Joes, Anthony James. *The War for South Viet Nam, 1954–1975*. Rev. ed. Westport, CT: Praeger, 2001.

Khoo, Siew-Ean, Bob Birrell, and Genevieve Heard. "Intermarriage by Birthplace and Ancestry in Australia." *People and Place* 17, no. 1 (2009): 15–28.

King, Nicola. *Memory, Narrative, Identity: Remembering the Self*. Edinburgh: Edinburgh University Press, 2000.

King, Russell. "Generalizations from the History of Return Migration." In *Return Migration: Journey of Hope or Despair?* ed. Bimal Ghosh, 7–55. Geneva: International Organization for Migration and the United Nations, 2000.

Kirmayer, Laurence J. "Landscapes of Memory: Trauma, Narrative, and Dissociation." In *Tense Past: Cultural Essays in Trauma and Memory*, ed. Paul Antze and Michael Lambek, 173–198. New York: Routledge, 1996.

Klausner, William J. "Valuing Cross-Cultural Marriage." *The Nation*, June 24, 2004, 12A.

Krall, Yung. *A Thousand Tears Falling: The True Story of a Vietnamese Family Torn Apart by War, Communism, and the CIA*. Atlanta: Longstreet Press, 1995.

Kwon, Heonik. *Ghosts of War in Vietnam*. Cambridge: Cambridge University Press, 2008.

Laird, Joan. "Women and Stories: Restorying Women's Self-constructions." In *Women in Families: A Framework for Family Therapy*, ed. Monica McGoldrick, Carol M. Anderson, and Froma Walsh, 427–450. New York: W. W. Norton & Company, Inc., 1989.

Lam, Andrew. *Perfume Dreams: Reflections on the Vietnamese Diaspora.* Berkeley: Heyday Books, 2005.

Lam Quang Thi. *The Twenty-Five Year Century: A South Vietnamese General Remembers the Indochina War to the Fall of Saigon.* Denton: University of North Texas Press, 2001.

Larsen, Wendy Wilder, and Tran Thi Nga, *Shallow Graves: Two Women and Vietnam.* New York: Random House, 1986.

Lefèvre, Kim. *Métisse blanche.* Paris: Bernard Barrault, 1989.

———. *Retour à la saison des pluies.* Paris: Bernard Barrault, 1990.

Levenstein, Aaron. *Escape to Freedom: The Story of the International Rescue Committee.* Westport, CT: Greenwood Press, 1983.

Lewy, Guenter. *America in Vietnam.* New York: Oxford University Press, 1978.

Leydesdorff, Selma, Graham Dawson, Natasha Burchardt, and T. G. Ashplant. "Introduction: Trauma and Life Stories." In *Trauma and Life Stories: International Perspectives*, ed. Kim Lacy Rogers, Selma Leydesdorff, and Graham Dawson, 1–26. London: Routledge, 1999.

Leydesdorff, Selma, Luisa Passerini, and Paul Thompson. "Introduction." In *Gender and Memory*, ed. Selma Leydesdorff, Luisa Passerini, and Paul Thompson, 1–16. New Brunswick, NJ: Transaction Publishers, 2006.

Libby, Jean. "Preface." In *Hoa Lo/Hanoi Hilton Stories*, ed. Nguyen Chi Thien, xi–xiv. New Haven, CT: Yale University Southeast Asia Studies, 2007.

Lone, Stewart. "Remembering Life in Urban South Vietnam, circa 1965–1975." In *Daily Lives of Civilians in Wartime Asia: From the Taiping Rebellion to the Vietnam War*, ed. Stewart Lone, ed. 219–246. Westport, CT: Greenwood Press, 2007.

Long, Lynellyn D. "Viet Kieu on a Fast Track Back?" In *Coming Home?: Refugees, Migrants, and Those Who Stayed Behind*, ed. Lynellyn D. Long and Ellen Oxfeld, 65–89. Philadelphia: University of Pennsylvania Press, 2004.

Ly Thu Ho. *Au milieu du carrefour.* Paris: Editions Peyronnet, 1969.

Manderson, Lenore, and Margaret Jolly, eds. *Sites of Desire/Economies of Pleasure: Sexualities in Asia and the Pacific.* Chicago: University of Chicago Press, 1997.

Marr, David G. *Vietnam 1945: The Quest for Power*. Berkeley: University of California Press, 1995.

McGoldrick, Monica. "Sisters." In *Women in Families: A Framework for Family Therapy*, ed, Monica McGoldrick, Carol M. Anderson, and Froma Walsh, 244–266. New York: W. W. Norton & Company, Inc., 1989.

McKelvey, Robert S. *The Dust of Life: America's Children Abandoned in Vietnam*. Seattle: University of Washington Press, 1999.

———. *A Gift of Barbed Wire: America's Allies Abandoned in South Vietnam*. Seattle: University of Washington Press, 2002.

McNally, Richard J. *Remembering Trauma*. Cambridge, MA: Belknap Press of Harvard University Press, 2003.

Metzner, Edward P., Huynh Van Chinh, Tran Van Phuc, and Le Nguyen Binh. *Reeducation in Postwar Vietnam: Personal Postscripts to Peace*. College Station: Texas A&M University Press, 2001.

Millman, Marcia. *The Perfect Sister: What Draws Us Together, What Drives Us Apart*. Orlando, FL: Harcourt, 2004.

Min, Suzette. "Remains to Be Seen: Reading the Works of Dean Sameshima and Khanh Vo." In *Loss: The Politics of Mourning*, ed. David L. Eng and David Kazanjian, 229–250. Berkeley: University of California Press, 2003.

Ministry of Foreign Affairs. "Interview granted to AP by Vice Foreign Minister, Chairman for Overseas Vietnamese Nguyen Phu Binh." (Hanoi: Bo Ngoai Giao Viet Nam Ministry of Foreign Affairs, March 18, 2005): http://www.mofa.gov.vn/en/tt_baochi/nr041126171753/ns050509142713.

Mishra, Vijay. *The Literature of the Indian Diaspora: Theorizing the Diasporic Imaginary*. London: Routledge, 2007.

Modjeska, Drusilla. "Introduction." In *Sisters*, ed. Drusilla Modjeska, vii–xiii. Sydney: Angus & Robertson, 1993.

Morrison, Toni. *Sula*. London: Picador, 1991. London: Chatto & Windus, 1980.

Morris-Suzuki, Tessa. *Peeling Apples*. The Australian National University: Pandanus Books, 2005.

Nguyen, Cam. "East, West, and Vietnamese Women." *The Journal of Vietnamese Studies* 5 (1992): 44–50.

Nguyen Chi Thien. *Flowers from Hell* (Hoa Dia-Nguc), trans. Huynh Sanh Thong. New Haven, CT: Council on Southeast Asia Studies, Yale Center for International and Area Studies, 1984.

———. *Hoa Lo: Hanoi Hilton Stories*. New Haven, CT: Yale University Southeast Asia Studies, 2007.

Nguyen Du. *The Tale of Kieu: A Bilingual Edition*, trans. Huynh Sanh Thong. New Haven, CT: Yale University Press, 1983.

Nguyen Hung Quoc. "Vietnamese Communist Literature (1975–1990)." In *Vietnamese Studies in a Multicultural World*, ed. Nguyen Xuan Thu, 120–143. Melbourne: Vietnamese Language & Culture Publications, 1994.

Nguyen, Kien. *The Unwanted*. Sydney: Pan Macmillan, 2001.

Nguyen, Nathalie Huynh Chau. "Eurasian/Amerasian Perspectives: Kim Lefèvre's *Métisse blanche* (White Métisse) and Kien Nguyen's *The Unwanted*." *Asian Studies Review* 29, no. 2 (2005): 107–122.

———. "Landscapes of War: Traumascapes in the Works of Kim Lefèvre and Phan Huy Duong." In *Francographic Literature: Remapping Uncertain Territories*, ed. Magali Compan and Katarzyna Pieprzak, 88–103. Newcastle: Cambridge Scholars Publishing, 2007.

———. "War through Women's Eyes: Nam Phuong's *Red on Gold* and Yung Krall's *A Thousand Tears Falling*." *Intersections: Gender, History and Culture in the Asian Context* 11 (2005): 32 paragraphs, http:wwwsshe.murdoch.edu.au/intersections/issue11/nguyen.html, http://intersections.anu.edu/issue11/nguyen.html (accessed April 2008).

———. "Writing and Memory in Kim Lefèvre's Autobiographical Narratives." *Intersections: Gender, History and Culture in the Asian Context* 5 (2001): 13 paragraphs, http://wwwsshe.murdoch.edu.au/intersections/issue5/nathalie.html, http://intersections.anu.edu/issue5/nathalie.html (accessed April 2008).

———. *Vietnamese Voices: Gender and Cultural Identity in the Vietnamese Francophone Novel*. DeKalb: Southeast Asia Publications, Center for Southeast Asian Studies, Northern Illinois University, 2003.

———. *Voyage of Hope: Vietnamese Australian Women's Narratives*. Altona, Australia: Common Ground Publishing, 2005.

Nguyen Thi Hanh Nhon. "Thu Moi Hop Mat Nu Quan Nhan Hai Ngoai" (Letter of Invitation to a Meeting of Overseas Servicewomen). *Dac San Cuu Nu Quan Nhan QLVNCH: Ky Niem Ngay Hoi Ngo NQN 12 Thang 8 Nam 2001* (Magazine of the Servicewomen of the Republic of Vietnam Armed Forces: Special Bulletin of the Reunion of Servicewomen on August, 12, 2001): 5.

———. "Phat bieu cua Dai dien Ban To Chuc Hoi Ngo Nu Quan Nhan Hai Ngoai Ky IV" (Speech of the WAFC Committee Representative delivered at the Fourth Overseas Reunion). *Dac San Cuu Nu Quan Nhan QLVNCH: Ky Niem Hoi Ngo NQN Ky IV 25-26 Thang 8 Nam 2007 Tai Nam California* (Magazine of the Servicewomen of the Republic of Vietnam Armed Forces: Special Bulletin to commemorate

the Fourth Reunion of Servicewomen on August, 25–26, 2007, Southern California): 4–5.

Nguyen Trieu Dan. *A Vietnamese Family Chronicle: Twelve Generations on the
Banks of the Hat River*. Jefferson, NC: McFarland & Company, 1991.

Nguyen Van Canh. *Vietnam under Communism, 1975–1982*. Stanford, CA:
Hoover Institution Press, 1983.

Oxfeld, Ellen, and Lynellyn D. Long. "Introduction." In *Coming Home?:
Refugees, Migrants, and Those Who Stayed Behind*, ed. Lynellyn D.
Long and Ellen Oxfeld, 1–15. Philadelphia: University of Pennsylva-
nia Press, 2004.

Passerini, Luisa. "Memories between Silence and Oblivion." In *Contested
Pasts: The Politics of Memory*, ed. Katharine Hodgkin and Susannah
Radstone, 238–254. London: Routledge, 2003.

Paulson, Daryl S. "War and Refugee Suffering." In *The Psychological Impact
of War Trauma on Civilians: An International Perspective*, ed. Stanley
Krippner and Teresa M. McIntyre, 111–122. Westport, CT: Praeger,
2003.

Penny, Janet, and Siew-Ean Khoo, *Intermarriage: A Study of Migration and
Integration*. Canberra: Bureau of Immigration, Multicultural and Population Research, 1996.

Perks, Robert, and Alistair Thomson. "Advocacy and Empowerment:
Introduction." In *The Oral History Reader: Second Edition*, ed. Robert
Perks and Alistair Thomson, 447–455. London: Routledge, 2006.

Personal Narratives Group. "Truths." In *Interpreting Women's Lives: Feminist Theory and Personal Narratives*, ed. Personal Narratives Group,
261–264. Bloomington: Indiana University Press, 1989.

Pham Duy Khiem. *Légendes des terres sereines*. Paris: Mercure de France,
1951.

———. *Nam et Sylvie*. Paris: Librarie Plon, 1957.

Phan Huy Duong. *Un Amour métèque: nouvelles*. Paris: L'Harmattan, 1994.

Pham Van Ky. *Frères de sang*. Paris: Editions du Seuil, 1947.

Phung Thi Hanh. *South Vietnam's Women in Uniform*. Saigon: Vietnam
Council on Foreign Relations, 1970.

Pflugfelder, Gregory M. *Cartographies of Desire: Male-Male Sexuality in Japanese Discourse, 1600–1950*. Berkeley: University of California Press,
1999.

Riessman, Catherine Kohler. *Narrative Methods for the Human Sciences*.
Thousand Oaks, CA: Sage Publications, 2008.

Ripault, Ghislain. "Pour présenter Duyên Anh." In *Un Russe à Saigon*, ed.
Duyên Anh, trans. Jean Mais and Ghislain Ripault, 9–17. Paris:
Pierre Belfond, 1986.

Robinson, W. Courtland. *Terms of Refuge: The Indochinese Exodus and the International Response*. London: Zed Books, 1998.

Rose, Stephen. *The Making of Memory*, London: Bantam Books, 1993.

Sanders, Robert. *Sibling Relationships: Theory and Issues for Practice* Basingstoke: Palgrave Macmillan, 2004.

Schafer, John C. *Vietnamese Perspectives on the War in Vietnam: Annotated Bibliography of Works in English*. (New Haven, CT: Yale University Council on Southeast Asian Studies, 1996): http://www.yale.edu/seas/bibliography/home.html.

———. *Vo Phien and the Sadness of Exile*. DeKalb: Southeast Asia Publications, Center for Southeast Asian Studies, Northern Illinois University, 2006.

Seidel, Michael. *Exile and the Narrative Imagination*. New Haven CT: Yale University Press, 1986.

Skultans, Vieda. "Narratives of Displacement and Identity." In *Narrative Research in Health and Illness*, ed. Brian Hurwitz, Trisha Greenhalgh, and Vieda Skultans, 292–308. Malden, MA: Blackwell Publishing, 2004.

———. *The Testimony of Lives: Narrative and Memory in Post-Soviet Latvia*. London: Routledge, 1998.

Smith, Ann B. Interview with Ann B. Smith, June 23, 2004. Ann B. Smith Collection. The Vietnam Archive, Texas Tech University.

Summerfield, Penny. *Reconstructing Women's Wartime Lives: Discourse and Subjectivity in Oral Histories of the Second World War*. Manchester: Manchester University Press, 1998.

Tai, Hue-Tam Ho. "Afterword: Commemoration and Community." In *The Country of Memory: Remaking the Past in Late Socialist Vietnam*, ed. Hue-Tam Ho Tai, 227–230. Berkeley: University of California Press. 2001.

———. "Faces of Remembrance and Forgetting." In *The Country of Memory: Remaking the Past in Late Socialist Vietnam*, ed. Hue-Tam Ho Tai, 167–195. Berkeley: University of California Press, 2001.

Taylor, Sandra C. *Vietnamese Women at War: Fighting for Ho Chi Minh and the Revolution*. Lawrence: University Press of Kansas, 1999.

Templer, Robert. *Shadows and Wind: A View of Modern Vietnam*. London: Abacus, 1999.

Terry, Susan. *House of Love: Life in a Vietnamese Hospital*. London: World Books, 1966.

Thai, Hung Cam. *For Better or For Worse: Vietnamese International Marriages in the New Global Economy*. New Brunswick, NJ: Rutgers University Press, 2008.

————. "Clashing Dreams in the Vietnamese Diaspora: Highly Educated Overseas Brides and Low-Wage U.S. Husbands." In *Cross-Border Marriages: Gender and Mobility in Transnational Asia*, ed. Nicole Constable, 145–165. Philadelphia: University of Pennsylvania Press, 2005.

Thomas, Mandy. *Dreams in the Shadows: Vietnamese-Australian Lives in Transition*. St Leonards: Allen & Unwin, 1999.

Tran, Barbara. *In the Mynah Bird's Own Words*. Dorset, VT: Tupelo Press, 2002.

Tran, Barbara, Monique T. D. Truong, and Luu Truong Khoi. "A Note to the Reader." In *Watermark: Vietnamese American Poetry and Prose*, ed. Barbara Tran, Monique T. D. Truong, and Luu Truong Khoi, 224. New York: Asian American Writers' Workshop, 1998.

Tran Thi Nga. "Famine." In *Shallow Graves: Two Women in Vietnam*, ed. Wendy Wilder Larsen and Tran Thi Nga, 156–157. New York: Random House, 1986.

Tran Tri Vu. *Lost Years: My 1,632 Days in Vietnamese Reeducation Camps*. Berkeley: Institute of East Asian Studies, University of California, 1988.

Tranviet, Thuy. "Introduction." In *The Industry of Marrying Vietnamese*, ed. Vu Trong Phung, trans. Thuy Tranviet, 9–21. Ithaca, NY: Southeast Asia Program Publications, Cornell University, 2006.

Trong, Lucien. *Enfer rouge mon amour*. Paris: Editions du Seuil, 1980.

Truong Dinh Tri and Albert de Teneuille. *Bà-Dâm: Roman franco-annamite*. Paris: Fasquelle, 1930.

Tumarkin, Maria. *Traumascapes: The Power and Fate of Places Transformed by Tragedy*. Melbourne: Melbourne University Press, 2005.

Turner, Karen Gottschang. *Even the Women Must Fight: Memories of War from North Vietnam*. With Phan Thanh Hao. New York: John Wiley & Sons, 1998.

United Nations High Commissioner for Refugees. *The State of the World's Refugees: Fifty Years of Humanitarian Action*. Oxford: Oxford University Press, 2000.

The Upanishads, trans. Swami Nikhilananda. New York: Harper, 1949–1959.

Valverde, Kieu-Linh Caroline. "From Dust to Gold: The Vietnamese Amerasian Experience." In *Racially Mixed People in America*, ed. P. P. Maria Root, 144–161. Newbury Park, CA: Sage Publications, 1992.

Viviani, Nancy. *The Long Journey: Vietnamese Migration and Settlement in Australia*. Carlton: Melbourne University Press, 1984.

Vo, Linda Trinh. "Managing Survival: Economic Realities for Vietnamese American Women." In *Asian/Pacific Islander American Women*, ed. Shirley Hune and Gail M. Nomura, 237–252. New York: New York University Press, 2003.

Vo, Nghia M. *The Bamboo Gulag: Political Imprisonment in Communist Vietnam*. Jefferson, NC: McFarland & Company, 2004.

Vu Trong Phung. *The Industry of Marrying Europeans*, trans. Thuy Tranviet. Ithaca, NY: Southeast Asia Program Publications, Cornell University, 2006.

Vuong-Riddick, Thuong. *Two Shores/ Deux Rives*. Vancouver, BC: Ronsdale Press, 1995.

Wajnryb, Ruth. *The Silence: How Tragedy Shapes Talk*. Crows Nest: Allen & Unwin, 2001.

Webb, Nancy Boyd. "The Impact of Traumatic Stress and Loss on Children and Families." In *Mass Trauma and Violence: Helping Families and Children Cope*, ed. Nancy Boyd Webb, 3–22. New York: Guilford Press, 2004.

Wiesel, Elie. *Ethics and Memory*. Berlin: Walter de Gruyter, 1997.

Wilde, Oscar. *De Profundis*. 43rd ed. London: Methuen & Co., 1925.

Yeager, Jack A. "Kim Lefèvre's *Retour à la saison des pluies*: Rediscovering the Landscapes of Childhood." *L'Esprit Créateur* 33, no. 2 (1993): 47–57.

Zhai, Qiang. *China and the Vietnam Wars, 1950–1975*. Chapel Hill: University of North Carolina Press, 2000.

INDEX

About the Author

NATHALIE HUYNH CHAU NGUYEN holds an Australian Research Fellowship from the Australian Research Council at the Australian Centre, the School of Historical Studies, the University of Melbourne. A graduate of the Universities of Melbourne and Oxford, she is the author of *Vietnamese Voices: Gender and Cultural Identity in the Vietnamese Francophone Novel* (2003) and *Voyage of Hope: Vietnamese Australian Women's Narratives* (2005), which was shortlisted for the 2007 New South Wales Premier's Literary Award.

Also by Nathalie Huynh Chau Nguyen

Voyage of Hope:
Vietnamese Australian Women's Narratives

Vietnamese Voices:
Gender and Cultural Identity in the Vietnamese Francophone Novel